MOBILE CITY

MOBILE CITY

Emerging Media, Space, and
Sociality in Contemporary Berlin

Jordan H. Kraemer

CORNELL UNIVERSITY PRESS **ITHACA AND LONDON**

First published 2024 by Cornell University Press

Library of Congress Cataloging-in-Publication Data

Names: Kraemer, Jordan H., 1978- author.
Title: Mobile city : emerging media, space, and sociality in contemporary
  Berlin / Jordan H. Kraemer.
Description: Ithaca : Cornell University Press, 2024. | Includes
  bibliographical references and index.
Identifiers: LCCN 2024029762 (print) | LCCN 2024029763 (ebook) | ISBN
  9781501778698 (hardcover) | ISBN 9781501778704 (paperback) | ISBN
  9781501778711 (epub) | ISBN 9781501778728 (pdf)
Subjects: LCSH: Social media and society—Germany—Berlin—History—21st
  century. | Online social networks—Germany—Berlin—History—21st
  century. | Digital media—Social aspects—Germany—Berlin. | City and
  town life—Germany—Berlin—History—21st century. | Social
  change—Germany—Berlin—History—21st century. | Place
  attachment—Social aspects—Germany—Berlin. | Spatial behavior—Social
  aspects—Germany—Berlin. | Group
  identity—Germany—Berlin—History—21st century. | Berlin
  (Germany)—Social conditions—21st century. | Berlin (Germany)—Social
  life and customs—21st century.
Classification: LCC DD881.3 .K73 2024 (print) | LCC DD881.3 (ebook) | DDC
  303.48/30943155—dc23/eng/20240724
LC record available at https://lccn.loc.gov/2024029762
LC ebook record available at https://lccn.loc.gov/2024029763

I dedicate this book
to my parents, Ross and Michael Kraemer
and
to my children, Julian and Eleanor Kraemer Moore

Contents

Acknowledgments

A sentiment I often heard in graduate school was that scholarly writing is a notoriously lonely endeavor. Despite that expectation, I found writing and preparing this book to be a highly collaborative process involving many interlocutors and opportunities for input, feedback, and discussion with mentors, colleagues, friends, editors, and others. This book has been in the making for many years, from its inception during graduate school at the University of California, Irvine, with the guidance of Tom Boellstorff, Keith Murphy, Mei Zhan, and Paul Dourish, and through the following decade. In that time, I navigated an increasingly difficult academic job market, my first post-PhD fellowship, adjunct teaching, a global pandemic, and eventually, my departure from academia for tech policy research in civil society. Accordingly, many people have shaped or influenced the trajectory of this book.

My foremost debt is to my many interlocutors and friends during three fieldwork visits between 2007 and 2015, primarily in Berlin. For confidentiality, I will not name them individually, but I am endlessly grateful for their patience, generosity, and willingness to share their lives with me, and their perspectives that shaped this book. Ethnography, like much social research, risks being an extractive endeavor where one person represents the experiences of others. When recognized, however, as the mutual production of knowledge, always temporary and contingent, it can also furnish a fuller understanding of human lives and worlds. I also thank Jörg Niewöhner, Falk Blask, and the late Stefan Beck, all at the Institut für Europäische Ethnologie at Humboldt-Universität zu Berlin at the time, who provided a scholarly home for me during my fieldwork in 2009–10.

After completing additional fieldwork in 2015, I revised and rewrote much of the original manuscript, on the basis of the incisive, generative, and sometimes difficult-to-hear feedback from readers and colleagues. The anonymous reviewers at *Anthropological Quarterly* and *HCI* all read prior versions of material that appears here, and their critiques improved my analyses and thinking immeasurably. I am grateful to them and to the full manuscript reviewers who engaged closely with the work, helping me refine its core contributions and pushing me to widen my understanding of identity and citizenship, of what this book is about and why it matters.

Many colleagues read portions during the book's development and contributed invaluable feedback. These included participants at Wesleyan University's

2014–15 Center for Humanities seminar series on Mobilities; participants at New York University Department of Anthropology's Science Studies Ethnography workshop in 2016 (where I had the misfortune to present shortly after the presidential election), at the generous invitation of Emily Martin and Rayna Rapp; and members of the EASA Media Anthropology listserv who attended the Media and Mobility E-seminar in 2017. I presented the material in this book at numerous conferences and invited lectures, including at Wesleyan's Center for the Humanities in 2014 and at Bard College on two occasions in 2017 (one virtual), the latter thanks to Jonah Rubin. At Wesleyan, I am especially grateful to Ethan Kleinberg, then director of the Center for the Humanities, and Betsy Traube, who guided me through a difficult but ultimately productive reader report of what became chapter 4. My students during my fall 2014 seminar on the anthropology of social and mobile media helped refine my thinking further, pushing me to understand critical texts and analyses in new ways (while letting me in on the secrets of anonymous campus social media). Tim Choy's insights into media as doubly material and signifying helped crystallize my thinking on media's dynamic materiality, while Ilana Gershon provided ongoing encouragement for the book and my work generally, reviving my morale with her excellent advice as did Alexander Dent and Susan Tratner.

I am especially grateful to my colleagues at NYU's Tandon School of Engineering, where I taught feminist science and technology studies and digital anthropology as an adjunct in the Technology, Culture and Society department from 2019–2021. Danya Glabau, director of the Science and Technology Studies program, provided me a scholarly home as I juggled revising the book, teaching, consulting, and parenting. Mona Sloane invited me to collaborate with her on a digital ethnography of the 2020 pandemic in New York City and has been a font of excellent advice, not to mention panache. Both have modeled scholarly and personal generosity, and I could not wish for better coconspirators.

This book owes its existence in no small part to Roger Sanjek, a gracious mentor whose interest in my research revived my commitment to it, when I despaired of finding a place in academia. Roger reached out when seeking contributors for his volume on ethnography in a digital era, *eFieldnotes: The Makings of Anthropology in the Digital World* (2017), and shared the initial manuscript with Peter Agree at the University of Pennsylvania Press. Roger and Peter infused the work with their confidence in its worth and steered it through the initial stages of proposal and review, although I did not ultimately publish with Penn. I am also grateful for the encouragement of Daniel Miller, who invited me to the 2016 book-launch workshop, "Issues in the Study of Social Media Today," for the University College of London series "Why We Post." My editor at Cornell, Jim Lance, took up this project after Penn Press was no longer able to publish it; his guidance and the reader reports he solicited clarified what I wanted to say and how to say it.

The work would not have been possible without the financial support of multiple funders, including the German DAAD, which supported ten months of dissertation fieldwork in Germany, and the Mellon Foundation, which funded my postdoctoral fellowship at Wesleyan, including a final fieldwork visit in January 2015.

No such undertaking is achievable without the grace and forbearance of friends and family. My academic coconspirator Jennifer Carlson can be found throughout many pages of this book, in spirit and, in a few places, in name. Her deft and evocative writing on everyday life, especially her attention to mood and ordinary objects, expanded my understanding of what ethnographic writing could be and could accomplish. I have also depended at every step on the wellspring of patience and love provided by my partner, Channing Moore, who probably knows more now about ethnographic theory than he ever wanted to know. My parents, Ross and Michael Kraemer, made this work possible through their unwavering support throughout the years, even when they deemed other paths more sensible. This work was bookended in some ways by my two children: Julian, who was born a little over four weeks after I received my PhD, and Eleanor, who was born while I was revising the manuscript in 2018, not long before I ended my academic job search. Their unbounded joy, mischief, and acceptance have been a balm during the darkest times and give me hope despite the seemingly insurmountable challenges in the world. I dedicate this work to my parents and to them.

MOBILE BERLIN

On a rainy night in March 2010, I stood outside the graffiti-plastered facade of
a prewar building in central Berlin—the art commune and nightclub Kunsthaus
Tacheles, where musicians I knew were performing. Tacheles, said to be Yiddish
for "straight talking," was founded when a group of artists occupied the abandoned building in the months after German reunification in 1990, saving it from
demolition. Built in the early twentieth century as an arcade and department
store (the Friedrichstrasse-Passage; Stewart 2002), the monumental building
housed an SS headquarters during the Nazi era and later a cinema, before falling
into disrepair in the 1970s. For the twenty-two years following the *Wende* (the
Change—that is, the fall of the Berlin Wall and eventual reunification of Germany from 1989 through 1990), Tacheles was home to scores of artists producing experimental, kitschy, or outsider art, featuring studios, event spaces, a café,
and a theater.[1] In many accounts, Tacheles symbolized the transitional period
after the Wende as one of openness, licentiousness, and experimentation, where
residents were committed to decidedly anticapitalist politics (Stewart 2002; Ward
2019). By the early 2000s, however, this period of *Zwischennutzung* (transitional
use) in repurposed spaces was ending, being replaced by feelings of loss and
nostalgia—not unlike the nostalgia for life in the former East in the 1990s (Berdahl 1999). By 2009, the surrounding neighborhood of Berlin-Mitte had transformed dramatically from a gentrifying area known for quirky shops, cafés, and
art galleries to an upscale district of international chains, glossy high-rises, and
boutique hotels. According to Alex, the DJ and promoter who had invited me,

Tacheles was no longer cool or authentic—club nights there attracted "tourists" looking for an imagined version of Berlin long since gone.[2]

That night, I ducked into the building's main foyer to get out of the rain and checked Facebook for directions to the show. The event page directed me up a flight of worn concrete stairs, layered with graffiti art. At the entrance, I found Alex standing with a small knot of people. He gestured for me to come inside to a table where another friend, Pascal, sat collecting the entrance fee. It was after 1:00 a.m., and the headlining performers had yet to take the stage. I circulated in the capacious, unfinished space, reminiscent of the underground parties of twenty years prior,[3] and found a musician I knew, Viktor, preparing for his set. Viktor, Alex, Pascal, and others, such as Annika, a studio artist, and Friederike, a freelance photographer, were close friends, part of what they called a *Freundeskreis* (friend circle). Some had met growing up in West Berlin; others became friends during university or since moving to former East Berlin. Most had joined Facebook within the past year or so, and it had become a key site for articulating local and translocal connections.

By the late 2000s, Berlin was undergoing a further transition: the accelerated urbanization of an emerging "knowledge" class and the rise of social media. I begin here, in the middle of the once-divided city, to chart the relationship between emerging media and the making (and unmaking) of social space at multiple scales. Berlin once symbolized Europe's Cold War divides between capitalist West and socialist East, as well as state socialism's later collapse, the city as synecdoche for the nation's sundering and rejoining and for the larger project of European supranationalism (Partridge 2012; Borneman and Fowler 1997; Boyer 2005; Bunzl 2005). But by the early twenty-first century, for younger middle-class residents in this and other friend circles, Berlin equally constituted a site of cosmopolitan connection and transnational aspiration associated with networked digital media. Social media, like Berlin, were seen as hip places to participate as urban, middle-class Germans and other EU Europeans. Social media, in conjunction with mobile networking, brought together collective formations at different spatial scales—from local ways of living to regional practices and national subjectivities—in new configurations. Despite the global, often placeless imagery associated with the internet, social media reworked experiences of the city and of German and European identity in ways linked to class and broader economic transformations.

This book charts a period from 2007 to 2015, during the late capitalist transition to an information economy (e.g., Florida 2004; Castells 1996), when many young people moved to Berlin as part of this nascent knowledge or "creative" class.[4] Berlin in the early 2000s attracted young people from many parts of the world, including students, visitors, "club" tourists (Garcia 2013b, 2016), and migrant workers (such as Indian information technology [IT] workers, Amrute 2015), who often got by through flexible and informal work. My account focuses on these mobile young Germans and other EU Europeans, largely but not exclusively white, composing a segment of this emerging creative class. Many aligned themselves with Berlin's countercultural legacies, such as underground art and music scenes. Young people from both western and eastern Germany moved to still-gentrifying central districts of Berlin such as Kreuzberg in the former West and Friedrichshain in the former East, where regional and class distinctions continued to shape social life.[5] Newfound mobility, especially for those from small towns, accompanied the adoption of incipient social network sites like Facebook (which became widely accessible in 2007), along with smartphones and other mobile media. Like Berlin, social and mobile media were associated with new forms of spatial and social mobility, particularly transnational circuits of popular culture such as indie and electronic music. These technologies were equally linked to capital's mobility through an influx of developers, internet start-ups, and a new class of techies and freelancers seen by some as threatening Berlin's countercultural, often anticapitalist ethos (Bauer and Hosek 2019).

Urban and digital spaces alike became new sites of contestation over class mobility and identity at multiple spatial scales, generating new mobilities. In this context, social and mobile media reconfigured these spaces and scales by entwining local, national, and transnational formations and selves, bringing Berlin ways of living online while integrating transnational linkages into the spaces of the city. Berlin's *Weltoffen* (cosmopolitan, literally "world-open") ethos drew these mobile, often counterculturally minded young people, for whom both Berlin and social media were sites of cosmopolitan mobility and interconnection. But Berlin's reputation for creativity and tolerance equally laid the groundwork for postunification investment and development that drove up housing costs. In consequence, many residents moved out of these central districts, which many had viewed as "voids" during the first years after the Wende (Huyssen 1997). Not long after that night at Tacheles, investors approached the artists and squatters to entice them to leave. By 2012, the remaining occupants were evicted by the city government.[6] As this book recounts, the scalemaking projects of the late twentieth century fused imaginaries of technology, particularly networked media technologies, with the scale-expanding imaginaries of late capital: a vision of world peace and economic cooperation through digital global interconnection. In Berlin, scalar transformations were lived out through ordinary practices—online and copresent—that reconfigured daily sociality, translocal encounters, new forms of mobility, and experiences of urban space. Against teleological visions of scale expansion, I argue that media technologies, situated at the nexus of materiality and signification, reworked space and place, fashioning emergent scales like the global and supranational yet ultimately enabling their breakdown and potential for European disintegration and illiberalism.

Emerging Media and the New Berlin

I arrived in the fall of 2009 in time for the twentieth-anniversary celebrations of the *Mauerfall* (the fall of the Berlin Wall in 1989). Since reunification in 1990, the divided city had undergone extensive reconstruction to attach the two halves (the three former Allied sectors and a fourth Soviet sector), demolishing much of the Wall and combining the dual transit systems.[7] By the late 1980s, many buildings and spaces had been neglected or abandoned, from nineteenth-century apartment buildings (*Altbauen*) pockmarked by bullet holes to the infamous Death Strip. In the first years after the Wall came down, many Berliners (from East and West) left en masse, largely for work in West Germany. Questions of ownership and jurisdiction meant that the status of many buildings was ambiguous (Ward 2019; Sark 2019). An influx of West German capital began to transform the spaces of the Wall, reconnecting the city and reestablishing Berlin as the capital of the New Germany. During much of the late 1990s, the city center was under construction, from cranes for the glittering high-rises of Potsdamer Platz to the razed German Democratic Republic (GDR) Palace of the Republic (Huyssen 1997; Boym 2008; Sark 2019). This destruction was seen as necessary for engendering the "New" Berlin and the reunified nation's capital, evacuating and then filling in what Andreas Huyssen called the "voids of Berlin," empty spaces available for creative appropriation (Huyssen 1997). This metamorphosis from marginal borderland to global metropolis intensified experiences of gentrification and contributed to perceptions that the city's center was shifting (Bauer and Hosek 2019, 2).

The rubric of scalemaking calls attention to the broader spatial processes at stake in stitching together the bifurcated city or fashioning the supranational institutions and regulatory regimes of the European Union. The transition to the New Berlin took place in the context of larger temporal and spatial shifts in Europe, especially the project of post–Cold War European integration and the expansion of the European Union (Goddard, Llobera, and Shore 1994). As Helga Leitner (1997) argues, the history of European integration, particularly the EU, represents a contestation over the scale of supranational institutions and policies, such as those governing citizenship and migration. The postwar era in western Europe saw the formation of predecessor institutions to the European

Union, such as the European Economic Community, while the economic policies of the then newly established World Bank and International Monetary Fund
underpinned the globe-spanning "world economy" of the postimperial era. This
world economy entailed the global circulation of capital over a system of interde-
pendent nation-states, a shift from the German economic theory of ordoliberalism, which operated at the level of the nation, to the neoliberal propositions of
Friedrich Hayek and other economists who envisioned an economic constitution
at the scale of the world (Slobodian 2018).[8]

Digital media technologies have been construed as a key means of compress-
ing space and time for these scalemaking projects (Harvey 1989), by enabling
global flows of communication (Appadurai 1996; Castells 1996; Urry 2000; but
cf. Tsing 2000). Few ethnographic studies, however, have examined how emerging media practices shape the mobile, urban middle class organized around
creative knowledge work, such as my interlocutors in Berlin. The centrality of
media to placemaking has been documented in extensive scholarship, going back
to twentieth-century histories of nationalization and mass media (e.g., Gellner
1983), most notably Benedict Anderson's *Imagined Communities* ([1983] 1991).
While some scholars of media and globalization predicted that digital technologies would give rise to supranational and global imaginaries (from McLuhan's
[(1964) 2003] "global village" to Castells's "space of flows"; see also Morley and
Robins 1989), the practices I observed countered narratives of spatial scales
expanding from local to national to global. Social and mobile media, rather than
superimposing new transnational identities on local spaces, reworked the meaning and experience of local, regional, and national connections in everyday life.
Cultural geographers such as Neil Brenner (1998, 2001) argue that geographic
scale itself (such as the "local" versus the "global") entails social constructions
of space, linked to the circulation of capital and its dominant territorial form,
the nation-state. In this book, I tack between digital or online spaces (primarily
social media) and copresent or "actual" spaces (Boellstorff 2012) through which
my interlocutors moved (homes, parks, cafés, music events, schools, or work-
places), to map the scalemaking practices that interwove online mobilities with
copresent ones.

In this book, I locate these emerging media practices in their everyday, material specificity. Where media technologies are often imagined as forging global
and transnational linkages, I show instead how they reworked experiences of the
city and how the city reworked life online. Historians and anthropologists have
long charted Berlin's many transformations as contested sites of placemaking,
from the upheavals of the Wende (Weszkalnys 2010, 15; Berdahl 1999; Borneman 1992; Huyssen 1997; Boym 2008) to struggles over citizenship, race, and
class, especially in the context of global migration (e.g., Mandel 2008; Partridge

2012, 2013; Amrute 2015), and the arc of gentrification and displacement since the early 2000s (Bauer and Hosek 2019; Sark 2019; Ward 2019). The fall of the Wall had symbolized the failures of Soviet socialism, as Daphne Berdahl (2000, 1) argued, underpinning narratives of "capitalist 'triumphalism'" and a forward march toward market societies (see also Verdery 1996). The city's (and nation's) reunification in this context was often framed as inevitable, part of capital's territorial expansion, enabled by new technologies and necessary for a future of peace and cooperation. As Katherine Verdery contends in her work on European postsocialism, 1989 marked not the beginning of a transition from socialism to capitalism and democracy but a transformation of actually existing economic practices and political institutions that would reorder the world spatially and temporally, in "a thoroughgoing reorganization of the globe" (1996, 16).

For many in Berlin and East Germany after the Wende, reunification was experienced not as a conjoining of equal halves but as a western takeover or annexation that consigned East Germany to the past. Gina Weszkalnys describes this period in Berlin as a "profound temporal and spatial upheaval" (2010, 15; see also Borneman 1992, 319; Kilborn 1993). In Daphne Berdahl's ethnography of an East German border village in the 1990s, the Cold War boundary (what many Germans call the "Mauer im Kopf," the Wall in the mind) persisted long after the physical barriers came down. Life in East Germany was described in temporal terms as *früher* (earlier) or *damals* (back then), terminology I heard used by those who had grown up in East Germany for a devalued past often associated with embarrassment and backwardness. In Berdahl's account, borders—metaphorical or literal—helped generate national identities, themselves a site of creative cultural production where identity is fluid and processual rather than split or fragmented (Berdahl 1999). These ethnographies of postsocialist Europe contradict linear, teleological narratives of scale expansion and unification that naturalize the relationship between technology and globalization.

In this context, the New Berlin entailed not just a rejoining of segmented halves but an economic transformation into a late capitalist "creative city," enabled by mobile, tech-savvy knowledge workers who were often imagined as laptop-toting freelancers. Huyssen's "city of voids" rapidly disappeared as sites like Alexanderplatz and Potsdamer Platz were rebuilt, instigating new contestations over public space. Alexanderplatz, a plaza and transit hub in East Berlin and the site of the iconic Soviet television tower, the *Fernsehturm*, became central to tensions in urban planning between socialist and capitalist world-making projects, which asserted competing understandings of space and time (Weszkalnys 2010, 17). Weszkalnys describes how "imagineers," a new class of designers, such as developers, journalists, and academics, displaced city planning professionals in urban planning. In

Alexanderplatz's redesign, neoliberal governance worked through the ordering of urban space and a reimagining of the social, in negotiation with city officials, planners, activists, community groups, and inhabitants, for whom planned space and lived reality did not always align (17; see also MacDougall 2011).

Berlin's reunification had taken place under the signs of freedom, peace, and unity, all on display at the twentieth-anniversary Mauerfall celebrations. These symbols aligned Berlin's spatial reordering with the scalemaking projects of national unification and European integration (the European Union was established a few years after the Wall fell, in 1993). But, as scholars like Damani Partridge maintain, rhetorics of freedom and universal rights excluded noncitizens, including Turkish Germans denied citizenship under guest worker regulations and Muslim and nonwhite residents, such as Black Germans (many with legal citizenship). Government regulation of citizens, especially through biopower, produced racialized noncitizens, not only through juridico-legal means but through cultural and bodily practices, as Partridge (2012) argues. Partridge terms these practices "exclusionary incorporation" to analyze the limits of citizenship and tolerance, in the context of nationalization and supranationalism predicated on "universal" rights—in Germany, white East and West Germans equally gained citizenship rights, as did non-German EU citizens, to a degree. The same processes that produced white Germans as national subjects rendered nonwhite *Ausländer* nonnormal, from the hypersexualization of Black men to the sexual unavailability of veiled Muslim women, denying them forms of care and life accessible to citizens.

The shift to knowledge work in the early 2000s equally made visible new forms of racialization through economic ordering, as Sareeta Amrute details in *Encoding Race, Encoding Class* (2015). A visa program in 2002 paved the way for migrant Indian tech workers who simultaneously embodied racialized outsiders and aspired to be middle-class subjects in the diaspora, appearing as both threatening migrants and emblems of Germany's globalized "technological modernity" (Amrute 2015, 6–7). Despite the imagery of knowledge work as cognitive and disembodied, Indian workers inhabited racially marked bodies, through which postgenomic understandings of race were marshaled to justify their suitability to IT work. Indian tech workers instead refused their position in these coding economies, resisting the neoliberal organization of work and life. As Partridge and Amrute both show, citizenship and knowledge work are structured by race and class, rendering digital technologies and spatial mobility sites of such contestations. Berlin has occupied a central place in German postwar imaginaries in which a cosmopolitan, postnationalist identity was necessary to move past National Socialism and forge a modern multicultural democracy (Mandel 2008). According to Ruth Mandel, Berlin in particular has been semiotically overdetermined as a site of renewed German cosmopolitanism: "It represents an experiment in the making of a distinctive German national narrative through the (re) constitution of a late- or even postmodern cosmopolitan city" (2008, 5).

As Mandel and others contend, Berlin has long served as a hub of cosmopolitanism and bohemian counterculture, since at least the Weimar era of the 1920s (Mandel 2008; Bauer and Hosek 2019). For some Germans, however, the guest workers (*Gastarbeiter*, predominantly Turkish Ausländer not eligible for citizenship) who arrived in the 1960s and made possible the postwar "economic miracle" (*Wirtschaftswunder*), particularly Muslims who have become Europe's current Other (Boyer 2005; Bunzl 2005), were seen as threatening German identity. Turkish Germans in Mandel's ethnography conceived of themselves as creative transnationals, part of a legitimate national minority, rather than as outsiders. Despite Turkish Germans' experiences of transnational mobility, discussions of German cosmopolitanism frequently focus on white European youth and creative professionals. Constructions of class identity in the 2000s in Berlin must be understood in this context, in which knowledge or cognitive work is often associated with unmarked, white bodies.

In this context of renewed German cosmopolitanism and postnational European citizenship, emerging technologies entailed and intersected with new forms of social and spatial mobilities. Transnational mobility (for some) eased further through the Schengen Agreement in 1985, allowing some EU and European citizens to travel without visas.[9] But forging the New Berlin meant, ultimately, building over the open spaces of the 1990s to make way for new high-rises and luxury condos, emptying squats and art communes like Tacheles, and establishing the city as a new site for investment and tech start-ups. By 2009, a new nostalgia was crystallizing for the early days after the Wende, a period Katrina Sark dubs "Babylon Berlin": "Berlin's nostalgic turn emerged in response to the systematic gentrification and rebranding of the city throughout the 1990s and 2000s, the gradual disappearance of its open spaces, and the increasing impossibility of utopian dreams, desires, and longing for alternative modes of existence and creativity in a globalized and reconstructed city" (2019, 26).

In Sark's view, it was this "pioneer" phase in the 1990s, seen in retrospect as a time of limitlessness, openness, and creativity, that generated Berlin's cultural capital. The arrival of "hipsters" in the late 2000s was seen by some as "the end of an era" (Sark 2019, 37), in which the punk and anarchist squatting cultures of the 1990s were replaced by "branding culture and the creative economy of the New Berlin" (39). *Time* magazine in 2009 declared "Hip Berlin" to be "Europe's Capital of Cool."[10] Berlin had been poised in its refashioning to capitalize on the new information economy, as Boym notes in her ruminations on nostalgia. In the late 1990s, she reflects, Berlin was on the brink of metamorphosizing through incipient digital technologies, becoming a "capital for the second millennium" that was "for some ten years the most virtual city in the world" (2008, 176–78).

Digital Placemaking among Mobile Youth

Like Berlin, social media were viewed by many in my research as hip spaces for cosmopolitan and transnational connection. The friend circles I studied were part of this emerging creative class, but many expressed ambivalence about Berlin's transition from countercultural borderland to "capital of cool," an ambivalence often aimed at those they perceived as tourists or hipsters. Most had recently arrived in central Berlin, except for a core of friends who had grown up in former West Berlin. Annike and Rike, for example, had gone to secondary school together and were now living in Kreuzberg, where Annike lived out of her art studio, while Rike pursued freelance photography. Their circle comprised mainly young people from West Berlin or West Germany and "EU-Ausländer" linked by shared interests in art and electronic music subcultures, such as Alex, a DJ and grad student; Viktor, a musician from Denmark; and David, who ran a record shop. These smaller friend circles were connected to broader networks in places like Amsterdam and Copenhagen; in chapter 1, I frame these connections as translocal for the ways they spanned localities. A second friend circle was living in East Berlin districts like Prenzlauer Berg and Friedrichshain after having grown up together in Saxony-Anhalt, a rural region in former East Germany. They maintained close ties to friends and family in the regional capital, Magdeburg, and in small rural villages where their families lived. Shared regional origins shaped the contours of this circle and their larger networks, but they were similarly enthusiastic about Berlin's nightlife; that was especially true for Jörg, a DJ and music journalist, and Sabine, also a music journalist. For this circle, both Berlin and social media were places to meet Ausländer and participate in life as hip, urban Germans.

Along with placemaking practices in Berlin, nascent social and mobile media shaped the construction of this emergent middle class. The broader media landscape or ecology (Gershon 2010; Madianou and Miller 2013) changed rapidly in Germany during the period of my fieldwork. From 2000 to 2010, the number of households in Germany with a computer doubled, from 47.3 percent to 85.7 percent. Similarly, the number of self-reported Internet users over age 14 grew from 37 percent in 2001 to 72 percent in 2010, reaching 94 percent in 2023, a much steeper rise in the first decade of the century than in the second. From 2000 to 2010, the number of inhabitants with a mobile cellular subscription more than doubled as well, from 48.2 percent to 109 percent (that is, there were more subscriptions than people), leveling off at 125 percent by 2023. Fewer of these subscriptions included mobile broadband, however, which did not become widely accessible until after my fieldwork, and relatively few people had fixed broadband internet in their households.[11] These numbers illustrate that, over the course of the 2000s, internet and mobile phone access increased dramatically. At the same time, social media sites (platforms and services organized around content sharing and interlinked personal profiles)[12] like Facebook, MySpace, and Twitter gained popularity rapidly in Germany, as in much of the world (see D. Miller et al. 2016). Facebook became the most popular among young people, displacing previous sites like MySpace. Facebook's market share in Germany jumped from 11 percent in May 2009 to over 63 percent in December 2009, while MySpace dove from 23 percent to nearly 0.[13] By 2014, 72 percent of German residents had a Facebook account, and 45 percent had used it within the past month.[14]

In some ways, this book is a study of urban youth culture and countercultural "cool" during this transitional period in Berlin, but my approach departs from prior framings of youth subcultures. Many of the young Germans and Europeans in my research were participants in alternative, countercultural lifestyles or "scenes" that were more amorphous and porous than the punk, mod, or Teddy Boy subcultures described by Stuart Hall, Tony Jefferson, Paul Willis, Dick Hebdige, Angela McRobbie and others of the Birmingham School in the 1960s and 1970s. Rather than focus on style—which varied greatly within the same friend circles—I track clusters of friends across online and copresent contexts. For Hall and others, youth style was a site of resistance to class domination, but for this burgeoning knowledge class, aesthetic tastes and practices were more often ways of participating in hip cultural circuits associated with digital worlds and translocal music scenes—that is, of aspiring to cosmopolitan connections as urban Europeans. Their media practices parallel those of other middle-class youth documented by anthropologists, such as youth in Hanoi for whom social media produced new public spaces to articulate emergent forms of political agency (Geertman and Boudreau 2018), multiethnic young Muslims in Chicago for whom Black culture in the United States is a source of cool that allows racialized Arabs and South Asians to resist US racial hierarchies (Khabeer 2016), or young Indonesians articulating cosmopolitan identifications through *bahasa gaul*, an emergent youth language linking coolness to social and economic mobility (Smith-Hefner 2007). These studies draw on anthropological approaches that take youth as a flexible cultural category (e.g., Wulff and Amit 1995; Bucholtz 2002; Durham 2004), framing media and cultural consumption as central to the construction of emergent middle-class youth culture (e.g., Liechty 2003; Luvaas 2010).

Prior ethnographic studies of youth culture and online fan communities have demonstrated the multiplicity of social connections in digital spaces and described how participants navigate tensions between relationships grounded in shared interests and those linked to place (e.g., Baym 2010; boyd 2014; Gray 2009). New media technologies have, historically, incited new anxieties and ambivalences, especially about youth, and disrupted existing social arrangements (e.g., Marvin 1990; Briggs and Burke 2009). Anthropologists and science and technology studies scholars have repeatedly shown that new media do not emerge as stable artifacts but instead represent new arrangements or assemblages of peoples, objects, and practices—products of rather than precursors to social relations (Latour 1993; Bijker, Pinch, and Hughes 1989; MacKenzie and Wajcman 1999; Escobar et al. 1994). Many social media scholars have been attentive to these anxieties, particularly to moral panics around youth, showing instead how youth creatively appropriate emerging media (e.g., Ito et al. 2010).

Social network sites like Facebook were designed to articulate and enhance social networking and social capital (boyd and Ellison 2008; boyd 2008; Donath 2007; Wellman 2001; Humphreys 2007). While some early studies of social media considered the potential benefits of generating social capital for users (e.g., Haythornthwaite 2005; Ellison, Steinfield, and Lampe 2006, 2007, 2011; D. Williams 2006), others quickly recognized that such benefits largely accrue to those who already have it (Hargittai and Hinnant 2008; Zillien and Hargittai 2009). Critics of social media have increasingly analyzed interactivity and participation online as new, often gendered modes for extracting value from users' unpaid labor (e.g., Jarrett 2016; Fuchs 2010). Other social media scholars analyzed distinctions between geographic and interest-based communities (e.g., Ellison, Steinfield, and Lampe 2006), while recent literature attends to the role of digital media in everyday placemaking. Critical and ethnographic approaches emphasize situating media practices in their everyday contexts, calling attention to how actual places, such as urban space, are constructed through such practices. Media technologies contribute to shaping class formations (Weidman 2010; Berger, Funke, and Wolfson 2011; Chesluk 2004), producing the local through news media (Udupa 2012), developing urban imaginaries (Melhuish, Degen, and Rose 2016), transforming ways of moving through urban space (Humphreys 2010; Hjorth and Pink 2014; Licoppe 2016), and generating the "digital city" (Halegoua 2020).

This book situates emerging media in placemaking practices among this nascent middle class in Berlin to examine reconfigurations of selfhood and sociality at contingent geographic levels. Accounts of digital and social media sometimes distinguish between "place-based," or geographic, social networks and virtual communities and collectives formed around shared tastes or interests (e.g., Ellison, Steinfield, and Lampe 2006, 2011; Ellison, Lampe, and Steinfield 2009; Baym 2010; see also Bernal 2014), although this perspective has shifted as social and mobile media have become more integrated into daily life. As anthropologists, historians, and cultural geographers have explored, building on the work of LeFebvre (1991) and others on the social production of place, especially urban and public space (e.g., Low 2000, 2009, 2017), media equally contribute to diverse experiences of place and placemaking. Setha Low (2014, 35), for example, argues that place and space are constructed—and contested—in ideologically, power-laden ways.

In contrast to those who predicted that global or transnational media would destabilize national selfhood and identities (e.g., Morley and Robins 1989), I explore ways that emerging media are neither placeless nor deterritorializing but instead refigure place-based identities at multiple geographic scales. Prior studies of mass media have shown repeatedly that film, radio, television, advertising, recorded music, and the internet contribute to new ways of participating in the imagined community of the nation (Abu-Lughod 2005; Bernal 2014; Mankekar 1999; Mazzarella 2004; Spitulnik 1996; see Anderson [1983] 1991). For my interlocutors, social media in Berlin frequently offered new means of enacting cosmopolitan selfhood as urban Germans (or other Europeans). Although digital media sometimes evoke rhetorics of placelessness or disembodiment (such as William Gibson's fictional conception of cyberspace in *Neuromancer*), many scholars examine ways that space, place, and bodies are constituted online (e.g., Boellstorff 2008; Dibbell 1999; Hayles 1999; Stone 1991; Stryker 2000). Feminist approaches to digital embodiment, for example, contend that communication technologies enable new forms of virtuality. Sandy Stone (1991) argues that the interactional possibilities of networked spaces reconfigure the boundaries between matter and information and between bodies and semiosis (see also Kraemer 2021b), while Katherine Hayles (1999) examines how digital texts are no more or less material than analog ones, but differ in their material qualities.

Just as digital technologies can be sites of embodied materiality, they can equally constitute real places. Tom Boellstorff's (2008, 2012) account of the immersive virtual world Second Life demonstrates how indexical relationships—through linguistic signs that point to or reference shared reality—render online worlds places in their own right: "The spatially and temporally specific social realities are no longer limited to the physical world; the processes of moving through space and establishing common grounds can now take place online as well as offline. Confronted with multiple embodiments, and thus with indexical *fields of reference* that are multiple in a new way, we thereby face the virtual as an emergent set of social realities that cannot be straightforwardly extrapolated from the physical world" (2012, 52).

Social media differ from online or virtual worlds because they enable movement between social connections and formations at multiple geographic levels, generating these scales in the process. This book, then, asks how emerging media practices produced social spaces online and offline in ways that produced—and reconfigured—the spatial scales of everyday life, from the local of Berlin to translocal music scenes and cosmopolitan forms of nationalism, in the context of European integration.

Methods

My primary field site, or sites, comprised friend groups of young people who had moved to central neighborhoods of Berlin like Kreuzberg and Friedrich-shain in the early 2000s and who were increasing their time on social media like Facebook and Twitter. The research took place between 2007, when I began preliminary fieldwork in Berlin in July and August, and January 2015, when I revisited the friend circles documented in this book. I conducted sustained participant observation—that is, I closely observed and spent time with people in their daily lives—between October 2009 and July 2010. I had met some contacts at music festivals and in Berlin in 2007 and others through mutual friends connected to the same electronic and underground music scenes. In Berlin, I met up with the circle of music fans weekly, often multiple times a week, first at music events and art galleries and later at cafés and homes for small gatherings, dinners, or birthdays. I visited musicians in their home studios, accompanied one student to class, volunteered at a record shop, and attended another student's design exhibition. I also traveled to meet friends in the circle elsewhere in Germany and extended networks of music fans in Amsterdam and Copenhagen. I met my roommates, from rural Saxony-Anhalt, through a room-share website and was invited to join them in shared activities—weekly gatherings around the kitchen table, group meals, birthday dinners, weekend outings to parks or flea markets, and informal time at home. I also accompanied my roommates to visit their home village, where I met their families, and joined a music journalist on a work trip to Hamburg. Overall, I conducted nineteen semistructured interviews and five open-ended follow-up interviews, not to mention countless informal conversations. In interviews, I sought to understand how my research participants viewed these technologies and their role in their everyday lives, particularly how they thought about questions of identity and place. I asked about their use of digital technologies like social and mobile media, currently and in the past, their access to the internet and online spaces, the people they interacted with online, and their personal and professional interests.

Along with copresent fieldwork methods, I conducted extensive research in online or virtual contexts. I considered Facebook, and other online spaces, part of my field site and created a specific group to aggregate my contacts in Berlin and Europe in a single feed. I checked Facebook daily, typically throughout the day, and saved screenshots (first as images, later as complete files) for review and analysis. I followed the friend circles in Berlin and across Europe, including a group of primarily Dutch people in Amsterdam, on Facebook and also over chat (mainly Facebook Messenger and Skype). Facebook was the primary site of engagement among these friend circles, but some used Twitter, followed music blogs, shared their photography, or participated in online forums and boards (some of which were restricted and difficult to access). Anthropologists and other internet researchers have adapted and devised holistic ethnographic methods to study social life in networked and virtual contexts. Initial studies of virtual spaces reworked ethnographic methods for text-based contexts such as MUDs (multiuser dungeons, an early platform for immersive online worlds) and bulletin boards (e.g., Ito 1997; Escobar et al. 1994; Hakken 1993, 1999; see also Wilson and Peterson 2002). While some research, and popular rhetoric, construed online life as more mediated and less real than offline life, many anthropologists and internet ethnographers examined how digital technologies produced online worlds as separate "spaces or places *apart from* the rest of social life" (D. Miller and Slater 2000, 4; see also Hine 2000).[15]

As online media and internet technologies became more integrated into daily life for more people, especially from the early 2000s on, many researchers revised their methods to study online practices in situated contexts, "as continuous with and embedded in other social spaces" (D. Miller and Slater 2000, 5; see also Burrell 2012). As Gabriella Coleman observes: "To grasp more fully the broader significance of digital media, its study must involve various frames of analysis, attention to history, and the local contexts and lived experiences of digital media—a task well suited to the ethnographic enterprise" (2010, 488–89). Anthropologists also began contending broadly with the growing ubiquity of digital and online media in their field sites and in their own lives personally and professionally. My methodological approach combined classic ethnographic methods—sustained, immersive observation and participation, semi- and unstructured interviewing, and detailed daily field notes—with new approaches to studying online worlds as spaces in their own right (see Boellstorff 2008, 2012). I conducted online participant observation, which involved participating in the same online spaces as my interlocutors, like Facebook, where I could observe online activities, and created digital records such as screenshots of social media and other websites and chat logs, including materials I dub "digitalia" (Kraemer 2016, 127; see also Pink, Horst et al. 2016 on digital ethnography). Comparing practices I observed directly, on-screen and off, with people's descriptions of their activities provided further insight into experiences of placemaking through emerging technologies. I also included a time-diary study, although few people were able to participate in an intensive logging of their daily habits, and visited the Archiv für Alternativkultur at Humboldt University, where I examined independent media and do-it-yourself zines of West Berlin's alternative social movements. These works provided further context for the role of media in constructing communities and sociality at multiple scales in Berlin.

Remaining connected to online worlds back home, however, raised issues of what constitutes the "field" in digital ethnography, a tension I navigated by immersing myself in multiple connections online and in Berlin, parallel to the practices of those alongside whom I studied (see Kraemer 2016 for more in-depth discussion of navigating digital fieldwork methods). The field came to be constituted by my attention to it, as I often shifted between "home" and "the field" by switching between chat windows, between conversations with friends and family and those with research participants. Defining such participants was not clear-cut either, as I met potential interlocutors through friends and extended social networks. I only recognized partway through my fieldwork, for example, how central regional connections were to my roommates and their friends. I had set out to understand the relationship between emerging media and scalemaking, but the production of scales such as the regional was not immediately visible until I began reflecting on how place and identity were constituted among those I knew. For me and my interlocutors alike, digital technologies brought disparate social worlds into close proximity. In other ways, however, mutual proximity provided insight into online practices and understandings of space, such as mobile phone use at a party or the implicit content of a Facebook post that references a copresent interaction.

Scaling the Mobile City

The public commemoration of the twentieth anniversary of the Mauerfall, in November 2009, included a celebratory Festival of Freedom in front of the Brandenburg Gate, where the Wall had once run, a free public event with speeches by various political figures and music performances before a large crowd gathered on Pariser Platz. The festivities included a large art installation of enormous dominoes, approximately eight feet tall (about 2.5 meters), each individually painted by different students and artists.[16] Frequent themes included hearts, peace signs, the globe, and Berlin. On one domino was painted the words:

GEMEINSAM
GEGEN OST-WEST DENKEN
WIR SIND EIN
VOLK

[Together / Against East-West Thinking / We are one people]

FIGURE 1. Festival of Freedom dominoes. Photo by author, 2009.

Another showed a silhouette of a map of Berlin in blue, with the words for *freedom* in English, French, German, and Russian (after the four sectors of post-war Berlin), along with a peace symbol, white dove, German flag, rampant bear (mascot of the city), and heart. On the side of a third was a small picture of the globe, divided by a black line, underneath a bright red X. Above and below it read "Unsere Welt ist Geteilt," which can mean "our world is divided" but also "our world is shared." These images linked the territory of the city and imagery of the globe—as a whole—to peace, love, and freedom. Like the European Union, reunified Berlin symbolized scalar projects of unification and wholeness that would bring about future peace and prosperity. Near the end of the evening, the organizers began a countdown and, after a few false starts, set the wall of dominoes in motion. The crowd cheered, and fireworks exploded over the iconic gate.

These images of scalemaking evoked a teleology of scale expansion, charting an imagined course through history from alleged tribalism and parochialism to greater political and geographic unity, first through nationalism and supranationalism and then through global or transnational connection. Media technologies have been central to these visions of global peace and cooperation, as illustrated

FIGURE 2.   A Festival of Freedom domino. Photo by author, 2009.

by the fictional *Star Trek* universe. In the series, which features a liberal human-ist fantasy of the future inflected by Cold War politics, technological advances do away with struggles for resources and lead to a money-free, peaceful society dedicated to scientific exploration and cultural pluralism.[17] Earth becomes a uni-fied polity and, with three other advanced planetary civilizations (modeled on the four Allied powers after the Second World War), helps found the United Federation of Planets after a major interplanetary war. Like the European Union, the Federation expands over time to include more planets and eventually makes peace with a longtime enemy, the Klingon Empire, which stands in for the Soviet

Union. But as scholars of globalization remind us, the link between technology and scale is not given. Instead, as Anna Tsing writes:

> In these times of heightened attention to the space and scale of human undertakings, economic projects cannot limit themselves to conjuring at different scales—they must conjure the scales themselves. In this sense, a project that makes us imagine globality in order to see how it might succeed is one kind of "scale-making project"; similarly, projects that make us imagine locality, or the space of regions or nations, in order to see their success are also scale-making projects. The scales they conjure come into being in part through the contingent articulations into which they are pushed or stumble. In a world of multiple, divergent claims about scales, including multiple, divergent globalisms, those global worlds that most affect us are those that manage tentatively productive linkages with other scale-making projects. (Tsing 2005, 57–58)

Economic projects—such as the workings of global finance—are invested in conjuring this global scale for the circulation and accumulation of capital. Yet narratives of scale's expansion naturalize the connection between technology and territorial ordering and between identity and place.

This books tracks, in contrast, a multiplicity of scalemaking practices online and in Berlin to contest assumptions about the world-making tendencies of digital technologies. The following chapters examine ways that emerging media reworked local, regional, national, and transnational connections and ways of being for this nascent middle class, intensifying movements between social formations at different scales. Facebook, for example, brought together social worlds at multiple scales, under the sign of "Friendship," a US English term that did not translate seamlessly to German conceptions of *Freundschaft*. Where Facebook and other social network sites reworked social space online, mobile media such as smartphones transformed experiences of urban space in Berlin, facilitating dominant forms of middle-class atomized mobility yet also at times enacting shared, embodied, and collective ways of being mobile. The national scale did not disappear in these contestations over class, space, and identity but became increasingly imbricated in local, regional, and translocal connections: being a certain kind of urban middle-class German meant being online, enmeshed in translocal or transnational circuits. National selfhood was negotiated through language practices online, such as mixing national, regional, and online-specific ways of speaking and writing. National identity also took shape affectively through news-reading practices and other ways of being German, as an acceptable form of nationalism situated in hip, cosmopolitan Berlin. Next, I address how material media infrastructures structured scalemaking practices, belying fantasies of deterritorialized global connection and often requiring informal logistical labor to manage. Media infrastructure also shaped public space in Berlin through provisional and ad hoc ways of managing its unevenness. These media practices fostered unspoken forms of mutuality that recalled the tactics of Berlin's late-1990s underground cultures, comprising forms of creativity and experimentation that drove but also exceeded the workings of capital.

Chapter 1 begins with friend circles in Berlin for whom Facebook became a new site to articulate translocal and transnational connections. On Facebook, it was possible to inhabit local ways of living in the same online spaces where many pursued interests in music and maintained friendships that spanned multiple locales, constructing local, translocal, and regional communities and formations. Facebook's particular capacities—understood as Elisabetta Costa's "affordances-in-practice" rather than fixed technological features—intensified movements between different spaces, allowing people to alternate rapidly among contexts rather than necessarily collapsing them. But many also preferred Facebook to other social network sites—like one for German university students, Studi.vz, or previously popular US-based sites like MySpace—precisely because it was imagined as a transnational, cosmopolitan space. Rather than tack between the local and global online or foster a new transnational space for communication, social media practices in Berlin reworked translocal and transnational encounters, local experiences of place, and regional friendships, linking the perceived cosmopolitanism of Facebook or Twitter to life in Berlin.

While social media reworked everyday life online and in Berlin, mobile media—such as mobile devices and networks—reshaped, and were shaped by, ways mobile young people moved through urban space. In chapter 2, I examine the emerging forms of mobility, in the sense of culturally meaningful movement, that mobile media encoded and enabled—or foreclosed. The design of mobile handsets reflected normative understandings of late modern mobility as transnational and discretionary—the acceptable movement of legitimate, middle-class subjects, in contrast to the threatening mobility of labor migrants and war refugees. Smartphone apps such as recommendation services, fitness route mappers, or transit planners plotted class-specific ways of moving through the city. Yet, while mobile media recapitulated imaginings of capital's mobility as liquid (Sheller and Urry 2006) or quicksilver (Maurer 2000), mobile devices supported more collective forms of sociality by making the circles of friends available to one another. These alternative experiences of mobility contrasted with liberal constructions of personhood as discrete and indivisible. Many also perceived mobile phones, often called "Handys," as bodily extensions, social and communicative prostheses. Like prostheses, Handys could extend agency for some, yet such discourses glossed over forms of injury and disability the same technologies produced (Jain 1999; Goggin 2006) for those excluded from acceptable mobility—whether factory workers in the Global South, noncitizens, unauthorized migrants, the poor, or people with disabilities.

Along with shifting experiences of mobility and urban space, language practices were key to managing relationships and audiences at multiple scales, as I discuss in chapter 3. Many Germans and Europeans in Berlin, for example, spoke and posted in English, particularly in European varieties of global or "Euro" English. Euro English located music shows and events taking place in Berlin within transnational cultural circuits, rendering speakers hip and urban. At other times, informal speech registers, such as internet idioms or regional *Ostfälisch* speech, in English or German, referenced and fostered intimacy and closeness. Switching between platforms and language idioms—a practice similar to what Mirca Madianou and Daniel Miller (2013) term *polymedia*—made it possible to manage friends and publics at multiple levels of intimacy and scale. Language switching and mixing in these ways aligned users with different social worlds, from intimate circles to national publics and transnational connections. But on Facebook, originally an English-language site, German users navigated incommensurable translations between US conceptions of friendship—a range of social relationships of varying intensity—and *Freundschaft*, which many perceived as a more enduring, reciprocal bond. Despite this contrast, many young urban Germans preferred to negotiate diverse worlds on Facebook because, like Berlin, it represented a cosmopolitan, multiscalar space.

In chapter 4, I address in more detail how national forms of identity and belonging were transforming among young people in Berlin. Few young Germans and other Europeans articulated national identity verbally, describing themselves instead in nonnational or postnational terms (and nationalism in Germany was of course particularly fraught). But other ways of being and feeling German took shape online and in Berlin, linked to acceptable forms of national selfhood. Those who preferred Facebook for local and translocal friendships, for example, daily checked national news websites like *Spiegel Online* (while few read print news); French, Danish, and Dutch nationals similarly preferred national news sources. Among the friend circle from Saxony-Anhalt, some expressed discomfort with their rural East German origins, which they saw as backward or parochial. But when preparing communal meals during *Spargelzeit*, the springtime season for white asparagus, they enacted warm feelings toward *Heimat* (home). In these examples, reading national news, like eating German foods, incited acceptable if unspoken feelings of Germanness—an affective form of selfhood joined to the nation.

Chapters 5 and 6 turn to the material and regulatory infrastructures of media technologies that shaped space, place, and scale and the unique position of media technologies as both material and symbolic. Chapter 5 explores the uneven communications system that many people in my fieldwork managed in creative ways. A constellation of national regulatory policies, international licensing agreements, and municipal service providers could make it difficult to get online or access transnational media, from YouTube videos to foreign television programs. This chapter approaches these media infrastructures, from WLAN networks to copyright restrictions, as engagements with the lively, contingent materiality of routers, wires, and computing hardware. Rather than construe this materiality as durable, fixed, or constraining, I consider creative, tactical ways young people in Berlin managed and interpreted the limits—and possibilities—of geographically specific telecommunication systems. Some shared WLAN networks across multiple apartment floors, while others relied on mobile data "surfsticks" to get online inexpensively and without contracts (which require official forms of documentation and residence). Most young people streamed video illicitly to get around international licensing restrictions that prevented the legal streaming of music videos and foreign television shows in Germany, belying images of unfettered global flows. Navigating uneven infrastructure and new technologies, however, involved not just technical competence but new forms of managerial labor that I term *logistical labor*: increasingly bureaucratic work that emerging technologies bring into home life.

Ways of managing media infrastructures also shaped public space. In chapter 6, I link longtime ways of getting by in Berlin to public and semipublic media practices that produced new experiences of urban space. In the days after the Wende, and to some degree before, young people in Berlin had repurposed abandoned and neglected spaces for art communes and dance parties, improvising ad hoc media setups and sound systems. By 2009, most underground dance parties were indeed licit, although venues like Tacheles continued to cultivate the rough, unfinished aesthetics of the 1990s. But other semi-licit events, like a warehouse showing of an indie foreign film or the projection of the 2010 World Cup matches on a sidewalk in Kreuzberg, reprised these tactics in repurposing public space. Similar tactics like guest-listing—getting friends and contacts into events for free—fostered feelings of mutuality in underground nightlife scenes, which cohered temporarily in a fluid solidarity Luis-Manuel Garcia (2013a) terms "liquidarity." Together, creative and improvisational ways of consuming media remade experiences of public space, locating translocal music scenes in Berlin or, conversely, making national sentiment acceptable in hip, urban, cosmopolitan settings. Media infrastructures also reasserted the national scale in other ways, such as through national subsidiaries of mobile service providers. Everyday media practices thus generated new geographic formations that were fleeting, embodied, and tenuous, cohering only temporarily.

One theme this book treats in less depth is how gender structured social media practices in relation to scalemaking. Gendered practices became evident in how research participants understood themselves as appropriate subjects of techno-logical expertise in chapters 1 and 5 and in how they expressed affect—for exam-ple, when preparing seasonal white asparagus (*Spargel*) together (in chapter 4). I analyze these questions in depth elsewhere, largely because they surfaced sepa-rately from this book's focus on space, place, and scalemaking. Social media—and technology generally—were key sites for enacting and encoding understandings of gender, and many of those in my fieldwork contested normative articulations of masculinity or femininity through online practices (see Kraemer 2021a). The interface design of platforms like Facebook and Twitter, for example, encoded implicitly gendered design idioms, such as cool color palettes and angular fonts associated in some design literature with masculinity, even as they presented themselves as putatively neutral social spaces. These design choices recapitulated ways technology has historically been constituted as a site of masculine compe-tence, excluding women and expressions of acceptable femininity. Image-based sites like Etsy or Pinterest, in contrast, were marked as domains of feminine domesticity, representing a shift not only to visual communication but to visual modes of interaction. Many young people in my research rejected hegemonic notions of gender, but social media became a site where gender itself was consti-tuted and stabilized, defining what it meant to be a cosmopolitan young man or woman. Additionally, I argue that gender itself was produced through interac-tions with digital technologies as material interfaces that reworked the relation-ship between the virtual and the material (Kraemer 2021a, 2021b).

By the time I returned to Berlin in 2015, the world had changed again, as the epilogue details. The sovereign debt crisis brewing during my fieldwork in 2009–10 had been partly stanched, with Germany agreeing to an EU bailout of Greece, but at the cost of draconian austerity measures that chipped away at Greece's and other nations' social welfare systems. Many more people had begun using social media in the early 2010s, with platforms like Facebook and Twitter becoming popular among older adults in the United States and Europe and among diverse users internationally.[18] In 2011, multiple new social movements, such as the Arab Spring uprisings in Egypt, Tunisia, and Libya (for example, Abu-Lughod 2012), took place on, or at least incorporated, Facebook and Twitter in highly visible ways. In Syria, attempts to overthrow authoritarian president Bashar Al-Assad ended in a violent crackdown and protracted, bloody civil war. Violence and instability in Syria, Iraq, and elsewhere in North Africa and the Middle East pushed many people to flee, leading to increasing numbers of refugees in Europe. At the time, many scholars and activists expressed optimism about the possibili-ties of social media for fomenting and supporting revolutionary change.

Social media practices began to change as well, in part because of attempts by Facebook and news media to monetize news-reading practices and to incorporate them into Facebook (especially on its mobile app, a primary way people visited the site). By 2015, far-right anti-immigrant sentiment was building. Campaigns like #PEGIDA (Patriotic Europeans against the Islamization of the West [Patriotische Europäer gegen die Islamisierung des Abendlandes]), an anti-Muslim protest movement, along with counterprotests, unfurled on Twitter and in public spaces in new ways, as I observed firsthand in the wake of the *Charlie Hebdo* shooting that January (see Kraemer 2016, 2017). Many of those I had known from 2009 to 2010 became motivated by these movements and began sharing politically charged news stories and commentary, protesting PEGIDA, and participating in refugee assistance efforts, often articulating a shared sense of Europeanness. In numerous follow-up interviews, however, I discovered that many of the close friend circles had dissolved. Some of the friends had become consumed by successful careers related to music, while others had moved in with new romantic partners and, in some cases, married and had children. The cost of living had also increased in central Berlin, as tech professionals moved in and wealthy foreign investors bought sleek new condos. New "sharing economy" services, like Airbnb and Uber, became widespread, correlating with both accelerating gentrification and increasingly precarious employment (Cansoy and Schor 2017; Cócola Gant 2016; Guttentag 2014; Rosenblat 2018). The following year, 2016, the United Kingdom voted to leave the European Union ("Brexit"), and a far-right, autocratic leader was elected president in the United States.[19]

The epilogue explores the idea that scalemaking processes are never inevitable or determined by technological change. The scales of the nation and the globe may have been forged in part by the circulation of capital. But, as this book shows, emerging social and mobile media participated in a multiplicity of place- and scalemaking projects. The knowledge workers described in this book were mobile not only because they moved through the city or traveled transnationally—in acceptable, class-specific ways—but because, on and through social media, they moved across multiple spaces, networks, and connections, both online and in Berlin. Berlin—like Facebook—became a multiscalar space of local living, translocal and transnational collectivities, and urban, cosmopolitan forms of nationalism. The city became mobile in new ways because, like the friend circles, it inhabited and forged—if temporarily—this multiplicity of ways of understanding and experiencing space.

By 2015, when I returned for a follow-up field visit, rising rents and new developments were driving out the artists who had arrived in the 1990s and early 2000s.[20] The city's population growth was comparable to that of much larger cities, and rents rose more than 80 percent between 2007 and 2017.[21] Berlin, as

Karin Bauer and Jennifer Hosek (2019) contend, was particularly susceptible to this pattern of renewal and gentrification precisely because the circumstances of its reunification left so many empty spaces for rebuilding. Spaces like Tacheles came to represent the transition from open and in-between (celebrated by some yet excluding many others) to passé, touristy, and commodified.[22] More broadly, the future of European integration and other liberal scalemaking projects remains in question today, exemplified by the United Kingdom's 2020 "Brexit" from the European Union. I hope to show here how the futures that media practices make possible depend on but are never fully determined by the cultural and economic contexts in which they are situated. Technology's role in scalemaking is a product of late capital's drive to naturalize its own expansion rather than any guarantor of a peaceful, equitable future.

LOCATING EMERGING MEDIA

When I arrived in Berlin in the fall of 2009 to begin fieldwork on emerging media practices, social media were popular primarily among teens and fan communities. Accordingly, I built on prior connections with circles of fans interested in underground and experimental electronic music, initially conceiving of my research as a study of these social networks online and in person. I arrived just before an annual music festival, Musikfest (a pseudonym), in a small town in western Germany, that was popular among these fans. Musikfest involved three days of live performances by industrial and electronic musicians, followed by all-night DJ sets. The event was small enough that attendees often became well acquainted and returned yearly. Most hailed from Germany, but some traveled from the Netherlands, the United Kingdom, France, or elsewhere in the European Union, and a few came from the United States. As at many linguistically diverse European events, English served as a common language. Although I had attended similar festivals before and exchanged email addresses or messenger handles with new acquaintances, I had rarely stayed in close contact with those I met.

This time, however, it quickly became clear that the media landscape had changed significantly since my initial fieldwork two years prior, in 2007. A US friend and DJ living in Berlin introduced me to some of his close friends, through whom I quickly met others, including a circle of friends from the Netherlands. It was not until after returning to Berlin, however, that I realized how pervasive social media—especially Facebook—had become in articulating social connections among these translocally dispersed fans. That evening, returning to the room I was subletting in central Berlin after meeting up with some of my new acquaintances, I discovered that a flurry of activity had taken place on my Facebook page, even though I had hardly logged in during the festival. An affable German DJ and promoter, Alex, had sent me a friend request (asking to be reciprocal Facebook contacts, *Freund* in German), followed by a request from Zach, a grad student from the United States studying Berlin's techno music scene. In my turn, I added Sal, an electronic music producer, and David, who owned a record shop, when their names came up in posts and comments about the festival. Other new acquaintances commented on my profile (at the time, my Facebook "Wall") and tagged me in videos and photos. When one musician tagged me and others in a video of his performance, I suddenly received numerous email notifications, one for every comment on the video. One person connected with me over email, but most activity was on Facebook.

Over the next few days, Musikfest attendees uploaded digital photos, tagged one another, and commented back and forth. Facebook became a place for this geographically dispersed collective of music fans to reinforce connections and friendships established during the event while integrating online activities into their daily interactions. Media are not new to music subcultures or fan communities, of course, nor are the ways that tastes structure friendships and relationships across multiple locales. But Facebook—and social media broadly—differed from prior media in its capacity to bring together collectives at different spatial levels, enabling more rapid switching or alternating between social contexts in the same online spaces. Facebook, combined with mobile media, brought translocal relationships into the same spaces where music fans and others posted updates about their daily lives, planned events with friends in Berlin, and interacted with smaller circles, often called *Freundeskreise* (friend circles), of close friends.

These capabilities intensify (and are produced by) the multiscalar complexity of social connections and capital's global circulation. Media technologies have long contributed to placemaking, accelerating communication across distance in ways that were foundational to the production of the modern nation in the eighteenth and nineteenth centuries, in Europe and elsewhere, and to these globalizing processes. Narratives of technological progress often link new technologies to the expanding scale of social and political organization, from local to national to global. But among these young people in Berlin, emerging media reworked local, national, and transnational connections in ways that interrupted narratives of global communication flows, remaking experiences of place. I approach the relationship between media and place here as a scalemaking project, a contingent way of ordering social space, rather than taking spatial or geographical scales as given. What does it mean to call into question the "local" or the "global" as ways of understanding space? If Facebook practices did not exclusively foster connections at expanding scales, how did they rework the local, translocal, regional, or other spatial assemblages? In what follows, I investigate how social media practices produced translocal music scenes online and in Berlin, enabled new ways of inhabiting "the local," and articulated regional connections. Facebook not only brought together spatial connections in new ways, it produced new experiences of space that linked the cosmopolitanism of life in Berlin to these emerging online worlds.

Scalemaking on/through Social Media

On a typical day, young people in the friend circles I followed posted updates about happenings in Berlin, musicians or albums, travel, and other aspects of daily life, commenting back and forth in ways that forged local and translocal connections. Alex, for example, praised a music show organized by David: "It was great to see so many lovely people gathered to celebrate Berlin's premier talent in bass. . . . The bike ride home towards the sunrise was just the sugar coating on an already perfect night:)." The next status update in my News Feed announced that "Sophie and two other friends commented on [Friend 1]'s status." Sal, who had performed at the event Alex mentioned, posted: "thank you Berlin! sleep well!" Another person asked for travel advice: "Hello traveler friends; can anyone give me some good advice where to stay and what to see when I'm in Tel Aviv?" Shortly thereafter, Alex posted for international apartment-finding recommendations: "Yo, facebook friends. Whats the most common (international) home-page for finding shared flats, like wg-gesucht.de in Germany? Besides Craigslist." Someone tagged Sal in a photo from his performance. Meanwhile, a close friend of his living in Hannover wrote about music: "Once again I have to tell you that I am deeply in love with a band called The Cure. Maybe you've heard of them already. Where's the mascara?" These updates all garnered various comments, mostly from close friends who commented frequently.

Since their inception, the internet and online media have supported fan communities and subcultures—that is, collectives or associations formed around shared interests, often in fringe or underground cultures. Initial research on online or virtual communities often concerned sites like the WELL (Whole Earth 'Lectronic Link), which predate the public internet (Rheingold 1993; Turner 2005). According to Fred Turner (2005), the WELL formed around shared countercultural interests in computers, homesteading, and tinkering—an electronic counterpart to counterculture figure Stewart Brand's Whole Earth Catalog (itself an early virtual community, albeit print based). By the early 2000s, as Nancy Baym recounts in her study of Swedish indie music fans, fan communities online were shifting from email lists, websites, and Usenet to social network sites like MySpace, blogs, and the online radio site Last.fm (Baym 2007).[1] She describes this shift as typifying what Henry Jenkins (2006) called "convergence culture," "in which popular culture materials and texts take form across multiple interlinked platforms," building a dispersed community through a network of sites and platforms (Baym 2007). Baym contends that the Swedish indie music scene was more "place based" than fandoms organized around global pop, because Swedish indie labels and bands primarily took place and performed in a cluster of Swedish cities. As indie music fans congregated on diverse online media, incorporating "a complex ecosystem of sites" such as blogs, social networks, discussion forums, and messaging and media-sharing platforms, the fan community became more dispersed and distributed. In Baym's view, this form of online community had "more in common with geographically place-based communities than previous online communities of interest" because they encompassed a variety of online spaces.

The experiences of my interlocutors, however, raise questions about what "place based" means, as social media brought connections at multiple scales into the same online spaces. Some studies of online communities initially contrasted "place-based" collectives linked by shared places like a college campus or neighborhood (e.g., Ellison, Steinfield, and Lampe 2006) with those linked by shared tastes or interests. Taste, however, especially consumer taste, is both a marker of and means to reproduce class distinctions (a thesis most famously elaborated by Pierre Bourdieu [1984]). Studies of youth culture—notably the theorists of the Birmingham school, such as Hall and Jefferson ([1975] 1993) and Hebdige (1979)—repeatedly demonstrate how consumer tastes entail and instantiate class difference. They described postwar British youth cultures such as Teddy Boys, mods, and punks as resisting class subjugation through style and performance, particularly through bricolage and pastiche (Hebdige 1979). For middle-class youth counterculture in the late 1960s, shared taste in music and style offered a means to form communities that rejected place-based identities and family networks, in the context of growing middle-class mobility. By the late nineties to the aughts, many alternative and underground music scenes comprised middle-class youth for whom taste structured community formation and reproduced class distinctions (e.g., Thornton's 1996 study of British dance club cultures; on situating music scenes, see Kruse 2003).

The class entailments of taste-based communities do not preclude shared geography, of course, nor are all music scenes middle class. Many early online fan communities were composed of middle-class users (DiMaggio et al. 2001; Pfaffenberger 1988; Porter 1997; Wilson and Peterson 2002); as danah boyd (2011b) argues, middle-class young people fled MySpace for Facebook precisely because of class- and race-based distinctions, a digital form of "white flight" instigated in part by growing access to online spaces.[2] For the friend circles in my research, music and related tastes reproduced and instantiated middle-class cosmopolitan aspirations to transnational worlds. Enacting this urban middle-class cultural belonging involved shared tastes and interests as well as linguistic competences (as I address in chapter 3), social media know-how, and, for some, fluency with music-production tools.

These friend circles, and the wider worlds in which they were enmeshed, were neither primarily place based nor primarily interest based; rather, they reconfigured the distinction between mutual connection grounded in geography, on the one hand, and that established by shared taste, on the other. Since the rise of social media, researchers have been grappling with the complex ways these platforms support multiple connections and relations. Where text-based multiuser dungeons (MUDs), bulletin boards, and immersive virtual worlds made possible online relationships and collectives (e.g., Boellstorff 2008), social network sites created new spaces to articulate existing friendships and other relationships. Where earlier studies distinguished between connections made online or offline (e.g., boyd and Ellison 2008; Ellison, Steinfield, and Lampe 2006), later research has called into question this distinction, as online and offline worlds increasingly overlapped (e.g. Ellison, Steinfield, and Lampe 2011, 2006; Subrahmanyam et al. 2008), such as through diverse "connection strategies" or ways of communicating (Ellison, Steinfield, and Lampe 2011, 874). Online communications in these studies comprise a diverse set of communicative practices, from the "lightweight interactions" that often characterize social media friendships to the multiple channels used by close friends, including messaging, video chat, and voice calls.

On social media, geographic multiplicity emerged in ways that neither shared geography nor shared tastes can account for fully. The features and capacities, sometimes called affordances, of social media coproduced this multiplicity. Scholars have proposed numerous affordances for social media, including programmability, popularity, connectivity, and datafication (Van Dijck and Poell 2013); persistence, visibility, spreadability, and searchability, in the context of teen use (boyd 2014; see also boyd and Ellison 2008); metavoicing (reacting to others' content), triggered attending, network-informed associating, and generative role taking, in the context of online knowledge sharing (Majchrzak et al. 2013); and "pervasive awareness" in relation to producing social capital (Lu and Hampton 2015; see also Bucher and Helmond 2019 for a review of social media affordances, such as social versus communicative affordances; Vertesi 2019). These affordances, often located in the technical and design features of social media, better support some practices and understandings over others.

Yet this notion of affordances—as an alternative to deterministic ways of thinking about technology's effects—does not adequately account for the diversity and complexity of social media practices around the world, as Elisabetta Costa (2018) and others argue (e.g., Miller et al. 2016). Costa contends that affordances take shape through interactions with technological interfaces rather than constituting immutable properties users must negotiate. In her research with Turkish young people on Facebook, she finds that, unlike in many US and European contexts, the architecture of the site did not merge disparate social worlds through "collapsed contexts" (boyd 2014, 30–31, more often termed *context collapse*). Instead, Costa's ethnographic subjects appropriated Facebook's privacy settings and other features to reproduce existing social divides. Rather than resisting an implicitly Western interface design, as "practices of resistance to a rigid architecture that constrains and limits its users" (Costa 2018, 3644), Turkish users interpreted their practices as normal and obvious and, on the contrary, expressed surprise that European users maintain single accounts under their legal names.

As Costa demonstrates, these diverse and sometimes unexpected ways of using social media require rethinking affordances as technical properties that facilitate some practices over others. She advocates instead refining understandings of affordances, seeing them instead as "situated patterns of usage," as she explains: "The concept of affordance has often been used to describe situated patterns of usage within particular Anglo-American social contexts, as if they were stable properties of a platform. By contrast, my findings advocate for a perspective that views social media as a set of practices that cannot be defined a priori, and are not predetermined outside of their situated everyday actions and habits of usage" (Costa 2018, 3643).

Rather than take such patterns of usage for granted, Costa proposes situating "the practices of usage" in their particular social and cultural contexts, what she calls "affordances-in-practice" (2018, 3643). Although the possibilities of a given platform are not limitless, Costa's analysis offers insight into how the capacities and properties of social media emerge from culturally specific engagements with mutable, open-ended technologies, comparable to what science and technology studies scholars call "socio-technical arrangements," which are constituted through practice. In my research, Facebook's architecture supported friend circles and collectives at multiple geographic levels in ways that reflected and cocreated existing social practices, such as norms around friendship. Music subcultures and fan communities, for example, long predate online media, but in concert with the properties of emerging platforms, their media practices generated new possibilities for overlapping worlds and multiple experiences of place.

More than facilitating various collectives or communities and experiences of space, social media brought these worlds into new socio-spatial configurations. In the rest of this chapter, I locate emerging media in everyday practice to examine what constitutes "shared geography" for the mobile, often transnational Europeans and other young people in these friend circles. Scale, an analytic I borrow from cultural geography, offers a way to rethink assumptions about geographic levels, like the local or national, as containers of space (Brenner 1998, 2001; Cox 1998; Marston 2000; Marston, Jones, and Woodward 2005; Swyngedouw 1996, 2004; also Tsing 2005, 57–58). Anna Tsing, writing about the globalizing effects of capital, argues that projects such as nationalization or globalization do not take place at a priori geographic levels but produce those levels: "the economic projects [of global finance] cannot limit themselves to conjuring at different scales—they must conjure the scales themselves" (Tsing 2005, 57–58).

While ethnographers tend to tack between the local and the global (as Clifford Geertz 1974 phrased it),[3] both globality and locality are ways of ordering space, what Tsing calls "scale-making projects": "I argue that scale is not just a neutral frame for viewing the world; scale must be brought into being: proposed, practiced, and evaded, as well as taken for granted. Scales are claimed and contested in cultural and political projects. A 'globalism' is a commitment to the global, and there are multiple, overlapping, and somewhat contradictory globalisms; a 'regionalism' is a commitment to the region; and so on" (Tsing 2005, 58).

Communication technologies have long played a role in organizing social space, making possible shared identities and imagined communities across distances, most notably print media and nationalism in the eighteenth and nineteenth centuries (Anderson [1983] 1991; see also Gellner 1983). Scholars of globalization have similarly analyzed how capital's global circulation—and accelerated accumulation—engenders new forms of territorial ordering (e.g., Harvey 1989; Massey 1993). Harvey argues that under late capitalism, accelerating global capital compresses time and space through high-speed transit and communication technologies (Harvey 1989, 328). For cultural geographers like Neil Brenner, the local, national, or global scales are always contested and in flux, despite temporary fixes, what he terms "a complex, socially contested territorial scaffolding upon which multiple overlapping *forms of territorial organization* converge, coalesce, and interpenetrate" (1998, 464). In examining the spatial entailments of social media, I consider the local, regional, or transnational levels to be contingent formations produced through situated media practices, reworking experiences of place and place-based identities.

Attention to scale makes evident the multiplicity of placemaking projects that took shape through emerging media, beyond the binary of local versus global. Facebook practices, for example, intensified possibilities for alternating among local friends, regional ties, and translocal or transnational connections in the same online spaces. Such activities created spaces on Facebook that made these movements possible. These possibilities included ways of local living specific to Berlin, regional affiliations that spanned Berlin and rural eastern Germany, and emerging translocal formations, such as music scenes spanning locales in and beyond Germany. This multiplicity further demonstrates that such scales were never inevitable but depended on contingent histories—of capital's circulation, of Berlin's divides and imagined voids, of youth cultures and social movements. On Facebook, a multiplicity of connections took place in close proximity, constituting new transnational and cosmopolitan configurations of selfhood, sociality, and place.

Producing the Translocal

While the friend circles primarily lived in Berlin, they participated in broader music and social scenes I consider translocal, contingently linking people and places without falling "between" the local and transnational, like nested containers (on this notion of translocal, see Zhan 2009, 8). Some of their closest friends, for example, lived across Germany or Europe, in Hannover and Hamburg, Amsterdam and Copenhagen. They pursued and maintained ties with friends and contacts who shared their music interests across these multiple locales, often in the same online spaces, and they visited one another regularly. Their tastes in music and style were not homogenous but did inform the contours of these scenes, such as subgenres of electronic music, like breakcore or dubstep, which often overlapped or permeated one another. Sometimes these tastes informed their identities, but constructing subcultural identities such as those described by Hall, Hebdige, and others often mattered less than participating in these scenes, such as listening to music or attending events. Marc, a Dutch music promoter, for example, described his social life in Amsterdam and online this way: "Music, everything revolves around music, electronic music of course. The music scene, of course, the DJing, the [event] organizing, helping other people organize."

For Marc, Facebook became a place to aggregate these translocal connections, adding friends of friends he might encounter later, perhaps at music festivals:

> I use my Facebook like a general thing. I will add people—I don't know— if there's a connection. Facebook, it's maybe 60% [contacts also known in person], maybe more. Almost like 70%. If I know a person, maybe I'll meet them later on through a music festival. People I don't know well, but have heard of—maybe I'll meet you later. It's great for expanding your contacts. To accept a request—I have to recognize a name, or look at friends in common. I'll give someone a chance if we have common friends.

He determined who might be potential friends by who participated in the same scenes and networks. In the language of social network analysis, friends of friends are considered "weak" or "latent" ties (e.g., Donath 2007; Ellison, Steinfield, and Lampe 2011; after Granovetter 1973), but for Marc, not all latent ties were equal. Instead, music tastes and shared connections generated feelings of belonging that linked close circles of friends with others across multiple places, primarily northern and western Europe, the United Kingdom, and the United States. These loosely structured networks and scenes raise further questions about what it means to describe such collectivities as communities, as in analyses of fan communities.

Fan communities are typically dispersed groups whose members share enthusiasm for (and often, detailed knowledge of) popular culture, such as television series, books, or music, going back at least to *Star Trek* fandom in the late 1960s and 1970s and likely to science fiction readers in the 1920s.[4] As with youth subcultures, scholars often describe fan communities as communities of interest organized around shared practice and consumer tastes, a concept rooted in Jean Lave and Etienne Wenger's work on situated learning (Lave and Wenger 1991; Wenger 1999). For Lave and Wenger, shared practice fosters both learning and common identity among what they termed "communities of shared practice," not the other way around. Linguistic anthropologists have developed similar notions of shared language and semiotic practice to understand how youth subcultures are formed and constituted, especially how youth construct shared identities (e.g., Bucholtz 1999, 2000, 2002; see also Eckert 2006 on sociolinguistic approaches to communities of practice). Penelope Eckert, for example, describes such collectivities as engaged in "mutual sense-making" (2006, 1). Emphasizing shared practice and meaning making offers insight into how participation in music scenes creates communities that are not necessarily grounded in shared place, such as online and virtual communities.

Such notions of community, however, risk demarcating or foreclosing the bounds of social formations in ways that are vaguely defined and undertheorized. Vered Amit and Nigel Rapport argue that anthropologists have made "communities" our locus of research when moving away from small-scale, place-based societies (Amit and Rapport 2002). In their view, "community" comes to stand in for collectives bounded in time and space but can be better understood as an artifact of ethnographic methods that circumscribe their subject. In the context of transnationalism and increased mobility, the notion of community evokes a stable, bounded formation. But for mobile, transnational subjects, the contexts in which they forge connections are increasingly partial, ephemeral, and context dependent. Amit and Rapport ultimately contend that while mobile people, including labor migrants and urban knowledge workers, may ground feelings of fellowship in shared experience, "these forms of consociation are often partial, ephemeral, specific to and dependent on particular contexts and activities" (2002, 6).

The loosely interconnected music scenes I studied can be better understood as partial, temporary consociations that came into being on and through media. In many cases, such scenes predated the commercial internet: print and electronic media, such as fanzines and mixtapes in the 1970s and 1980s, previously played central roles in facilitating youth and music subcultures (and fandoms) (Willis [1981] 1990; Gildart et al. 2018). Recorded music and print media circulated translocally before the internet and digital media, while music festivals and events have long brought together music fans from diverse places. Online media differ not because they make possible translocal circulations or virtual communities but because they intensify and accelerate possibilities for interchange and communication.[5] The advent of online platforms that articulated social networks did not generate wholly new geographic formations or experiences of place. Instead, I argue, their particular capacities and properties—coalescing in affordances-in-practice—intensified movements between social contexts, from the everyday spaces of Berlin to online spaces.

As Costa argues, these affordances represent and entail culturally specific understandings and interpretations of Facebook's features, emerging from situated practice rather than fixed technical properties. Music events such as festivals often elicited flurries of activity as people uploaded photos and videos, added and tagged Facebook friends, and commented on one another's updates. Before Facebook, in my prior fieldwork, festivalgoers shared photos through dedicated online gallery platforms, although fewer people had digital cameras; those who did were more likely to be professional photographers or at least serious enthusiasts. With the advent of mobile phones and social media, participants could take and upload digital photos directly and share them with their network of friends. Facebook differed from previous platforms like email lists, bulletin boards, and fan websites because of how users integrated checking and updating Facebook into their daily lives, with consequences for how they experienced urban space and place-based connections. While few people had smartphones during my fieldwork in 2009–10, most owned laptops and checked Facebook at regular intervals throughout the day, which contributed to the ways people were active on the site during Musikfest. Facebook's continually updated News Feed feature played a central role in this daily practice as well. Introduced in 2006, a few years after the site's inception, it transformed how users perceived and engaged with their reciprocal list of Facebook friends, by centralizing and making visible users' activities.

The News Feed, unlike the main pages of earlier social network sites, publicized users' activities and actions on the site to their friends, bringing together everyday practices at different geographic scales. Before its introduction, activities such as status updates and comments took place on a user's Wall, or profile page. During my fieldwork, the News Feed constituted the main screen users visited when they checked Facebook, although they also saw updates through the Notifications feature (which linked directly to new comments and "mentions"—that is, when their profile was tagged by someone else). The News Feed announced ordinary happenings on the site, actions solicited by the interface, including ones users might not intend to broadcast. Adding a new friend, "liking" a musician's page, or responding to an event listed with Facebook could all appear in aggregation on others' News Feeds. In a typical example, Facebook collated activities such as Sal adding two new friends, Andreas joining a group showcasing a friend's photography, Viktor "liking" the page for rap performer Missy Elliott, and a friend who ran a monthly knitting circle at a bar called the StrickenClub responding to an event invitation and adding twelve new friends. I recreate these updates below to demonstrate how they appeared in my feed:[6]

> **Sal** is now friends with [**Friend 1**] and [**Friend 2**]
>
> **Andreas** joined the group [**Friend 3**'s photography]
>
> **Viktor** likes Missy Elliott
>
> **StrickenClub Berlin** and **David** are attending [Music event] @ [Club name]
>
> **StrickenClub Berlin** is now friends with **Agathe** and 11 other people

These pronouncements alternated with status updates—that is, brief posts users composed by filling out a field with the prompt "What are you doing right now?" (in the German language version, "Was machst du gerade?"). At the time, automatically generated actions constituted close to half of the items in my News Feed, though sometimes fewer. On an individual Wall, a field at the top prompted visitors simply to "Write something . . ." Doing so automatically created a News Feed item, as when Erik's friends wished him happy birthday. The good wishes of our mutual friends appeared in my News Feed, with an arrow to indicate who was posting on whose Wall:

> **Pascal** > **Erik**: happy birthday!
>
> **Sal** > **Erik**: haaaaaaaaaaaaappy birthday!!!

The News Feed aggregated these updates and activities in a centralized place. While it was nominally chronological, its contents depended on proprietary algorithms that Facebook continually updates and alters.[7] Through Facebook's privacy controls, users could modify which friends saw what, to a degree. In practice, few people I interviewed calibrated these settings, beyond limiting their account's visibility to their Facebook Friends (so their posts and photos, for example, could only be seen by those they had added as Friends). The News Feed, in consequence, pulled together in the same online spaces disparate activities and updates that might at times refer to life in Berlin or to US popular culture or at others to someone in the Netherlands joining a photography group or to friends in Berlin sending birthday greetings to someone in Hannover. In an interview, Marc, the Dutch music promoter, distinguished between friends at varying geographic and affective distances, contrasting people he met "abroad" with his close "inner circle" (similar to German Freundeskreis) of mainly Dutch friends. He explained that he primarily used his Facebook account with friends who shared his interests in music, clubs, and shows:

> Music, yeah, my old Facebook is mainly musical friends, and that kind of stuff, or people I've met at festivals, or traveling. It's mostly people you share . . . you go out with partying, or you share the common interests of music. And also, the topics are . . . well for chatting, it's music or just daily stuff, or maintaining friendship or trying to get an appointment with somebody or arranging the appointment. . . . Or talking [about] what's going on in your life . . . it's not really . . . focused on that kind of stuff. Or it's not so narrow.

Marc viewed Facebook as an appealing tool for connecting with people he met through industrial and noise music scenes; as he phrased it: "It's great for expanding also your contacts." But in practice, he communicated on social media most often with his "inner circle" of close friends in Amsterdam. He described his online network as located "all over," then qualified that most lived in Europe or the United States: "Well, depends, it's all over, not Asia, but for the rest, it's Europe, and the US, mostly. I don't have Russians; I had some Asians but they were only posting their updates in their native character sets . . . so that was a little complicated" (for more on moving between languages on social media, see chapter 3). "All over" entailed not global connection per se but linkages between particular places—Amsterdam and Berlin, the United Kingdom and California—in emerging translocal articulations (comparable to Karen Ho's critique of narratives that locate global finance in particular cities, like London and Tokyo; Ho 2005, 86). Facebook, with its centralized News Feed, integrated these translocal connections into spaces of daily encounters with both (geographically and affectively) close friends and those geographically dispersed. Travel, such as going to music festivals, could strengthen translocal relationships, and Marc and his friends regularly visited other friends in Berlin.[8] Such translocal scenes and collectivities were not new but unfolded on Facebook alongside local and regional formations, as I turn to next, in ways that intensified movement between—and produced—locality and the translocal.

Inhabiting the Local Online

On social media, translocal connections unfolded alongside daily interactions in Berlin, even as local living took place online. By local, I mean the contingent scale of geographically proximate people, places, and relations, often contiguous with the scale of the city in my research. In Arjun Appadurai's work, the local scale, extending to the national, can obscure translocal and transnational circulations of capital: "The locality (both in the sense of the local factory or site of production and in the extended sense of the nation-state) becomes a fetish that disguises the globally dispersed forces that actually drive the production process" (Appadurai 1996, 42). As identity became deterritorialized under globalization, "mediascapes" (images, narratives, and other cultural productions) provide resources for fashioning identity. In this account, the local and global remain in tension as the grounds for cultural production. By attending to scalemaking, I consider further how the local itself was constructed spatially through everyday practice (see also Udupa 2012). Among my interlocutors, *local* meant the central districts of Berlin they inhabited on a day-to-day basis, linked by the city's dense public transit network, and the people they encountered there, especially their circles of close friends. Locality was further stratified by race, class, and other forms of cultural difference. Students and mobile professionals interacted with peers, colleagues, classmates, and sometimes family and frequented cafés, restaurants, nightclubs, and shops that catered to their interests and budgets. Mobile technologies, as described in chapter 2, exacerbated these divides further by facilitating class-specific ways of moving through urban space. Especially in gentrifying central districts like Prenzlauer Berg, Friedrichshain, and Kreuzberg, trendy boutiques, cafés, and organic grocers mixed with traditional bakeries, mobile-phone shops, and neighborhood bars or snack shops, serving clientele of different socioeconomic means and ethnic backgrounds. Kreuzberg, for example, is the center of Berlin's Turkish German community, with many Turkish specialty shops and businesses that cater to both Turkish and non-Turkish Germans (see Pécoud 2002, 2004).

Tension between localness and transnational connection has long been a theme of migrant experience in Berlin, as many anthropologists detail. After reunification, some young Turks in Germany, such as university students in Jenny White's research, felt themselves to be simultaneously "Berliners and Europeans, but not German"—a racialized category they could never inhabit (White 2004). But they rejected Turkish identity as well, aligning themselves with a more global sense of being "oriental": "Their identity of place is simultaneously local and transnational" (2004, 24). Cosmopolitanism is also part of what constitutes being a Berliner, whether German or not, as Antoine Pécoud argues. In his work on Turkish

German business owners in Berlin, he found that they managed racialized discrimination and disadvantage through flexibility and cultural competence navigating multiple cultural milieus (Pécoud 2002). Cosmopolitanism "as a practice embedded in concrete daily interactions" offered a means to manage these structural inequalities, not through cultural hybridity between two discrete cultures but by movement between cultural contexts (2002, 8). Media often play a central role in constructing the local and transnational for migrant Berliners, as Barbara Wolbert, Kira Kosnick, and others contend. For Wolbert, photographs among Turkish Germans fostered "virtual neighborhoods" that sustained transnational connections between Germany, Turkey, and elsewhere: "Virtual neighborhoods are then the elementary particles of contemporary social networks that are discussed as 'transnational communities'" (Wolbert 2001, 31). Visual media in this instance produced the local and the translocal (see also Kosnick 2007).

Among my interlocutors in Berlin, who similarly felt themselves to be urban and transnational but rarely embraced national identity, the local scale coalesced through shared practices, movements, aesthetics, and histories. Many central districts of Berlin in the early 2000s were dominated by graffiti-covered Altbauen (an imposing style of late nineteenth-century worker housing), sometimes repurposed as communes and squats filling in the voids of the postwar era, alongside monumental concrete Soviet architecture. In gentrifying areas, shops and cafés often featured kitschy, vintage decor while nightclubs like Berghain and Tacheles embraced a raw, unfinished industrial look, with bare concrete and exposed pipes. Before reunification, neighborhoods like Kreuzberg in West Berlin had served as a locus for numerous left-alternative movements, including activists who had fought to retain the neighborhood's mix of housing and work (MacDougall 2011). They linked the built environment of Kreuzberg to the city's nineteenth-century past, as a place "whose politics, sociability, and culture marked the built landscape" (2011, 167). As Carla MacDougall explains: "Their defense of the old urban fabric that dominated the physical look of Kreuzberg proceeded not simply in terms of the architectural merits of the buildings, but in the 'presence of a past that is for us far from over'" (2011, 166).

Among these friend circles, the local in Berlin similarly constituted aesthetics and ways of living specific to the city's history, especially those of particular neighborhoods. One of the music fans, David, co-owned a record shop in Friedrichshain, a rapidly changing area in former East Berlin, across the river Spree from Kreuzberg. The shop exemplified the industrial look of many clubs and art spaces in post-reunification Berlin. He and a friend had opened the shop, which supplied many Berlin DJs and electronic music fans. Berlin was renowned for its techno scene (Nye 2013) but was home to lesser-known forms of electronic dance music as well, such as industrial, experimental, and dubstep. They had recently moved the shop to a new location near the border of Prenzlauer Berg, a neighbor-hood that had seen an influx of young people—and capital—from the West in the 1990s and had become much more expensive by the early 2000s.

The shop occupied a commercial space on the ground floor of a nondescript modern apartment building on a main artery connecting Friedrichshain to Prenz-lauer Berg, near an optometry office, a Vietnamese takeout restaurant, and an insurance agency. A few blocks away was Friedrichshain's main shopping street, Simon-Dachstrasse, lined with vintage shops, boutiques, and bustling outdoor cafés. But this block saw little foot traffic, was more residential, and was farther from the nearest metro (U-Bahn) stop. Concrete steps led up to the entrance, frequently tagged with graffiti. Inside, the decor was minimal—plywood stands holding crates of vinyl and CDs, fluorescent lighting, simple displays of album covers and posters on the wall, and a single worn loveseat near the register. Behind the counter hung a small number of T-shirts for sale, while an aging iMac sat on the counter near stacks of event flyers, new releases, and headphones for a listening station where customers could preview records. In the back of the shop was a combination of cluttered office space and storage for additional stock, haphazardly furnished. One of my interlocutors worked there part-time, and I volunteered there over a number of weeks as part of my fieldwork.

The shop's look was not found only in Berlin at the time; spaces in Hamburg, London, and Brooklyn have all embraced minimalist, industrial style at some point. But the worn, bare concrete and repurposed materials recalled the semi-licit clubs and spaces of Berlin's underground dance parties in the 1990s, as well as squats and activist spaces like Kunsthaus Tacheles, the artists' collective, and club space in a prewar shopping arcade in Mitte.[9] By the mid-2000s, the graffiti-covered, multistory edifice had become a destination for people Alex denigrated as "tourists" (on Berlin's "techno-tourists," see Garcia 2016), partly because of how it preserved an imagined underground past, even as the surrounding neighbor-hood became an upscale shopping district (in chapter 6, I further discuss Berlin's nightlife and creative appropriations of shared space through media practice).

The record shop invoked this history through its aesthetic sensibility, locat-ing the shop, and the music sold there, in Berlin's history of underground music and parties. The local here refers less to a position on a grid, in Michael Lam-bek's words, and more to a set of everyday rhythms, practices, and aesthetics with a temporal dimension (Lambek 2011, 198). "Local" for the circle of music fans in Berlin meant the industrial aesthetics and underground histories par-ticular to their experience of the city. Lambek contests conceptions that posi-tion the local as opposing the global—that point to a difference of perspective or scope. Instead, he challenges both the local and the global as a monolithic way of construing space—a homogenous grid of empty space, the spatial equivalent of empty, allegedly neutral time (after Benjamin 1962, 263, and Chakrabarty 2000, 265): "This grid of homogeneous space parallels Benjamin and Chakrabarty's elaborations of secular, homogeneous, and empty time. The power of the grid is now nowhere better epitomized than in the availability of GIS, Google Earth and other satellite images, and indeed in the whole configuration of the internet" (Lambek 2011, 204).

He proposes instead thinking of the local as singular, incommensurable instances of everyday living, ones that may not exemplify specific instances of something larger, abstract, generalizable, or transcendent: "A more appropriate opposition to the local than the global might be the everywhere and nowhere of objectivist Enlightenment thought, the ideal of escaping the particular, the specific, the immediate, or the immanent. That is, the opposite of the local may be the abstract or transcendental universal. In this respect the local describes the human condition, down here on earth. It exists at many levels of inclusion and scale" (Lambek 2011, 199–200).

Lambek's approach entails a shift away from envisioning the local as an instance of something global or universal and recasts cultural specificity as attention to the granular, contingent, and nonreplicable, worth understanding precisely because of its "density, texture, and incommensurability" (2011, 205). Lambek advocates instead recouping the temporal dimensions of locality, as places that must be continually made: "Humanly inhabited spaces have a temporal dimension of sedimented labor, work, acts, and their consequences. We must be attuned to the temporality and depth of the local" (208–9). The local in this sense is "constituted by the activities of its inhabitants, operating within specific traditions in some conjunction with one another" (216). As the product of particular rhythms and temporalities, as well as spatial dimensions, the local can be *inhabited*, lived out through particular practices rather than representing a fixed position: "The indexicality of the local means both that it is not fixed in space or time and that it can be invoked and inhabited at many levels of inclusion" (200). What was local about Berlin was not the geographic position of particular places but the styles and ways of living that linked people to contingent histories and experiences of Berlin, to ways of moving through the city. Berlin, or particular experiences of it, constituted an arrangement of places and practices, tastes and aesthetics that made it *their* Berlin (paraphrasing D. Miller and Slater 2000 on the internet's multiplicity).[10]

Berlin, from the perspective of many of my interlocutors, did not take place only in record shops, cafés, nightclubs, or homes but could also be inhabited online, through digital placemaking. Just as Facebook brought translocal connections into daily living, the rhythms, practices, and sensibilities specific to Berlin unfolded on social media. A bimonthly event called the Knitting Club (StrickenClub Berlin, a pseudonym) illustrates how these local aesthetics iterated online. The organizer was connected to the circle of electronic music fans, which included a number of young women interested in crafts, visual arts, and fashion (see Kraemer 2021a on gender, crafting, and social media). She had begun hosting knitting get-togethers at a bar in Kreuzberg to learn and practice knitting, for which she had created a personal Facebook account (rather than a page or group) under the name "StrickenClub Berlin." The account added numerous friends in May 2010 and used the Wall to notify them of upcoming meetups, as the description explained (in English): "The StrickenClub opens his doors every month somewhere in berlin. we keep you update for the next times! The StrickenClub is also knitting in the streets." The profile included the event's logo, a picture of a knitted blanket or scarf stitched with the name "StrickenClub" and the image of a pint of beer. While knitting was not a hobby associated with underground dance music, many of the music fans attended—the first time most had learned to knit, a practice more associated with their *Omas* (grandmothers). But interest in crafts (and the "DIY," or do-it-yourself, ethos of punk and squatter scenes) was popular, as was evident at the many craft fairs and flea markets popular with young people. The StrickenClub's Facebook profile recapitulated an aesthetic local to Berlin and brought the rhythms of the event—sometimes located in the same spaces as music shows—online.

As with the StrickenClub, the record store's presence on Facebook and the shop's website mirrored—and indexed—the actual store and its aesthetic. Through event updates, the store brought local temporalities into online spaces. Conversely, the shop operated as a nexus for translocal music scenes, attracting DJs and music enthusiasts, like a well-known dubstep producer originally from the United Kingdom and visitors from farther afield places like Japan, Hungary, and Israel, all with their own thriving local electronic music scenes. Through the same platforms where translocal connections commingled with daily living, mobile young people enacted the rhythms and temporalities of Berlin online.

Regional Affiliations: "Now Everyone Is On"

Along with local and translocal connections, regional origins structured online practices as well, remaking the experiences of Berlin. For a friend circle from rural eastern Germany, regional ties threaded through their closest friendships and broader connections. For example, my roommates Daniele and Katrine (whom I had found through an online room-share search) had recently moved to Berlin from the neighboring state of Saxony-Anhalt, along with other close friends from their home village or the regional capital, Magdeburg (where they had lived for a few years). Saxony-Anhalt is one of Germany's *Neue Länder*, one of the new federal states previously in East Germany, and the friends in this circle were children in the German Democratic Republic and remembered the fall of the Wall. Daniele and Katrine spent time most frequently with their neighbors Jörg and Dieter, who lived across the street, and others like Sabine and Anya, meeting weekly for kitchen get-togethers as well as visiting parks, flea markets, or clubs. In Berlin, they maintained close ties with each other, friends in Magdeburg, and family (mostly in their home villages). In the initial months of my fieldwork, Daniele and Katrine often visited their families on weekends, in what they called "*unser Dorf*" (our village), but these visits slowed in the ensuing months.

For Daniele, Katrine, and many of their friends, moving to Berlin coincided with or instigated joining Facebook. Online, Daniele had migrated from MySpace, while others previously used a social network site for German university students, Studi.vz (pronounced "shtudi-fau-zed"). As Daniele recounted: "Everyone had been using Studi.vz, MySpace, etc., before, but then I began to use Facebook with foreigners in Berlin, because it was easier to stay in touch with them."[11] Berlin, like Facebook, constituted a site of cosmopolitan connection, to meet and befriend Ausländer, typically those from the European Union, United States, and other Western nations. Daniele met Nathan, a UK national interning in Berlin, at a nightclub and began inviting him and his friends to the weekly kitchen gatherings (informal parties featuring beer and tea, usually around the kitchen table; compare to Boyer's (2006a) discussion of the more masculine *Stammtisch*, or "regulars' table," in Berlin pubs). Nathan introduced her to Facebook, which as she indicated, she joined to stay in contact with new friends and acquaintances.

Facebook constituted a shared space where multiple connections and relationships took place—for this circle, articulating regional formations alongside local and transnational ones. Daniele began checking Facebook regularly, eventually acquiring her own laptop to replace an aging one she had shared with Katrine. Our household also finally ordered WLAN (wireless internet; see chapter 5 on managing uneven internet infrastructures), after which she spent more time online. On Facebook, she read others' posts, only commenting occasionally: "I don't update my own often, occasionally I comment or change my profile photo." She kept up with Nathan and others this way but increasingly chatted over Facebook Messenger with her close friend Sabine, whom she knew from Magdeburg. She and Sabine typically posted updates in German, though not all of their Ausländer friends on Facebook understood German well. Sabine, for example, posted this snippet without context to her Wall:

mo, di, mi???? kriegen wir da was hin? [mon, tues, wed???? Are we going there?]

Such updates both indexed particular places ("going there"), typically in Berlin or sometimes in Saxony-Anhalt, and required shared knowledge to interpret, often referring to happenings within her regional friend circle (chapter 3 explores linguistic means of scalemaking in more detail). At other times, they relied on translator tools to communicate with those who did not speak or read German. There were also gendered dimensions to these practices; maintaining friendships on social media is a form of affective labor that often falls to women (a topic I explore further in Kraemer 2021a, 2021b). But among these circles, I observed similar practices among men and women.

Online, Daniele, Katrine, and their friends moved between cosmopolitan circuits with Ausländer in Berlin and networks of friends from rural eastern Germany, networks that spanned Berlin and Saxony-Anhalt but also encompassed friends from home traveling or living abroad. Their friend Kirsten, for example, was traveling through New Zealand and Australia for six months. She and Daniele chatted regularly over Facebook Messenger, and Kirsten often circulated digital photos from her travels. One evening, Daniele and Katrine were browsing Kirsten's newest photos on Facebook in the living room. Katrine exclaimed to Daniele, "echt richtig cool Bilder!" (really cool pics!). These Facebook messages and posts allowed Daniele and Katrine to maintain and articulate originally regional ties to friends across Berlin, urban and rural Saxony-Anhalt, and abroad.

Although this circle took shape primarily around shared regional ties, music interests shaped their online practices as well, enmeshing them in translocal and transnational music scenes, primarily indie rock and electronic music. Sabine and Jörg in particular (both music journalists; Jörg DJed as well) followed bands and music labels on Facebook, many of which were based in the United States or United Kingdom, and frequently posted about new albums or live shows. Jörg had long been interested in indie music, before moving to Berlin or joining social media, and had closely followed numerous labels in the United States. When living in Magdeburg, he had joined MySpace to follow various bands. Like his friends, though, he joined Facebook after moving to Berlin: "Well, I haven't even been that long on Facebook. I've only been there for a month. First I had a MySpace account, not, nothing personal. Only one for my band." He read music blogs and sites daily, like Needledrop, Stereogum, and Pitchfork, and posted album reviews to his own blog. He also ordered records online from sellers in Germany, the United States, and elsewhere, including various independent sellers, Amazon Marketplace in Germany, and shops in Berlin, like David's. As he explained of his friends and contacts online: "Most of the people I know online are in Germany, like [Person 1] from Needledrop. Andreas, my best friend from kindergarten, is now in New Zealand. I don't have many regular contacts abroad."

Between music journalism and his blog, he was often in contact with labels in Germany and the United States, and from them, he learned about upcoming shows in Berlin. He preferred bands from the United States, though, who he felt were "somehow cooler" than European bands:

> [I listen to] guitar music and electronic music, separate or together. Mostly I listen to American music, produced, recorded, and released in the US, and in Canada; it's somehow cooler than most stuff released in Europe. There's also a really cool electronic scene in Germany, even Europe, [the] UK, France. And I like the IDM scene, you can find everything at [David's shop]. There are other labels, German IDM labels. One is from a coworker, based in Berlin.

Sabine shared Jörg's interest in US indie rock and followed numerous English-language music blogs *"von andere Ländern"* (from other countries). She had similarly joined Facebook within the past year and still had a Studi.vz account, though she used it "very, very little." She preferred Facebook, which she used "to stay in contact with people, chatting and news." She rarely posted her own status updates, although she shared links and videos, liked band pages, and responded to related events. In one post, for example, she shared a live-recorded video of an indie rock band on YouTube, with English title and description, commenting: "jahahaaaa" (ahahahah). In another post, she shared a photo of a humorous chalkboard sign from her neighborhood, indexing the local of Berlin. When a mutual friend from Magdeburg updated her status to say, "weekend is coming and Berlin is calling. . . .)," she and other friends in Berlin "liked" the update.

For Sabine, Facebook connected her to transnational music scenes but was primarily a space for "real life" (*Echtleben*) friends: "All the people I've befriended, I already talk to in real life." For Sabine, Jörg, Daniele, and their friend circle, Facebook centralized disparate activities and connections in and across Berlin, Magdeburg, and elsewhere, interweaving regional friendships and transnational indie rock circuits. Katrine, for instance, coordinated plans with friends in Berlin and in Magdeburg, as well as with recently met Ausländer, in the same online spaces where Jörg reflected on new music and Sabine shared music or event videos. Berlin and Facebook alike constituted spaces where these regional and cosmopolitan connections intertwined without collapsing or dissolving geographic distinctions. Bringing regional and transnational circuits into the same online spaces transformed their experiences of Berlin and their regional identities as rural eastern Germans. Although Sabine and others sometimes expressed shame or embarrassment about "typically East German" speech or practices (see Kraemer 2018, 1397 as well as chapter 5 of this book), online they moved between regional selves and urban, cosmopolitan ones as a way of being young, urban

Germans. Their friends in Magdeburg followed suit, as Daniele reflected on the spread of Facebook among her friend circle, bringing them into this multiscalar space: "At first, not many others were there—now everyone is on."

(Re)Configuring Scale

Among these friend circles in Berlin, social media took shape as a new space for enacting relationships and worlds at multiple geographic scales. This space differed from prior online communities in its geographic multiplicity, bringing together (and producing) scales like the local, translocal, and regional in new configurations through features like the News Feed. At the same time, social media became entwined in daily life in new ways. Daily life and communication increasingly took place on and through Facebook and mobile devices (as described in chapter 2). This shift was owed in part to Facebook's adoption in Berlin and elsewhere, as Daniele recounted. But it also depended on greater access to broadband connectivity, allowing continuous high-speed internet access. Only 9 percent of German households had some kind of broadband internet access in 2003; by 2009, 65 percent did, and by 2020, that number peaked at 91 percent.[12] Over the period of my fieldwork, broadband access and social media use both expanded rapidly—in one year alone, 2009 to 2010, broadband access jumped 10 percentage points.[13]

Continuous high-speed internet contributed to shifts in what it meant to be "online" at all. As Marc, the music promoter, detailed, broadband access and smartphones rendered going online a more continuous experience, no longer as temporally and spatially demarcated as dial-up internet had been: "Cable, of course [brought about] a mentality shift, in that a computer is always on. A lot of people just leave the computer on all day—and integration with the phone, that helps." While the always-on nature of digital and social media is sometimes framed as hyperstimulation, paralleling the 24-7 cycle of cable news (see Kraemer 2017), this persistence created the conditions for a new social space to emerge. Friends and contacts no longer logged in for discrete periods of time but instead checked in intermittently throughout the day, whether on Facebook or for messaging:

> Instead of phoning, we now keep in contact the whole day. Chat has changed—you don't really say good-bye anymore. . . . We now have small bits of conversation, if you want to, you can spend an hour chatting, but it's more organic now. It used to be that nobody's only online, but now everyone's continuously online.

Scholars of virtual worlds point to the persistence of online spaces as a key affordance constituting them as separate worlds (Boellstorff 2008, 47; see also boyd

2014, 11).[14] An immersive world such as Second Life or a massive multiplayer role-playing game like World of Warcraft continues to exist whether an individual player is logged in or not. Before continuous connectivity, chat conversations ended when participants logged off (although chat rooms, channels on internet relay chat [IRC], or conversation threads on bulletin boards and Usenet could persist). But continuity, across devices like laptops and mobile phones and through broadband, allowed virtual conversational spaces on Facebook and chat to persist like a virtual world. Such spaces incorporated connections and encounters at multiple geographic levels into spaces of daily living, conjoining local rhythms, translocal consociations, and regional formations.

This geographic multiplicity did not dissolve spatial distinctions or create homogeneous global connections. On the contrary, social spaces on Facebook created new possibilities for interaction that brought local ties, practices, and rhythms into transnational and translocal circuits, parallel to ways Berlin constituted a cosmopolitan place. In the spring of 2010, Alex, the DJ, promoted and organized a show with his friend and collaborator Pascal in ways that evince this multiplicity. The headlining performer was a dubstep musician, a South Asian British woman based in Berlin. Dubstep, a broken-beat style of electronic dance music with signature wobbly bass lines, coalesced as a genre in London, arising out of the UK garage scene, then circulated translocally through Berlin, Copenhagen, the United States (where it was popularized by superstar DJ Skrillex, often to the chagrin of many longtime fans), and elsewhere. For example, many industrial and electronic musicians in Europe at the time were influenced by dubstep (and broken beat styles generally) and incorporated its sounds into their music.

Alex and Pascal promoted the show on Facebook and through print flyers and advertisements. They circulated these in Berlin while addressing an implicitly transnational audience in posts online. On Facebook, they posted about the event (where they were also DJing) in English on their pages and created an event page, also in English. Mixing English and German like this was common in Berlin, even for audiences that were mostly German speaking (as I discuss more in chapter 3 on language mixing). On the day of the show, Pascal updated his Facebook status with a link to the event page and reminded his contacts: "we're on at 11pm. dont be late!" Two users "liked" the update, as displayed by a small icon of a blue fist with a thumb up, next to the number of people who had clicked the Like button. A third person lamented, in colloquial English: "FUCK IM NOT IN BERLIN!!! Next time!"

Pascal playing tonight @ [Venue] Kreuzberg with [XX, XX DJs, XX XX, XX]

We're on at 11pm. dont be late!

9 minutes ago · Comment · Like

2 people like this

> [**Friend 1**] FUCK IM NOT IN BERLIN!!! Next time!
>
> 8 minutes ago

Alex is looking forward to the [Event name] world premiere later at [Venue] Kreuzberg! We're on from 11pm!

15 minutes ago · Comment · Like

Pascal and [**Friend 2**] like this.

Alex Big day!

5 hours ago · Comment · Like

Sal, [**Friend 1**] and [**Friend 2**] like this.

Earlier in the day, Alex simply posted "Big day!" Later, he updated to say he was looking forward to the show and added: "We're on from 11pm!" Pascal and Erik, in Hannover, clicked Like. Although Pascal and Alex anticipated that most attendees would come from Berlin and speak German, they addressed their wider circles of friends and contacts, including dubstep fans in other locales. At the same time, they indexed their location in Berlin by referring to the start time of the event with little context. Promoting events in English on Facebook connected a local (that is, Berlin-based) happening to translocal circuits that became visible when friends elsewhere commented or clicked Like.

That evening after their DJ set, Alex asked me to take photos of him and his friends backstage, which he later uploaded to Facebook. The following day, he and Pascal posted on Facebook about the show: the venue had been packed, and they were pleased with their success. Their updates referred, implicitly, to interactions that had taken place at the show, invoking the local. Pascal wrote: "crazy awesome good night out! playing good music, being paid and drinking for free. what could be better?" One friend quipped in reply: "If I was there?"

Pascal crazy awesome good night out! playing good music, being paid and drinking for free. what could be better?

7 hours ago · Comment · Like

[**Friend 1**] If I was there?

Indexing their experiences at the event located it, and them, in Berlin while making visible the geographic multiplicity of their Facebook contacts. They could inhabit the local online, but doing so brought the local into translocal encounters. Although boyd and others have described the colliding of social worlds on social media as "context collapse," such encounters did not create homogeneous social spaces in my fieldwork. It was precisely this geographic multiplicity, of being able to participate in transnational circuits online, that made Facebook appealing, especially compared to platforms like the German Studi.vz, or even the now-abandoned MySpace. For Alex, Facebook allowed him to share information with his friends in a decentralized, "dispersed way," as he explained:

> The most interesting thing about Facebook is that it's the first time that social interaction with my friends moved, basically, into the cloud, you know? Like . . . this Newsfeed is a dispersed way of communicating— you don't communicate, but you still get the information, and you know that the other people get the information. . . . I know that it's a more efficient way to get my message through, which is mostly silly kitten videos or, you know. . . . But, I still know that it's the most efficient way to address the people.

This indirect communication comprised lightweight engagement like "silly kitten videos" that fostered friendship and shared sociality as much as it conveyed a particular message (see Ellison, Steinfield, and Lampe 2011 on these "lightweight" encounters and weak ties). More so than on prior platforms, he and his friends brought such interactions "into the cloud," where life in Berlin unfolded in the context of translocal and transnational connections.

By bringing encounters online at multiple scales, Facebook became a space where it was possible to move between contexts such as close friend circles, translocal music scenes, and regional networks. Continuous online connectivity, especially on laptops and smartphones, brought these dense connections and social formations into sites of daily living, from living rooms to record shops and nightclubs. These emerging spaces formed through the intersection of Facebook's technical capacities or features, such as the News Feed, and the interpretive practices of users. Among many mobile young people in my research, these practices reflected normative, classed (as well as raced and gendered) understandings of sociality and selfhood. Inhabiting the local online invoked experiences grounded in aesthetics and temporalities specific to Berlin's post-reunification music worlds and art scenes, particularly for a predominantly white middle class. For these urban young people, participating in cosmopolitan worlds on Facebook and other social media was a means of enacting middle-class selfhood and mobility, not by moving geographically but by moving between scales in the same online spaces, in ways that constituted them as white, middle-class Europeans.

Moving between connections and encounters in these ways reconfigured local, regional, or transnational scales, making both Facebook and Berlin sites of cosmopolitan connection for an emerging European knowledge class. Such commingling was rarely seamless, however. Rather than collapsing distinctions like online and offline or global and local, it created tension, such as when people did not provide sufficient context for others to understand a reference. These reconfigurations are not unique to social media—virtual communities predate the internet (as Sandy Stone [1991] and others have shown), and print media fostered feelings of national belonging in the nineteenth century, as Benedict Anderson ([1983] 1991) has shown. Novels and newspapers were also technologies of mobility (as Jordan Frith [2018, 20] mentions), allowing passengers of new transportation technologies such as trains to participate in the burgeoning national imaginary while riding alongside mobile strangers.

On social media, participants moved between scales on and through these platforms in ways that intensified such alternations. In the same online spaces, translocal circulations, regional German affiliations, and local ways of living were interleaved at an accelerated pace. But, as Lambek contends, the local is not a concentric scale embedded within circles of nation and globe—that is, not a specific instance of some larger phenomenon but a way of living, made up of contingent and particular practices. Geographic multiplicity online reworked everyday experiences of space by integrating regional and translocal connections into spaces where the local—or rather, my interlocutors' experience of the local— was inhabited. Although Facebook activities did not homogenize geographic differences, such as aesthetics, rhythms of living, or place-based connections, they brought expressions of regional and rural identity into urban, cosmopolitan contexts online, enacted translocal worlds in everyday places and friend circles, and reshaped online experiences in ways specific to these middle-class social worlds in Berlin.

MULTIPLE MOBILITIES

A month or so into my fieldwork in Berlin, my roommates invited me to join their informal weekly kitchen gatherings. Some friend circles I knew met on weekends, but this midweek get-together was specific to the circle from Saxony-Anhalt. Most had moved to Berlin within the past year or two, primarily to neighborhoods of former East Berlin, like Prenzlauer Berg and Friedrichshain, that were popular with mobile young people. Recently, the circle had expanded to include newly met EU-Ausländer (foreigners mainly from other EU countries), such as Nathan, an intern from the United Kingdom. The gathering began around 8:00 p.m. each week at the apartment of their close friends Jörg and Dieter, across the street. As people arrived, they settled around the kitchen table, shedding coats and shoes, taking bottles of beer from the fridge, and then, almost automatically, removing their mobile phones from bags or pockets and laying them on the kitchen table, among plastic lighters and mugs of herbal tea. Mobile phones had been commonplace for some years (by 2006, there were more mobile phone subscriptions than residents in Germany),[1] although only a few of my interlocutors had smartphones, which were expensive. Mobile phones had become integrated into daily living, especially for coordinating with geographically proximate friends and maintaining affectively close ties, such as to family.

During the evening, people rarely looked at their phones, unless they received a call or text or a friend's phone rang or buzzed while they had stepped away. Mobile phone use, as much research corroborates (e.g., Licoppe 2004; see also Frith 2015; Humphreys 2007), correlates with people having shorter conversations and sending short messages to intimates, especially among those more likely to see each other in actual or copresent contexts. For many middle-class mobile young people in Berlin, mobile phones facilitated acceptable, legitimate forms of mobility, from ways of navigating the city (such as through recommendation apps) to state-sanctioned travel within and across borders (such as through route-finding apps). The design of mobile handsets and interfaces reflected and instantiated not just middle-class forms of mobility but acceptable forms of selfhood as discrete and indivisible. Mobile phones and service contracts, for example, typically assume a singular owner, with one phone number per handset (unlike landlines), for whom a phone functions as a productivity tool with a digital address book, calendar, and clock. On smartphones, these design norms extend to saving users' login information, making it difficult to share handsets.

Mobile devices in these ways encoded Western understandings of mobility and personhood, supporting and enabling middle-class mobilities and consumption practices. But they could also generate new mobilities, including counterhegemonic ones. During the weekly kitchen gatherings, I often saw friends answering one another's phones and leaving their own out. Doing so made the group communally available to calls by those not present, whether friends nearby or members of the friend circle who were more geographically distant. In these instances, mobile phones supported more collective, distributed forms of sociality. Among the friend circle from Saxony-Anhalt, most owned basic candy-bar or flip-style handsets with limited internet capabilities and mainly used them for voice calls and texts (SMS, or short messages). Only a few owned smartphones, owing to the costs of the devices and data plans. A few years later, when I returned, this situation had changed rapidly, as touchscreen smartphones became the main style available on the market.

Most of my interlocutors had acquired their first mobile phone before their own computer (most had used a computer at school or shared one with family) and before they had access to broadband internet. For a few, a high-speed mobile data plan was their primary internet connection at home. The relatively early adoption of mobile phones, compared to broadband internet, was typical among younger Europeans, as most European countries implemented mobile telephony, and the interoperable GSM standard, by the early 1990s. In German, however, the colloquial term for a wireless or mobile phone is neither *mobile* (as in the UK and many parts of Europe) nor *cellular*, as in the United States, but *Handy*— pertaining to one's *Hand* (possibly from the English *handheld*). The exact origin is unclear but likely owes to marketing campaigns in the early 1990s that termed the new device a "Handfunktelefon" or a "Handheld-Telefon oder [or] Handy."[2] Although German *Hand* and English *hand* are cognates, both *Handheld* and the suffix -*y* derive from English (although the plural is *Handys*, not *Handies*). More than once, the somewhat chagrined story I heard was that Germans thought

Americans used the term *Handy* and adopted it in mistaken imitation.³ Unlike *Handy*, the term *mobile phone* invokes the device's potential for movement, while the US-based *cell phone* indexes radio technology (cellular in contrast to wired). But the language of *ein Handy* (in opposition to a *Festnetz*, a fixed network) characterizes such devices in relation to the body—something you hold in your hand, with the promise of cosmopolitan connection.

One weekly kitchen get-together illustrated the Handy's potential for extending social relations in embodied ways. My roommate Daniele had left her phone on the kitchen table and stepped out onto the balcony. When it began ringing a little later, a friend reached for it and called out, "Daniele, dein Handy!" Daniele later explained that she kept her phone (a "*kleines Klapphandy*," little folding phone) "to make calls, and to be called" (*angerufen zu werden*). Among her circle of friends, Handys could circulate, making friends available to one another. Mobile technologies in these ways embodied many of the tensions and contradictions of emerging media among these young knowledge workers in Berlin. Their design entailed neoliberal notions of selfhood, individual and customizable, while facilitating acceptable, middle-class movement through urban space. The term *Handy*, adapted from English, itself indexed cosmopolitan aspirations to transnational cultural circuits, even as it grounded German-speaking users in relation to mobile devices, as bodily components that could extend shared sociality. I explore in this chapter the politics and ontologies of these constructions of mobility, as articulated through mobile phone design and practice, alongside the alternative and multiscalar mobilities such practices generated.

Multiple Media Mobilities

My interlocutors' framing of mobile phones as Handys requires rethinking the sense in which such technologies are mobile and what kinds of mobility they represent. Literature on mobility, whether of bodies, goods, or information, often equates it with movement, particularly transport and circulation. As anthropologists have repeatedly shown, circulation (of goods, practices, and people) has long constituted human cultural worlds, going back at least to Bronislaw Malinowski's ([1922] 2014) work on the Kula Ring (see also Munn 1986). Nationalist projects (and the modern nation-state system generally) depend on linking territory to identity and belonging, in a homology of one people, one culture, one place, through both legal and cultural citizenship (e.g., Gellner 1983; Hobsbawm 1992; A. Smith 1971). The classic Romantic works of German thinkers like Johann Gottfried Herder (1744–1803) forged this connection, which in turn influenced anthropologists like Franz Boas and Malinowski in their concept of culture, as *cultures*, plural and relativist (see Stocking 1966; also Wilf 2013). The notion of multiple cultures, however, risked construing culture as bounded, consonant with nationalist projects. Transnational migration, along with postcolonial critiques, pushed scholars to rethink these Romantic views of culture as bound to particular people and places (e.g., Appadurai 1996; Clifford 1988; Clifford and Marcus 1986; Gupta and Ferguson 1997; Eric Wolf 1982; see also Tsing 2005). As James Clifford laments, "Culture is a deeply compromised idea I cannot yet do without" (1988, 10).

A similar critique of national cultures underpins Liisa Malkki's (1992) analysis of refugee mobility and nationalism. Malkki argues that nationalist projects work by naturalizing the link between people and the territory of the nation, such as through metaphors of trees and rootedness or of blood and soil: "The metaphorical concept of having roots involves intimate linkages between people and place" (24). Discontinuous national territories become the naturalized counterpart of similarly discontinuous, segmented peoples and cultures. In what she terms a "sedentarist metaphysics" (privileging a rooted view of citizenship and belonging; 31), migrants, nomads, and refugees, among other mobile people, appear dangerous and pathological because they are uprooted and disconnected from the land, threatening the coherence of the nation-state. Among Hutu refugees from Burundi, exiled in Tanzania, however, she found diverse experiences of national identity, mobility, and space. One group of refugees living in a Tanzanian township, for example, developed a cosmopolitan, rhizomatic identity, in contrast to a second group of refugees in a more isolated camp. But this cosmopolitanism—more rhizomatic than rootless, in Malkki's terms—seemed impure to the camp refugees.[4]

While some people's movements can threaten the territorial integrity of the nation, capital's late modern acceleration provoked new questions of mobility and place in the context of globalization (Castells 1996; Hannerz 1996; Harvey 1989; Urry 2000). New transit and communication technologies played a central role in what John Urry calls "flows of time and space" (2000, 26), similar to Manuel Castell's (1996) "space of flows," a new conception of spatiality enabled by electronic and digital communication at a distance.[5] For Urry, Western social science's conception of bounded societies, closely coupled with nation-states, no longer inheres, if it ever did: "Society here means that ordered through a nation-state, with clear territorial and citizenship boundaries and a system of governance over its particular citizens" (2000, 9). He redefines the social in relation not to stable, discrete societies, the historical focus of sociology, but rather to mobility: emerging global networks and flows characterized by lateral interconnections and the "hybrid" agency of human subjects and nonhuman objects—that is, "complex mobile hybrids constituted through assemblages of humans, machines

and technologies" (4). In this context, emerging technologies enable and accelerate such flows, condensing time and space in new socio-technical arrangements
of people, capital, and states (what David Harvey [1989, 328] calls "space-time
compression"). States increasingly function to regulate not only their own citizens but also such mobilities. For Manuel Castells (1996), these new technologies
and flows undergird an emergent "network society" (see also Hannerz 1996), in
which economic production shifts to managing information rather than goods
or services (Castells 1996, 13–17).

In David Harvey's analysis of space-time compression, transit and communication networks facilitate (and are produced by) the accelerated circulation of
global capital. Global capital makes the world, as a geographical and historical
configuration, feel smaller. At the same time, scholars of globalization linked
increasing mobility and migration to processes of deterritorialization, in which
belonging and identity become detached from place (e.g., Appadurai 1996;
though as Malkki argues, national identities often reassert themselves for displaced and diasporic peoples). As a (relatively) new, networked communication
technology, the internet figures prominently in such imaginings as a placeless
space of networked flows. Geographer Mark Graham (2013), for example, argues
that the metaphor of "cyberspace," coined from William Gibson's 1984 cyberpunk
novel *Neuromancer*, invokes a spatial imaginary in which online communication
creates a "world apart." The cyberspace metaphor depicts a disembodied space,
what Graham calls an "ethereal alternate dimension which is simultaneously infi-
nite and everywhere . . . fixed in a distinct location, albeit a non-physical one"
(2013, 179). As a deterritorialized, placeless space (e.g., Harrison and Dourish
1996; Dourish 2006), the internet, according to those like Castells and Harvey,
manifests the space of networked, global flows.

In particular, emerging digital and online communications were seen to provide new means of constructing communities and identities detached from place.
Mobilities scholars, however, in what Mimi Sheller and John Urry (2006) consider a "mobility turn" in social thought, question the view that mobility and
placelessness represent an emergent postmodern, postnational condition. Sheller
and Urry argue that Western social science reflects a modern, colonialist view of
social organization that takes nationalism for granted (see also Urry 2000). Like
Malkki, they construe nationalism, in which a people and culture are bound to a
place, the territory of the nation, "bounded and authentic," as inherently "sedentarist" (Sheller and Urry 2006, 208–9). This sedentarism takes stasis as the norm,
linking stability and meaning to place.

Sheller and Urry take movement, instead, as key to organizing social life and
propose a "new mobilities paradigm" that sees stasis as temporary: "It is rather
part of a broader theoretical project aimed at going beyond the imagery of 'ter-

rains' as spatially fixed geographical containers for social processes, and calling into question scalar logics such as local/global as descriptors of regional extent" (2006, 209). Drawing on the work of Tsing (2005) and others, they call attention to "scalar logics," which produce concepts such as local or global. Tsing, for example, considers not just the hypermobility of capital but the material and social infrastructures necessary to enable and produce it, arguing that the scales of the national or global are culturally constructed orderings of space.[6] Sheller and Urry (2006) contrast their perspective with what they consider "postnational" accounts that focus on the speed of capital's mobility. This emphasis on flows and networks constructs modernity as heavy and solid and postmodernity as light and liquid, in which mobility is fast and flowing, what they term "liquid mobility" (201).

In this context of emerging technologies and capital mobility, mobile communications, from the postnational perspective, can deterritorialize social life further. Like previous new technologies that facilitated communication at a distance (from the telegraph to the telephone; e.g., Marvin 1990), mobile phones and wireless networks potentially intensify space-time compression. Telepresent communication is newly mobile and untethered from the wires of landlines and desktop computing. Nicola Green, in her work on mobile media and movement, sums up the view that mobile communications overcome spatial considerations: "Advertising presents mobile technologies as devices to transcend the 'limitations' of geography and distance" (2002, 282). The mobility these technologies purport to enable, whether mobile phones, laptop computers, or even portable music players and handheld game consoles, reflects the lightning speed of liquid mobility, near instantaneous and unimpeded (recalling Tsing's [2005, 5] discussion of how global flows were imagined to be "pervasive and unimpeded"). These assumptions about movement and mobility, however, are not neutral, as Tsing, Bill Maurer, Green, and others argue. In Maurer's (2000) account of capital's mobility, for example, he argues that narratives of finance's unimpeded, "quicksilver" flows serve to justify globalization and neoliberal policies of financial deregulation rather than describe them.

Mobile devices and infrastructures, then, do not simply enable or reproduce hyperfast mobility but rather encode and generate it, from handset design to service plans. For circles of young, mobile Germans and Europeans in Berlin, mobile phones at times supported cosmopolitan, middle-class forms of movement associated with quicksilver capital and liquid mobility. Erik, who worked in public relations in Hannover, visited friends in Berlin regularly and was close with a number of those in one of the friend circles I studied. He elaborated on a favorite recommendation app called Qype, which consisted of unpaid reviews contributed by users, typically of restaurants but of other businesses as well.

Qype, like its counterpart Yelp, initially featured only urban areas, and ratings were more likely to cover the kinds of restaurants Erik and his friends frequented. That is to say, not every corner *Imbiss* (literally "snack," typically a currywurst or falafel shop) or *Spätkauf* (convenience store) was reviewed, but establishments with younger, middle-class clientele tended to garner more reviews. For Erik, Qype guided him through Berlin on his visits, helping him find high-rated businesses, likely reviewed by others with similar tastes and interests:

> What I really like to use is—do you know Qype? It's geo-based; when you go to a restaurant, you can go there and review it on Qype.com. When I'm going to Berlin, it tells me what's around me, restaurants, shows me reviews, ratings from people. It's cool; a few of my doctors I found on Qype, and I got a cool app for the iPhone.

Apps like Qype mapped out the city according to the paths of other young, mobile, cosmopolitan visitors and residents who used the app (and left reviews).

Paul Dourish, Ken Anderson, and Dawn Nafus (2007) contend that dominant conceptions of mobility as discretionary and legitimate inform the design of mobile networking and computing. They argue, for example, that designers (and information design scholars) often imagine the city as the primary site of consumption and mobile users as young, affluent, cosmopolitan, and professional. They conclude that mobile technologies tend to "accommodate" the mobility of elite consumers and the ways they move through urban spaces: "The processes of making space a place through practice are the same, while [advantaging] those with more technologies designed to meet their needs" (110). Such conceptions of acceptable mobility as urban and cosmopolitan reiterate earlier analyses of legitimate movement. While Malkki explores tensions between rootedness and national belonging, on the one hand, and the pathological transgression of outsiders, on the other, Tim Cresswell (2006) concludes that movement is acceptable for middle-class Western subjects, as nation-states distinguish between legitimate mobility and the threatening transgression of transients and migrants. Cresswell charts, for example, the shifting framing of Chinese mobility in the late nineteenth- and early twenty-first-century United States; although Chinese immigrants were constructed as threatening and dangerous by the Chinese Exclusion Act of 1882, by 2001 such movement was reimagined as part of the narrative of US immigration and plurality (177). For Cresswell, it is typically Others' mobility that threatens the bourgeois nation, and mobility scholars must attend to "how mobility as a cultural resource gets to be unevenly distributed—how the raw fact of motion gets encoded with meanings and how these meanings affect practices of mobility" (178).

Similarly, in early twenty-first-century Europe, the Schengen Agreement enabled freedom of movement across (some) national borders, generating a supranational territory that European citizens can traverse. For immigrants within the Schengen area who do not have citizenship (such as many Turkish Germans and Muslim immigrants in Germany), their movement remains restricted (see Leitner 1997, 135). Mobile media similarly encoded and reproduced acceptable, normative mobility among my interlocutors in Berlin. The mobilities associated with mobile media and networking were, as Dourish, Anderson, and Nafus (2007) describe, voluntary and linked to professional and consumer activities. In the friend circle from eastern Germany, Jörg was one of the few in 2009 who owned an iPhone (originally launched by Apple in 2007). One evening, he demonstrated enthusiastically many of his favorite apps. He drew attention to an English-language GPS-based fitness app, Map My Ride, which records routes and other data while one is jogging or biking: "I use a jogging app for jogging and workouts; I put my iPhone in my pocket during jogs to record the route, the pace, distance, etc., all via GPS." He also showed me his preferred German transit app, a trip planner that covered public transit routes throughout Germany. Like Qype, these apps assumed—and generated—discretionary, acceptable forms of movement through urban space, such as jogging or able-bodied use of public transit, mapping the city in class-specific ways.

Although mobile devices like the iPhone enabled and accommodated acceptable middle-class mobility linked to citizenship and national belonging, they could also embody aspirations to participate in hip, cosmopolitan life. Jörg and Erik, who generally considered themselves technologically savvy and digitally connected, spoke of their devices with untarnished enthusiasm. As Jörg described his relationship to his phone: "[I use it] continuously. It's my alarm clock in morning; after I get up, I go online for radio, newspaper, football matches and results, and occasionally for phoning people and SMS." This set him apart from many of his close friends, whose handsets had only limited internet capabilities, which they used primarily for making phone calls and sending text messages. Yet most expressed optimism about the possibilities afforded by mobile and social platforms. Both Daniele and Sabine, for example, enumerated which devices they hoped soon to acquire—for Daniele, a MacBook (which she later received as a gift), and for Sabine, an iPod. Both imagined that these newer, lighter, faster models would connect them to the multiple cosmopolitan worlds they sought online and in Berlin, facilitating the quicksilver, liquid mobility of late liberal capital.

Multiscalar Mobilities

For many of my interlocutors, mobile phones and devices mapped and engendered middle-class, often cosmopolitan and elite, mobilities. More so than the emerging practices on social media, which most associated with transnational connection, mobile media tracked closely with the scale of the local. By local, I mean ways of living specific to the city and to these intimate social circles. While at times mobile media like smartphones could pull people out of the immediate space of copresent encounters (sometimes termed "absent presence"; e.g., Frith 2015, 20), at others, they generated new forms of engagement, as friends sought information and online encounters together. As Jordan Frith (2015) asserts, mobile media—primarily location-based "locative" apps and services—integrate layers of digital information into everyday spaces, particularly in relation to mapping and wayfinding. For Frith, mobile media facilitate different forms of mobility rather than creating placeless, homogenized spaces, constructing urban space in new ways. Such hybrid informational spaces meant that people could engage with other people and spaces at multiple geographic levels. For example, mobile media brought national and transnational connections into everyday living, while everyday practices of moving through the city shaped online practices. In this sense, mobile media participated in and fostered multiscalar experiences of daily life.

Sabine, a music journalist, was one of the few of her friends to own a smartphone, which she used frequently to check work emails, call coworkers, and research stories. Although she shied away from describing herself as tech savvy—unlike some young men who volunteered enthusiastically to participate in my research (see Kraemer 2021a on gender and social media)—it was quickly evident that she was well versed in wireless networking, social media, and other digital platforms. She checked her email and Facebook accounts regularly throughout the day, as she recounted: "I'm often online—checking Facebook updates, email, using Google, reading news." She owned a laptop but found it too "old, heavy, and difficult" to carry around, despite spending little time in an office. She therefore relied on her smartphone to chat with coworkers, schedule interviews, and conduct research. Even when home, she preferred her mobile phone for going online and relied on a prepaid USB "surfstick" to connect to the internet over mobile data.

One evening, she invited me and a few close friends to dinner at a nearby Korean restaurant. Daniele and I met Sabine at her apartment and then headed over together to meet up with two other young women, including one I had not met before, who was not close with Sabine's main friend circle. After ordering, Daniele and a friend stepped outside to smoke, and Sabine pulled out her smartphone. "I just had a message from a coworker," she explained briefly, and she wanted to read it and respond quickly. Her action left me and the woman I had just met sitting awkwardly across the table, uncertain what to discuss. Soon, the others returned, and Sabine completed the exchange with her coworker and rejoined our conversation. But the brief distraction, as Sabine moved her attention to her exchange with her coworker, seemed to intensify the awkwardness among her friends at the table.

Later that evening, smartphones played the opposite role. Sabine opted to go out for drinks next, so I searched on my phone and recognized a nearby bar. There, we seated ourselves in a cozy back room with couches and a low table. Not long after, Jörg joined us. As Sabine returned with the drinks, she asked whether we recognized the song that was playing. Simultaneously, Jörg and I reached for our phones, competing to retrieve the answer with a song recognition app called Shazam. Jörg beat me (by a second or two), and we discussed music and song lyrics while looking at his phone together. Later, Daniele asked about an upcoming event, and he researched the details, sharing his discoveries out loud while Daniele looked on. His phone, rather than isolating or distancing him from our celebration, incorporated online information into our conversation and facilitated planning a future get-together.

Although online encounters on Sabine's phone could draw her attention away from her immediate surroundings, they effectively created multiscalar spaces as she switched between contexts, on- and offscreen. Christian Licoppe (2016) considers the plural experiences of place generated by mobile media, particularly locative or "location-aware" platforms that overlay an online, on-screen experience of the same space the user is concurrently inhabiting (see also Frith 2015). Licoppe draws on Andy Crabtree and Tom Rodden's (2008) conception of "hybrid ecologies" to account for the multiple ways such technologies construct experiences of space and place, of one's environment, as well as design approaches that make explicit the breaks between virtual experiences and actual ones. Attending to the limits of digital tools and environments makes possible "seamful" rather than seamless user interface design (see Chalmers and MacColl 2003). For Licoppe, locative media potentially remake the experience of urban public space, once assumed by sociologists to comprise "strangers in motion," as in Erving Goffman's (1963, 1972) work. On location-aware apps like Foursquare, Grindr, or Tinder (which were not yet popular or even available to my interlocutors at the time), however, nearby "strangers" are potentially knowable through user profiles and profile pictures and accessible through built-in chat tools. According to Licoppe, these networked, mobile connections could eventually mean that "the augmented city becomes the sites of ceaseless encounters with pseudonymous strangers" (2016, 102).

Previously, Licoppe (2004) observed that young French mobile phone users primarily engaged in brief but frequent conversations, in contrast to how similar people had used landlines. Brief, frequent communication characterized intimate, geographically proximate relations most; distant friends and family still tended to speak for longer but less often. To some degree, mobile phone practices shifted because users were more likely to be away from the home when using them. Mobile devices are also designed in ways that reduce what he terms "ergo-nomic and logistical barriers to communication" (146): phone numbers are typi-cally saved, and those on the other end can access their device. These affordances allow for what Licoppe describes as the "continuous" mode of conversation, in which participants relay an ongoing, open-ended encounter over multiple calls. According to Licoppe, this continuous mode is foundational to sociability and the construction of shared worlds. Notably, these regular yet brief engagements, including text messaging, primarily concern short-term coordination and plan-ning or foster intimacy as a "phatic" mode of communication (after Jakobson 1963). In this sense, mobile communication took place primarily at the local scale and, in turn, produced the "local" as the scale of intimate, daily coordina-tion and connection.

As Erik explained in an interview, he mainly conversed with family on his phone or coordinated with friends in Hannover. His Handy was particularly valuable in offsetting his tendency not to be on time, as punctuality is a charac-teristic many Germans considered necessary for friendship:

> Mostly, with family, it's on the mobile phone, or friends when we meet each other (or want to meet each other and I'm late or somebody won't come) and we talk to each other—Oh no! I'm not *pünktlich* [punctual]! Just short calls, under one minute; I never talk much longer on the phone. I like SMS. I write quite a few, but they're so expensive, I hate it. So mostly with family or short messages to friends. E.g., "What about . . . pizza tonight?" "Yeah pizza!" So my communication behavior is much more . . . articulated on the web, and outside of the web, via phone, SMS, it's just on the surface. . . . I have had phone calls with friends that last an hour and we talked about life, but not that often. [So I talk with] people I know in per-son. Why should I short text someone I only know online? Doesn't make sense to me. I've got their mail address and Facebook, and that doesn't cost any money, and most of the time they'll read it faster than SMS.

This pattern emerged repeatedly in interviews and through direct observation. Almost everyone I interviewed reported daily phone calls or text messages with close friends and family, especially for, as Pascal put it, "short term planning." Sabine specified that she primarily called "friends in Berlin" and family (mainly in Magdeburg). Others, even those without family nearby, like Nathan, an intern from the United Kingdom, or David, an EU national from France, echoed these words. David, despite using his phone less frequently, specified making local calls.

At the same time, mobile phones, especially smartphones, increasingly brought relationships at other scales into everyday spaces. Licoppe suggests that the immediacy and availability of mobile phones becomes a "permanence of connection" that replaces "ordinary places," as mobile interactions become increasingly detached from place: "the management of this relationship tends to detach telephone interaction from the places in which it takes place" (2004, 147). Yet in practice, place often still matters quite a lot to mobile and online communication, shaped by when and where—and who—people are. As Frith (2015) argues instead, mobile phones—and information—rework place as "meaningful location," mediating mobility in new ways. From this perspective, "offline" or "offscreen" place is constructed as much as online spaces, through practice, movement, and built infrastructures.

Erik, for example, inhabited multiple spaces when posting to Twitter on the train to work, rendering the space of the train multiscalar. Sabine brought professional conversations into the intimate space of a birthday dinner with close friends when responding to messages on her smartphone. Small friend circles that spanned multiple places, such as Berlin and Magdeburg or translocal music scenes (as described in chapter 1), could remain available to one another by keeping their phones out during get-togethers. Mobile devices, primarily phones, fostered relationships at the most intimate, daily scale of living, through frequent, brief contact to make plans or strengthen connections through phatic messaging. At get-togethers among the friends from Magdeburg, mobile phones made others in the friend circle reachable and available, supporting and extending a more collective experience of sociality. But such devices also represented—and materialized—aspirations to cosmopolitan, transnational connection and enabled acceptable, normative movements through urban space. Smartphones and apps frequently enacted class-specific mappings of restaurants, cafés, and bars popular with the young, urban middle class in Berlin. Even as they did so, however, these technologies could equally generate alternative experiences and understandings of mobility, personhood, and place, as I discuss next.

Alternative Mobilities

In some ways, mobile media encoded normative assumptions about class, selfhood, and mobility, reflecting their design by (and often for) tech professionals. The first generation of smartphones, for example, began as handheld productivity devices or personal digital assistants (PDAs, such as the original PalmPilot), which combined "mobile office" features like a calendar and address book with email and a web browser. These PDAs were often advertised as personal organizers that required syncing with a computer. During my fieldwork, popular candy-bar and flip-style phones featured a similar suite of apps—calendar, address book, clock,

The connected organizer that keeps you in touch with your PC.

For more information, call 1-800-881-7256.

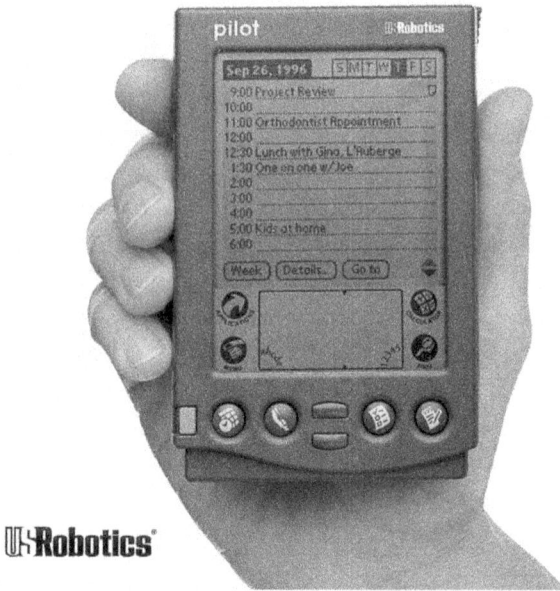

FIGURE 3. 1996 ad for the original PalmPilot, a PDA from US Robotics. From https://www.computerhistory.org/revolution/mobile-computing/18/321/1642, Jeff Hawkins. © U.S. Robotics, Inc.

simple games, and basic camera. With the small screens and discrete, numeric keypads (versus touchscreen keyboards), however, few people took advantage of capabilities like mobile web. These app suites catered to expectations of professional, middle-class productivity and the mobilities typical of knowledge workers. In other ways, however, mobile devices contributed to alternative experiences of mobility that exceeded or deviated from such assumptions, allowing for more collective forms of selfhood and social connection.

In this section, I analyze how user interfaces (i.e., the design, layout, and steps needed for particular actions) and phone plans encoded these normative under-

FIGURE 4. Mock-up of a Palm Centro ad from 2007, for a marketing class. Posted to DeviantArt by Andrew Jo of South Korea, https://www.deviantart.com /koreansensation/art/Palm-Centro-Magazine-Ad-70375854.

standings yet still allowed for counterhegemonic mobilities. The iPhone's operating system at the time included office productivity apps like a calendar, notes, a calculator, contacts, a clock, and weather, alongside web and media apps like YouTube, Safari, email, iPod (music player), and camera. The interface could be customized within limited parameters, such as setting an image for the lock screen (the default display in standby mode) or rearranging the icons on the screen, but the default apps could not be deleted. Like its precursors, the iPhone displayed these icons in a colorful grid, but it unified the look of the interface by requiring all icons to fit the same shape, a square with rounded corners. Media, internet apps, games, productivity tools, and utilities all took up the same amount of screen space and were organized visually the same ways, equalizing rather than hierarchizing different types of use. At the time, Apple's user interfaces simulated their three-dimensional counterparts, a design philosophy known as *skeuomorphism* (see Hayles 1999; Gershon 2010b). The notepad, for example, resembled a leather-bound ruled legal pad, the YouTube icon a retro midcentury television, and the Contacts app a spiral-bound address book, while the clock icon showed an analog face. These design choices entail "iterative, replicative change," referring back to analog materialities (Gershon 2010b, 17).

The popular mobile recommendation app Qype further exemplifies the ways interface design encoded assumptions about class and mobility, shaping mobility and the potential for cosmopolitan connection. Qype, similar to the popular US app Yelp, launched out of Hamburg in 2006 and later expanded to the United Kingdom, parts of continental Europe, and Brazil. The mobile app reiterated many of the stylistic and interactional features of the iPhone operating system, with similarly stylized icons, in a black, blue, and gray palette (see figure 5). The top categories reflected the presumed interests of its users, such as Eating & Drinking; Cafes & Coffee Shops; and Nightlife, Arts & Entertainment. Unlike

FIGURE 5. App screenshots from Qype's user interface (UI) developer showing the main categories and locations, in a blue, black, and gray palette, https://www.behance.net/gallery/764429/Design-for-Qype-Mobile-(iPhoneAndroid).

Yelp, however, it distinguished itself with multilingual tools that allowed users to set a default language for displaying reviews and offered separate versions for each country where it was available (e.g., Qype Germany or Qype UK). Despite these multilingual, country-specific versions, the German version sometimes mixed German and English, as screenshots published by the app's user interface designer show (see figure 6). It was possible to view Qype (including its categories and other interface features) in English, while other information remained in German (for more on language mixing and cosmopolitanism in Berlin, see chapter 3). When I searched reviews, I often found them in both English and German, perhaps because I had not created a user account and therefore had not set a language.

The interface design brought together the assumptions or expectations of designers, such as which categories to make primary, with the daily trajectories of users, such as which businesses to review (in contrast to more comprehensive, top-down directories). Erik was enthusiastic about the ways Qype allowed him to navigate Hannover and Berlin and followed some of the developers on Twitter. When he visited Berlin, he and Alex would shop for comics and organize

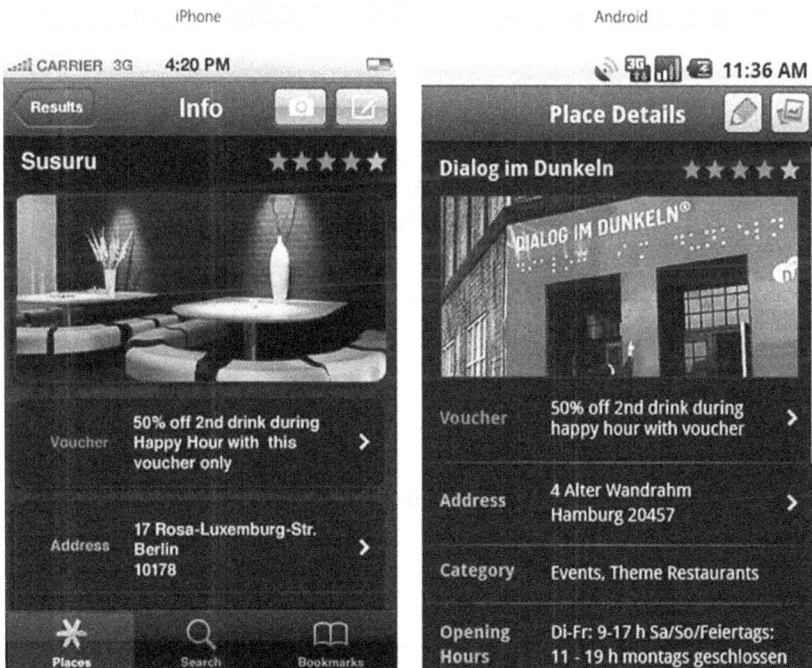

FIGURE 6. Screenshot of the Qype app from the UI developer showing the mixing of English and German, https://www.behance.net/gallery/764429 /Design-for-Qype-Mobile-(iPhoneAndroid).

FIGURE 7. Mobile phone advertisement on an intercity train in Germany. Photo by author, 2009.

dinner outings with friends. On one of these visits, for example, they invited me and others to a Vietnamese café in Kreuzberg with cheerful, bright decor that attracted a young, mobile clientele—a place typical of those Erik searched for and sometimes reviewed on Qype. For Erik, Qype opened up new possibilities for discovering places he might not have known about otherwise, especially in cities he did not know well, like Berlin. But the app did so by generating particular mappings organized around activities with specific class entailments, like eating at trendy restaurants, going to coffee shops and clubs, or shopping for music.

Mobile apps and operating systems mirrored—and generated—the presumed uses of an emerging mobile middle class, facilitating acceptable middle-class travel and movement through the city. But through user profiles and customization, the interface also encoded normative understandings of liberal Western selfhood as discrete, singular, and indivisible.[7] The possibilities for customizing devices like the iPhone implied an autonomous, singular user adapting default options to their individualized preferences. The Qype app, for example, required users to create an individual account to contribute reviews, save bookmarks, or create a personal profile (although it was possible to use the app without doing so). These features, typical of many mobile apps, rendered the phone specific to a singular user. Most apps or systems saved the login information and password for their primary user (often relying on system-wide security such as a code lock), keeping them logged in to email, social media, and cloud-based services. Saved user data along with customization meant that each handset was highly personalized and made it difficult to share devices between friends or family members.[8]

Anthropologists have long called attention to liberal constructions of personhood that contrast with diverse and often incommensurate understandings of the self in non-Western contexts (e.g., Sykes 2007; see also MacPherson 1962) and have broadly criticized Weberian methodological individualism. Marilyn Strathern (1988), most notably, compares individualist notions of personhood with what she terms "dividual" selfhood in Hagen, in the Western Highlands of Melanesia. Rather than view society as the sum of bounded, independent actors, persons in Hagen understood themselves as constituted by multiple circulating parts of others. In this sense, they were the product of social relations, not the precursor, as she explains: "We must stop thinking that at the heart of these cultures is an antinomy between 'society' and 'the individual'" (12). Instead, "the singular person, then, regarded as a derivative of multiple identities, may be transformed into the dividual composed of distinct male and female elements" (15), that circulated like gifts. Personhood and subjectivity in this sense were produced by circulation, rather than preceding it.

Like normative Western persons in Strathern's analysis, mobile phones, with their individualized interfaces and service plans, were not expected to circulate among users. Typical service plans, especially those popular with my interlocutors, assumed an individual user. Even shared family plans (which few used) were meant for multiple users with separate phone numbers. Those I knew in Berlin and elsewhere strongly preferred their mobile phones to fixed landlines, which require household members to share a line, even if they own multiple handsets. Most young people in my fieldwork lived in a room-share ("Wohngemeinschaft," or WG; literally "housing community") and either did not have or did not use a fixed line at home, even though such lines were less expensive for calling other fixed lines (for example, to reach parents who still used them). The cost structures of most mobile service plans were complex and charged by the minute for making (but not receiving) calls, depending on the service provider and other factors. Many, like Jörg, reported making calls regularly to close friends and family, as he described: "I call my friends, good friends, when I feel lonely, or to make appointments; also occasionally my granny (*Oma*) or mom; even my dad or brother. It's useful to reach people who don't check email as often or from anywhere [as he could with his iPhone]." He went on to add: "I don't have a landline; I don't need it." Transnational residents like Nathan, a student from the United Kingdom, or Viktor, a musician from Copenhagen, felt no need for a landline, as Viktor explained: "I haven't had a landline since I was 18."

Among those who did maintain landlines, most did so either for calling family or for work. Pascal, for example, described the landline he shared with his roommates: "Yeah, we actually have a landline, I hardly ever use it. We have it because we can make free calls to Festnetz, but . . . I think I only have one Festnetz number in my cellphone." But it allowed his mother to call him at home. Others lived either alone or with a romantic partner; for example, Sabine lived on her own, and Sal and David were music professionals who maintained home offices. Bettina, who had recently moved in with her boyfriend, imagined she would use the landline more often now that she no longer had roommates: "I may use it more soon, now that I'm in my own house and have a cordless." Mobile phones, in contrast, allowed both phone calls and text messages, which most people sent and received daily, and provided more privacy and autonomy.

In contrast to landline phones, mobile phones could circulate with the body of their owner and were mobile in that sense. But was this mobility the imagined flowing, liquid, quicksilver mobility of global capital, as Sheller and Urry (2006) or Maurer (2000) highlight? As Maurer contends, not all forms of movement and circulation are comparable or equivalent, and at times, mobile phones generated alternative experiences of mobility. In Maurer's account of global finance in the British Virgin Islands, he writes that discussions of globalization presume "that movement generates change, that movement is self-evident, and that increasing mobility characterizes the present" (670). He describes capital's mobility—or at least imaginings of it—as lightning fast, "quicksilver capital" (671). In this view, the movements of mobile phones, mobile persons, and other mobile objects represent the same kind of motion. Instead, Maurer asks how objects come to be mobile in the first place—that is, how mobile objects are produced as objects. Is a mobile phone simply a telecommunication device rendered movable by cutting the landline cord? Or, like Strathern's dividual persons, are mobile objects produced by certain kinds of movement and circulation?

Like Western persons, objects that circulate are often presumed to exist as ontologically stable things such as capital or commodities that are capable of movement. Maurer argues on the contrary that the objects of capital mobility come into being through the relations of capital, in which "the ontologies of moving objects of capitalism are never given in advance of relationships that produce and reproduce them, relationships that also interrupt teleologies of capital's advance, from its initial 'penetration' to its 'triumph' at the 'end of history' (Derrida 1994; Fukuyama 1992)" (2000, 690). Maurer's analysis suggests not only that the objects that circulate as capital are not necessarily equivalent but that not all forms of movement are alike. With its liquid mobility, capital is often portrayed as hard, quick, clean, and penetrating. Global finance networks, for example, purport to circulate capital at the speed of light, like a fiber optic network. Maurer seeks to interrupt this narrative of "the virtual objects of quicksilver capital zipping around the globe in networked circuits" (672) to explore instead alternative mobilities, such as the slow, seeping spread of killifish that reproduce in mud. As Maurer puts it, the species "oozes through the muck" (687). He asks instead how we might reconsider capital mobility as "less a fiber optic network; more like a lava lamp" (672).

Although mobile phones at times encoded normative forms of mobility—as discretionary, professional, and legitimate—at other times, they participated in alternative kinds of circulation and movement. One sunny spring afternoon, Jörg, Daniele, and some of their friends gathered in a nearby park. When

FIGURE 8.   A mobile phone, purse, cigarettes, portable speaker, and other objects scattered on a blanket in the grass at a park. Photo by author, 2010.

I approached the park entrance, I called Daniele to find them. A high falsetto voice answered instead, impersonating her. "Do you know who this is?" the voice finally asked, laughing. I guessed, correctly, that it was Jörg, and he guided me to their spot. Phones could circulate among this friend circle, fostering a more collective, dividual sociality.[9] As Daniele had explained, her phone, despite its lack of features, allowed her to be available to close friends and family. At kitchen and other gatherings, phones circulated among friends not because they were not seen as personal or individual devices but because they extended the reach of those immediately present to others who might be checking in or arriving. Mobile phones at times exceeded the professional, autonomous, middle-class forms of mobility (and personhood) for which they were designed. Instead they facilitated a more collective, distributed feeling of shared sociality, indexing the availability of subjects to one another.[10]

Prosthetic Mobilities

Although mobile phones could circulate among friends, some described their Handy as "like a body part," as one musician phrased it. Tropes of prosthetic extension figured frequently in discussions of these devices, echoing the collo-quialism of a Handy—that is, something handheld or pertaining to one's hand. As Jörg related, he reached for his phone first thing in the morning, then checked it throughout the day, keeping it on him while working or jogging. For others, the phone served a multiplicity of other purposes, like playing MP3 music or taking notes, useful because of their proximity to the hand or body. Sabine, who often traveled for work, described the continuity afforded by the constant companionship of her smartphone, being online "the entire day, and on my phone" ("den ganzen Tag, und auf Handy"). Prior analyses of mobile media examined the semiotic entailments of mobile phones, described, for example, by James Katz (2003, 1, 17) as being a "second skin" among young people, doubling as a communication technology and a cultural signifier. Mobile phones in this account were embedded in social life as both media and fashion accessory (see also Katz and Sugiyama 2006; Ito, Okabe, and Matsuda 2005). Theorists of technology and disability, however, have critiqued the tropes of prosthesis that often characterize discussions of bodily technologies, questioning the kinds of bodies and subjects they enable or disable.

The term *Handy*, suggesting bodily extension, stands in contrast with terms like *mobile*, indexing a phone's relation to a fixed network, or, in common US English, *cellular*, indexing the network technology. *Handy* implies a more intimate relation to the body, while simultaneously recalling the (imagined) English vernacular. In this sense, the term invoked participation in global cultural circuits, while representing an intimate, embodied connection to such devices. Human-technology interfaces often incite metaphors of prosthetic extension or cyborg hybridity, going back to Donna Haraway (1991) and Sandy Stone (1991), among others. Yet as disability scholars have repeatedly shown, such imagery depends on normalizing certain bodies and abilities, without accounting for how different bodies are produced (e.g., Kafer 2013; Goggin 2006; Jain 1999). Sarah Jain critiques the prosthesis trope in social studies of technology, examining multiple ways the same technologies can extend and injure: "My second concern is how a promising trope that might in some measure account for the technological extension of bodies can also take into account the variety of bodies and the social construction of abilities. Certain bodies—raced, aged, gendered, classed—are often already dubbed as not fully whole" (1999, 32). For Jain, needs and bodies are socially constructed in ways that highlight the harms of industrial technology production. Consumer economies depend on creating needs—and perpetual consumer dissatisfaction—as the history of car manufacturing, for example, shows. Similarly, Jain suggests that a prosthesis is better understood not as a technological extension but, after Derrida (1974, 144–52), as "that which supplies a deficiency" (Jain 1999, 33).

Jain notes that consumer marketing emphasizes the lightness and joy of tech products, eliding the real human pain of their production, in a reference to Haraway's pivotal 1990 essay on the cyborg: "Sunshine, open and free, recalls all those generic signifiers that are associated with consumption and fully dismembered from the exigencies of both material production and interfacial consumption" (Jain 1999, 49). The language of *Handy* as a body part, an indispensable extension of self, replicated this erasure, as when my interlocutors engaged in activities like finding hip new restaurants or joining conversations on Twitter. One person described how on Facebook, from his laptop, he mainly read others' posts. But on Twitter from his mobile phone, he was much more likely to post numerous updates: "Usually, if I really go on a Twitter frenzy, it's more from the mobile phone, I think." Erik, who had described Qype in enthusiastic detail, appreciated that some of the app's developers, based in Hamburg, also used Twitter: "I'm also following some of the developers on Twitter, I think they're from Hamburg, and it's cool." As prosthetic supplements, Handys enabled participation in the cosmopolitan worlds of social media and of Berlin. But their sleek, streamlined interfaces are produced under often harsh conditions, what Haraway once called "a matter of immense human pain in Detroit and Singapore" (1990, 153), typically not visible to consumers in places like Berlin. The imagined worlds opened by this prosthetic supplementation simultaneously foreclosed these new mobilities for those unable to access them.

New technologies may generate new mobilities, such as new ways of experiencing and navigating urban space. But they also raise further questions of bodily ability and social agency. Gerard Goggin (2006), for example, recounts how mobile phone design often presumes users imagined as normatively able-bodied, without hearing, visual, or mobility impairments. The early generation of analog mobile phones better suited the needs of some users with disabilities because they were compatible with TTY (Text to Telephone). The following generation of digital cell phones, however, displaced those analog systems with little regard for accessibility (2006, 95–96). Cell phones have since offered Deaf and visually impaired users new opportunities for communication—SMS, for example, allows Deaf users a new, rapid means of near-synchronous exchange—yet disabled people are still rarely imagined as normative or default users. Disabled users are excluded from who counts as users—and as cosmopolitan subjects—when these technologies fail to accommodate prior cultural arrangements, such as sign language rather than written communication.

Mobile phones, then, potentially extend agency for some—able-bodied, professional, often white and male. For Erik in Hannover, for example, his smartphone was an indispensable object that he used to check email and Twitter while commuting or to check in with his parents and brother back home: "I think [I use it] everyday when I'm on the way to the job; then when I'm sitting in the *Bahn* [train], I'm reading Twitter, or checking emails." As Goggin and others argue, mobile apps and devices equally create new forms of exclusion for those unable to access such technologies and interfaces, whether because of class competences and resources or because of bodily ability. One music producer who had grown up in eastern Germany contrasted his experiences in Leipzig, before he moved to Berlin and began using Facebook: "I haven't been on Facebook for very long, maybe a year? I began using it when I moved to Berlin, to find out when, where, what's happening. To be up-to-date. It's more relevant, more important than in Leipzig. In Leipzig, there was not so much going on. I used flyers, monthly magazines, city magazines [to find out about events]. Facebook is especially good because it's filtered [because there's so much more going on]." Mobile and social media in Berlin opened up access to new social worlds and art and music scenes, at the expense of those whose uses and abilities such technologies do not accommodate.

Mobile technologies in this sense not only construct some bodies and persons as socially and physically able; they enable social participation and agency for some—able-bodied, professional, middle class—over the poor, the aging, or those with hearing, visual, and mobility impairments. Celeste Langan argues that unequal transit systems render those who cannot use or afford cars "mass-transit dependent" (2001, 463), generating new forms of disability and inequality. She likens such dependence to "mobility disability," in which cars, like new communication technologies, become necessary prosthetics for moving or speaking freely. Like transit, mobile networking provided new means for navigating public space. Transit apps, such as the one Jörg preferred, provided instantaneous access to routes and timetables, recommending itineraries and taking some of the guesswork out of public transit. Frith terms this new urban inequality "splintered space," in which location-based apps (called locative media) create a two-tiered system (2015, 140). Those with full-featured smartphones and high-speed data (and the necessary tech competences) experience an overlay of digital information that produces "personalised, digitally infused streets" for elites (140). But creating new means of navigating urban space often excludes those whose mobility has been seen as dangerous or threatening.

At the time of my fieldwork, touchscreen smartphones—especially the iPhone, associated with tech-savvy professionals—signified affluence. An encounter one evening illustrated how controversial these mobile devices could be in Berlin's anticapitalist youth spaces. Alex had brought me to dinner after work at a local *Volksküche*, a communally run kitchen that provided low-cost vegan meals to the public once a week. While eating, he pulled out his iPhone to check something briefly. He had acquired it secondhand through a friend, who had bought it unlocked from Italy to avoid the expensive and restrictive multiyear service contracts required in Germany. I had previously borrowed this particular handset when I first arrived in Berlin, and I saw that Alex had reformatted it and was using a SIM card from a German provider, O2 (despite previous problems connecting on the device). Without thinking, I pulled out my own unlocked phone to suggest some apps and was immediately, if good-naturedly, rebuked: "Put that away or they'll think we're capitalist pigs!" (or an epithet to that effect). Although Alex appreciated the access the phone provided to email and information, he remained attuned to the class position it indexed, which was often at odds with the countercultural spaces he inhabited.

Mobile phones, especially smartphones, extended or supplemented agency for elite, able-bodied, normative subjects, offering new ways to navigate the city, according to particular mappings. For those who could afford them (or had the tech competences to use them inexpensively, such as illicitly jailbreaking secondhand devices or using cheaper prepaid plans), mobile devices produced cosmopolitan experiences of urban space, tracing paths between hip businesses, nightclubs, and gentrifying neighborhoods. They also made possible new ways of being accessible and able to participate in online life, contributing to a sense of being continually online. Continual access for many contributed to experiences of deterritorialization, potentially rendering urban spaces homogenous. But as Frith (2015, 25) argues, rather than creating placeless spaces, mobile technologies allowed for new hybrid experiences of urban space, integrating digital

FIGURE 9. Ads for the newly launched Apple iPad at a mobile service provider store in Hamburg, June 2010. Photo by author.

information into daily trajectories. Such new experiences were available differently, however, as mobile devices accommodated, and incited, normative, able-bodied subjects capable of extending agency online and in the city. These devices equally generated new forms of communicative and mobility disabilities, limiting how some people—poor, disabled, noncitizen—were able to participate in digital spheres. As Jain's argument suggests, the light, airy, colorful ads for the newly released iPad (see figure 9) collated dreams of technological freedom, possibility, and transnational belonging, but concealed the disablement, the social and physical dismemberment, of those manufacturing technological goods or of those unable to afford or interface with them.

MULTISCALAR PUBLICS

What was good about Facebook was that, with Berlin, I got a total new social sphere, which involves a lot of English-speaking people, and so I post things in English—and this is the difference, I realized—I have some friends on Facebook who have no English[-speaking] friends at all, but still post in English.

Alex, the German DJ and electronic music promoter, joined Facebook when he first moved to Berlin after university in the early 2000s, as did many of his friends. Through the then-incipient social media platform, he articulated and sustained a new sphere of friends and contacts. Many of his friends were fluent in English and had English-speaking friends, and increasingly, he posted in English on Facebook, having developed English competence online in his late teens and early twenties. But he was surprised to find some of his German-speaking friends posting in English, as he explained: "I have some friends on Facebook who have no English[-speaking] friends at all, but still post in English." In the early 2000s, English served as a shared idiom for many of my young, mobile, urban interlocutors in Berlin and elsewhere in Europe. English allowed Alex and his friends to participate in cosmopolitan social worlds online and in Berlin, where the events they promoted and attended were often advertised in English or a mix of English and German. English competence opened access to new spheres, yet at other times, it created barriers to participation and cultural citizenship.

Online, especially on social media, language choices provided a means to move between—and produce—social spaces, often on the same platforms. By switching between idioms, media channels, and platforms, it was possible to manage audiences at different levels of intimacy and scale. Navigating multiple audiences and publics this way allowed users to navigate the multiplicity of social spheres cohabiting online spaces, what danah boyd (2014, 11) and others call "collapsed contexts." But switching between idioms and registers also aligned users with social worlds at different spatial scales—as when they alternated between audiences imagined as transnational, national publics, and close friend circles. Increasingly, the friend circles in my research preferred Facebook for these interactions, opting to move between social circles and publics through linguistic and semiotic means rather than compartmentalizing worlds with different platforms for each (cf. Costa 2018 on Turkish users who created multiple accounts for managing multiple social worlds). Facebook, like Berlin, operated as a multiscalar space, imagined as cosmopolitan and transnational. This contrasted, however, with the ways Facebook's interface design entailed implicitly normative, US understandings of friendship and sociality, including the organization and categorization of friendship.

Social media and other online spaces produced new experiences of place among these young, urban Europeans, bringing relationships, networks, and collectives at different scales into daily living. In particular, a shared sense of cosmopolitan connection took shape through online and networked communications, alongside reworkings of national and regional identities, selves, and consociations. In this chapter, I examine signifying practices, specifically language and verbal communication, to consider how they produced space online. In this approach, however, I understand these semiotic practices as inseparable from dynamic materiality (as discussed further in chapter 5 on digital materiality, see also Hayles 2004; Dourish and Mazmanian 2013; Pink, Ardévol, and Lanzeni 2016). What distinguishes online and digital communications from other modes or channels, such as face-to-face interactions or print media, is not whether they are more or less material, or real, but what material qualities and capacities they invoke or require (as Katherine Hayles [2004] argues).[1] Signification here is not detached from an otherwise inert material substrate. Media inhabit, perhaps uniquely, interstices between materialness—as lively and dynamic—and signification.

Social media in this analysis comprise both technological platforms, such as Facebook, Twitter, or Instagram (themselves constellations of objects, practices, people, and technical capacities), and shared meaning-making activities (signifying practices, phatic expressions, affective entailments, and so forth). In this context, language practices, like choices about which platform to use, enabled movement between—and generated—transnational circuits, local friend circles, and other spatial scales. What some scholars call Euro-English, for example—a variant of global English specific to young, mobile Europeans—located hip Berlin worlds in broader transnational, cosmopolitan cultural circuits. Moving between national languages and other idioms, in contrast, proved a means of managing diverse publics without changing platforms, to navigate audiences at multiple scales and degrees of intimacy (comparable to Madianou and Miller's [2013] concept of polymedia). Language switching became a means to produce spatial scales online, articulating national publics alongside intimate friend circles and transnational music scenes. But language switching on Facebook took place on what began as an English-language platform, where translation to German and other European languages was never seamless. Instead, Facebook's interaction design introduced implicitly US-based norms of sociality and friendship, in which *friend* did not correlate precisely to German *Freund*. Despite these differences, many German users preferred Facebook over national German social media, precisely because it mediated between close friend circles and audiences or publics at multiple other scales. Intimate, daily life in Berlin simultaneously inhabited hip, transnational, cosmopolitan worlds through Facebook.

Euro-English: "This Is Berlin"

Alex worked part-time at a small record shop on a quiet stretch of one of Berlin's main thoroughfares in the eastern district of Friedrichshain. He often coordinated and promoted music events with David, who co-owned the shop with another electronic music enthusiast. As I described in chapter 1, they located themselves in Berlin's underground electronic music scenes, preferring genres like dubstep (a scene based in London), electronic industrial, breakcore, and IDM (a more experimental, less dance-oriented subgenre). Often aesthetically bleak, these syncopated music styles contrasted with the upbeat, "four-on-the-floor" rhythms of more popular genres in Berlin like minimal techno. The shop catered to electronic music fans and DJs more widely, however, both in Berlin and beyond. Alex's responsibilities included composing and distributing the shop's monthly email newsletter, sent to those who had signed up for it either at the store or on the website. Most of the time, he told me, he wrote it in English, although some customers regularly requested a German-language version, as he recounted in a conversation:

Alex: Even, for example, the newsletter I write for the record store, I regularly get emails asking that I should write it in German.

Jordan: You write it in English?

Alex: I write it in English, because we have a lot of English-speaking customers, but, I get a lot of requests, like, that I should write it [in German].

Jordan: Do you ever consider doing a dual version?

Alex: Uh, it's too much work and not enough money for . . . [*laughs*] Sometimes, if I'm, like, lazy or I want to do it fast, I just write it in German.

Writing two versions was time intensive, and more German-speaking customers were likely to read English than vice versa. But for Alex, composing in English required more effort. David explained that although most customers were not native English speakers, they were linguistically diverse and the majority could read English. Another close associate of Alex's, the electronic musician Sal, similarly reported composing Facebook posts and other online media updates in English, to reach a larger audience. They perceived English, especially Euro-English (Forche 2012), as having a greater reach in translocal music scenes, in Berlin and online.

Linguistics scholars often term English outside native-speaking contexts "global English" (e.g., Crystal [1997] 2003); "world English" (e.g., Brutt-Griffler 2002); or sometimes "New Englishes" (e.g., Platt, Weber and Ho 1984). David Crystal ([1997] 2003, 7–11) dates the global spread of English to at least eighteenth- and nineteenth-century British imperialism and industrial dominance. With the rise of the United States as a superpower in the postwar period, he argues, English predominated as the language of globalization—a shared language for mass media, science and technology, business and marketing, and so forth. For Crystal, emerging internet technologies in the 1990s contributed to English's role as a global lingua franca. Yet as Janina Brutt-Griffler (2002) clarifies, English dominates in many cases because of the hegemonic nature of Western, Anglo-American culture. She counters unidirectional narratives of English "spreading" from colonizer to colonized, which frame the latter as passive recipients. Instead, she argues that indigenous speech communities acquired English as a second language proactively, not simply as a response to Western territorial expansion: "English owes its existence as a world language in large part to the struggle against imperialism, and not to imperialism alone" (2002, ix). She resists reading world English as the inevitable result of British linguistic imperialism, arguing rather that English spreads as an ongoing process facilitated by the language acquisition of Asian and African speech communities, in particular.

Global English (or Englishes), in these accounts, entails a diverse, multiglossic, multidialectal language variety that belongs to its speakers around the world and that varies according to local and national contexts. From this view, English exists in numerous instantiations, operating as an official or semiofficial language; a dominant but unofficial language; a second language with a "special role," as Crystal terms it ([1997] 2003, 3); as a common language where there are numerous native languages; and as an international language. Crystal describes a common language as necessary to globalization, mirroring arguments that national languages are necessary for forging nation-states (e.g., Gellner 1983; Anderson [1983] 1991; see chapter 4 of this book), and argues that English predominated initially on the internet (Crystal 2001; see also Cook 2004), largely because the public internet began in US military and academic institutions. For Crystal, the internet and digital communications represent a potential "linguistic revolution" (2001, viii), in which new communication technologies further the spread of global English, and English competence in turn enables participation in communities beyond local or national boundaries.

But as anthropologist Eric Henry, writing about the anthropology of global English, contends, English can insert speakers into global and transnational circuits, cultivating aspirational selves enfolded in emerging scalemaking projects: "The desire to speak English doubles and reflects linked desires to be cosmopolitan and to be internationally mobile. It allows a feeling of connection to what would otherwise be alien and alienating global structures of power and capital" (2007, 40).

Certainly, among young Germans like Alex, English competence was key to accessing online worlds. For Alex, who first spent time online in the late 1990s, his nascent English "opened up" the internet, as he phrased it, in turn improving his abilities. As he explained, he visited the internet earlier than many of his peers: "[My family], we were also the first ones to have, like, access to the internet—1999 is, in terms of internet, not much, but in terms [of] German rural areas, it was. There was a German Net, but most of the stuff was English. [English] opened up . . . like, one of the main reasons you were able to use the internet is that you have [English], that your English was better than others." In contrast, his mother, who had moved to Germany from eastern Europe as an adult, found online media less accessible because of her limited English skills: "basically, she's still not able to navigate [it], because her English is not that good."

Alex's English capabilities enabled access to early internet communities such as online forums and web boards, often devoted to English-language media such as role-playing games: "And English, actually, my English improved through the internet, because I started to post to message boards and getting role-play games information. For example, *Vampire*, which we were playing back then, the books weren't all out in German, so we ordered them in English and we read a lot on the forums, like White Wolf forums and stuff like that."

Alex's experience was common among his friend circle of music fans, most from western Germany, former West Berlin, or other EU countries. The role of English has shifted rapidly in Germany and Europe since the 1990s, becoming more widespread in the early 2000s, in education, media, news, and business domains (Erling and Walton 2007, 116). Elizabeth Erling and Alan Walton, for example, found that German university students from 2001–2002 at the Freie Universität Berlin (FUB) valued English for connecting them to international and multicultural worlds in Berlin, online, and elsewhere. The young, mobile, middle-class German students they studied considered English key to modern, urban German and European selfhood, offering an "alternative national identity"

(123) that was hip and cosmopolitan, in contrast to the more shameful associations with German nationalism or East German communism. In her account, English competence was redefining Germanness, particularly through the social and media worlds such competence affords. This hip, urban German identity encompasses multiple geographic scales, including strong ties to Berlin and associations with Europe and world or global cultures.

For the friend circle of music fans, English as a common language connected them to translocal and transnational cultural worlds online and in Berlin. David, the music shop owner, and Sal, the musician, advertised and posted online in English to target audiences beyond Berlin, but they equally promoted events in Berlin in English. One Friday, for example, David updated his Facebook status in English to say he was "putting the last touches to his [DJ] set for tonight," with a link to more information about the event. He frequently booked shows at Berghain, a nightclub whose licentious techno parties and renowned DJs had cemented Berlin's reputation as the "techno capital" of Europe (e.g., Rapp 2010; Sicko 2010; see also Borneman and Senders 2000). David, however, typically booked events on Fridays, before the weekend-long bacchanals, catering to a smaller scene for experimental dance music.

As described in chapter 1, these electronic music scenes took place across multiple locales, linking Berlin to London and other sites, while social media brought local rhythms of living into online spaces. English similarly located events based in Berlin, and their participants, in these translocal scenes. As Alex explained, English was the language most commonly understood by the store's multilingual customers. But at David's music events in Berlin, most attendees I heard spoke German. This practical reality contrasted with multinational festivals like Musikfest, which attracted attendees from the Netherlands, Denmark, France, the United Kingdom, and elsewhere, and where English was spoken as a shared language as often as German. In fact, it was likely possible to promote events in German and still reach non-German speakers; key information on flyers and websites, such as dates, locations, names of DJs or performances, and sometimes genres of music, is recognizable with no or minimal German competence. But English on event flyers (see figure 10) or online linked happenings in Berlin to translocal music scenes, rendering spaces in Berlin multiscalar.

One fieldwork encounter illustrates how English had become local to Berlin, particularly among mobile young people like Guus, from Rotterdam in the Netherlands. I had met Guus and some of his close friends at Musikfest in Cologne the previous October and had stayed with friends of his in Amsterdam. They visited Berlin regularly, every few months, to attend all-night techno parties, typically sharing a car or taking the train and renting a furnished apartment. One afternoon, I accompanied Guus and two of his friends to a café on Boxhagener Platz

FIGURE 10. Event flyers at a café in Kreuzberg, Berlin in German and English. Photo by author, 2015.

in Friedrichshain, near their short-term flat, for coffee and a late lunch. Like many young Dutch people, he had learned German as well as English in school. German and Dutch are closely related languages, making German relatively easy to learn, and he spoke and understood conversational German. When we arrived at the café, however, Guus approached the counter and ordered in English. When he returned to our table, I asked why, since he could equally have ordered in German. He simply shrugged and replied, "This is Berlin."

For Guus, English was appropriate to the youth worlds he transited in Berlin, from nightclubs to cafés. He, like Alex, David, and many of their peers, did not perceive English as a foreign language but as a localized idiom that reflected and indexed the city's hip and cosmopolitan position. Like other global Englishes, this form of Euro-English does not precisely replicate the speech of native English speakers in the United Kingdom, United States, or elsewhere, instead taking on its own distinctive characteristics. Euro-English, according to Forche (2012, 453) incorporates features of continental languages, including tenses, vocabulary (e.g., *faux-amis* such as *actual* for current, *eventual* for possible, *possibility* for opportunity, etc.), colloquialisms like *Handy* for mobile phone, deliberate articulation, slow tempo, and numerous other morphosyntactic shifts (see also Ferguson 1992, xvi–xvii). Many of my interlocutors spoke English this way; for example, Erik added *s* to pluralize *email* (*emails* or sometimes just *mails*) or *info* (*infos*), a common feature of Euro-English in Forche's (2012) account. For many young Berliners, as Erling (2007) argues, this form of English positioned them simultaneously as educated and urban Germans, mobile Europeans, and global citizens. Euro-English offered an alternative way of being German that, like social media, connected them to translocal and cosmopolitan worlds.

At other times, however, ubiquitous Euro-English presented barriers to participating in cosmopolitan nightlife and middle-class worlds. Another of Alex's friends, Torsten, had grown up in East Germany before the Wende (the fall of the Wall) and moved to Berlin for university. One evening, we attended an art installation and dance party at a former indoor public pool in Wedding, a neighborhood of former East Berlin. Torsten often posted online in English but preferred speaking German in copresent situations. Alex and another friend were bantering in colloquial US English while Torsten looked on, refraining from joining in. Later, he shared with me his anxieties about speaking English: "Alex and Sal joke a lot in American slang, but I don't always understand all of it." Neither Alex nor Sal had lived in the United States or any other native English-speaking place. But they had adopted informal, sometimes vulgar English banter from online spaces and English-language media. Joking together in English—unlike on Facebook, where more German-speaking friends could read or use an online translator—risked excluding friends like Torsten whose education and access to online media growing up had provided fewer opportunities to learn the language.

These hurdles were even more pronounced among the friend circle from Saxony-Anhalt, in former East Germany. My neighbor Jörg, for example, wrote and spoke English with enthusiasm. He had honed his English partly through education and his work as a music journalist and partly through his long-standing passion for indie music from the United States and United Kingdom. He had followed numerous US-based music labels since living in Magdeburg, for example, and corresponded with a number of US bands, including one whose tour he had hoped to promote. In contrast, most of his friend circle spoke more limited English, posting and commenting on Facebook in German. Sometimes, like David, he promoted upcoming music events in English, as in this example where he announced a DJ set at a local indie and electronic club night:

Jörg is djing tonight @[Venue], 12pm. Only the best
post/punk/math/indie/pop/rock/electronica/idm/chillwave tunes. Come!
vor 3 Stunden · Kommentieren · Gefällt mir
Nathan, Jörg und **4 anderen** gefällt das.

[**Friend 1**] um 12pm muss ich schlafen.

vor 2 Stunden · Gefällt mir

Nathan chillllllllllllllllwave!

vor 2 Stunden · Gefällt mir

A German-speaking acquaintance responded in German, quipping "around 12pm I have to sleep," calling attention to Jörg's typo (and retaining the English way of writing time, rather than the German, 12h [for *uhr*, hour]). On other occasions, often when sharing and discussing music, he posted in German, as when commenting on a music video he shared from YouTube:

> **Jörg** kriegt nich genug und sich nich mehr ein! ["can't get enough and can't join in"]
>
> this drummer is at the wrong gig
>
> [www.youtube.com link]
>
> vor 5 Stunden · Kommentieren · Gefällt mir · Teilen
>
> **Daniele, Jörg** und **3 anderen** gefällt das.
>
> [**Friend 2**] ha, ha! wie das tier aus der muppet show. [like the animal from the muppet show]
>
> vor 5 Stunden
>
> [**Friend 3**] wenn er nicht aufpasst, hat er sich seine eigene zwangsjacke aus dem fetzigen goldenen fummel getrommelt! [If he's not careful, he'll have his own straitjacket out drummed to the groovy golden fumble]
>
> vor 4 Stunden

The video was a humorous clip in English of a US-based cover band, dressed up in gold sequin jackets and playing a rock song. The drummer played wildly, seemingly out of character with the more restrained bandmates. Jörg composed his comment in informal German typical of his online writing, dropping pronouns and spelling *nicht* without the final *t*.

Jörg's friends Daniele and Katrine were less conversant in English, especially in informal speech online. Daniele, as she recounted to me (see chapter 1), had joined Facebook to maintain contact with Ausländer (mainly English speakers from the United States, United Kingdom, and elsewhere) she met in Berlin, often at nightclubs, such as Nathan and his friend Emily. She and Katrine often relied on translation tools to chat online with new-met acquaintances and rarely posted or commented in English. One evening, for example, Katrine was messaging Emily over Facebook chat. She copied and pasted her messages into an online translator, which slowed down the otherwise synchronous flow of turn-based chat. At one point, she asked me instead how best to translate a phrase:

"Jordan, can you help me with this?" Later she asked my input on what a specific English word meant. Katrine never expressed resentment or frustration when speaking English rather than German with Ausländer friends (who often also spoke German or were learning). Like Guus, she viewed English as commonplace in Berlin, and she took advantage of digital tools to mitigate her limited English abilities (perhaps improving them in the process). Although the prevalence of Euro-English threatened to bar her from the cosmopolitan worlds of nightclubs and of Facebook, she approached these spaces with enthusiasm, integrating tech tools or friends' help to pursue new connections online and in Berlin and to inhabit cosmopolitan, urban Germanness.

Intimate Networks

Euro-English situated these electronic music scenes in translocal circuits and in cosmopolitan Berlin. When in copresent spaces, however, Alex, Sal, David, and others typically spoke German, often mixing in English words. As Alex observed, many of his friends who posted in English on social media primarily interacted with German-speaking friends and contacts online. To address different friends or audiences, some moved between platforms, such as between Facebook and Twitter, or between transnational and national social network sites, like Studi.vz. Even within platforms like Facebook, switching language registers and idioms made it possible to move between audiences, generating new publics, spatial scales, and levels of intimacy. Some people articulated their assumptions about their media practices, offering insight into what Ilana Gershon (2010a, 2010b) terms media ideologies, after literature on language ideologies (e.g., Gal and Irvine 2000; Kroskrity 2000). Language choices, explicit or not, also provide insight into how they imagined the transnational and translocal worlds they transited. In everyday practice, imagined audiences often deviated from those who actually contributed to online conversations, as became clear in my analysis of encounters on Facebook.

Many of those I interviewed frequented Facebook as their primary social network site, keeping in daily contact with both close and extended social circles. Among the music fans, Alex, Erik, Pascal, Annike, and others visited Facebook daily, from either a desktop computer or a mobile device, and reported knowing all, or at least the majority, of their Facebook friends (*Freunde* in German, as I will discuss) "in person" ("*persönlich*," personally—that is, having met offscreen at some point). As Niels, a music programmer, averred, "I know 80–90% of my Facebook friends personally." Pascal echoed this sentiment on when he would add someone on Facebook: "Usually if I know them then, and usually if I've exchanged more than a few sentences with them at some point, and I've known them for a while." Sabine similarly said, "Most are friends; I've met them all in real life" (*echtleben*, roughly "actual life"). Many contrasted Facebook, as a site for friendship and leisure pursuits, with blogs, which, as Sabine put it, were for "infos" but not chatting or commenting: "It has to be something that I'm really, really interested in . . . [otherwise] I have to already know someone personally to write a comment."

Knowing most of one's Facebook contacts, however, did not translate to guessing which friends might view any particular post. Over time, users typically acquired hundreds of friends, but the algorithm-based News Feed (introduced in 2006 [boyd 2008]) did not deliver posts in a chronological, unfiltered fashion.[2] It was difficult to ascertain, then, who scrolled through any particular posts, if they saw them at all. Instead, friends became visible only by commenting or liking an update or link. In this sense, an audience for any particular post constituted an imagined community in Benedict Anderson's ([1983] 1991) sense, produced by circulating shared texts with unseen but imagined others.[3] Posts and comment threads additionally brought together friends of friends, those whom one might not know directly but who could see one another's comments on a friend's post or wall. Sociality on Facebook in these instances coalesced around the stranger sociability described by Michael Warner (2002)—that is, publics constituted by the circulation of media texts among unknown others, potentially fostering feelings of communality (and in contrast to forms of sociability generated by intimacy or affect; see Berlant and Warner 1998).

In this context, alternating between languages or registers addressed, and created, publics at multiple scales and degrees of intimacy. The circle of music fans, for example, frequently discussed transnational media like music in English. In a characteristic exchange, Erik (the public relations consultant in Hannover) shared (that is, reposted from another user, using Facebook's Share button) a link to a website for a new album from a US music producer, Trent Reznor, known for popularizing industrial rock music, as well as for evocative film scores. In 2010, Reznor released a new album solely as a digital download, drawing media attention during a time when CDs were still common. Erik included his own commentary on the link, writing: "Trent Reznor is back." Alex liked the link, and they continued discussing the new album in English:

> **Alex**: Like it?
>
> **Erik**: Like it because it sounds like one of those sad/melancholic nin [Nine Inch Nails, Reznor's first project] songs that are based around the piano that I like so much (but with a twist because of the singer's gorgeous voice)—In fact, this is basically a nin song (the melody reminds me A LOT of "Right Where It Belongs" with a new singer. Anyway, like it.
>
> **Alex**: Yes, exactly . . . I hope the up tempo rock phase is over now and he gets back to the fragile and moody compositions, which were a bit neglected in his latest oevre.

As Forche and Erling have argued, Erik and Alex conversed in an international or global English, constituting an emerging Euro-English. They did not necessarily replicate the writing of native speakers; for example, the exchange "Like it? . . . Anyway, like it," which echoes German grammatical structures (e.g., "Gefällt's dir?"), does not reflect a native English vernacular. Global or Euro-English here located the conversation in a transnational sphere of popular music, rather than in either German or US publics. Yet when Erik visited Alex in Berlin, they spoke German (specifically colloquial *Hochdeutsch*, or "standard" German).

In an interview, Alex reflected on his tendency to post in English, which he described as reaching a wider audience: "I do post in English, because I have a lot of English-speaking friends, and I do only post German things which relate only to German [things]—like you know, none of my English speaking friends would understand anything of it." He reserved German for topics he deemed specific to other Germans, mainly topics of national interest, as I will address further (see also chapter 4). The musician Sal reiterated the sentiment that English posts and updates addressed a wider audience, especially online, explaining that he posted "in English, although I use German with non-English speakers online. But in general, English reaches a bigger audience." In interviews, most described Facebook as a public or semipublic site for hanging out with friends and peers, where leisure and personal interests typically structured such encounters.

Global English on Facebook, as in event promotion in Berlin, aligned updates and comments with a public space perceived as global and cosmopolitan. Language practices on Facebook, then, often contrasted with copresent conversations, as well as conversations on other digital platforms, such as one-to-one chat or instant messaging (IM). Many preferred Skype messaging and other IM programs (including Facebook Messenger, Apple's integrated text and chat platform, and AIM, AOL's legacy chat service) for conversing one-to-one with close friends. Alex, Sal, and others preferred Skype (better known for its video chat and voice-over-IP service) for messaging one-to-one, often replacing previous services like ICQ.

Erik, for example, enumerated his daily slate of computer programs: "I've got AIM, ICQ, no bullshit, Adium and iChat, and Skype—and I use it everyday. It's always—there are four programs I open when I boot the computer, it's Mail, Tweetie, Skype, and iTunes, most of the time. Three of those are just for communicating, and the rest is for listening." Similarly, Niels, another music producer in Berlin, reported leaving Skype running "all day long" (*alltäglich*). Nathan, an Anglophone friend of the circle from Saxony-Anhalt, characterized Skype as primarily for "friendship maintenance" with friends in the United States and Europe. A woman living in West Berlin who was connected to the same friend circle described switching to Skype from ICQ a few years prior, primarily for brief everyday exchanges with friends: "So, Skype is always up-to-date stuff, so you have an easy brief exchange, what you're doing right now."

Communication over Skype and other IM platforms often involved short-term planning and coordination, which unfolded in informal registers that connoted—and created—intimacy. Scholars of online and computer-mediated communication initially compared IM and other internet language to a hybrid of written and oral modes, a "hybrid language variety," as Akkaya argues in her 2014 review (see also Baron 1998; Crystal 2001; Werry 1996; Yates 1996). Many researchers have since shifted to analyzing online language as instances of discourse in a new context rather than an entirely new medium, emphasizing instead a "diversity of practices and ideologies" that prior approaches erased (Akkaya 2014, 286). Graham Jones and Bambi Schieffelin (2009a), for example, contend that for university students in New York City, IM lay on a continuum between writing and speech. Their approach diverges from accounts of "Netspeak" as a new and separate language hybrid (see, for example, Crystal 2001, 92) by identifying continuities between offline and online language. In a study from the early 2000s, they chart the emergence on IM of the phrase "be + like" ("he was like") to enquote others' talk (shifting, for example, from "he said"). IM, they argue, gained popularity in the early 2000s as a typewritten genre approximating oral speech, through synchronous temporality, informal speech, and turn taking, "a technology and genre distinctive in its close relationship to spoken communication" (Jones and Schieffelin 2009a, 80). But unlike previous analyses of online speech, they distinguish IM from email (intimate and informal among close associates, but not synchronous) and chat rooms (which involve turn taking and other talk-like features but usually among anonymous participants and which are therefore less intimate and informal).

Like the university students Jones and Schieffelin studied, the circle of music fans messaged one another regularly, often daily, alongside reading email, browsing Facebook, and checking news media. As we became better acquainted, Alex and Sal began messaging me, usually during the day from their computers (often while working or hanging out online). These encounters offer insight into how language practices over IM signified and fostered closeness. One afternoon, for example, Sal messaged me over Skype, and we discussed weekends plans. He incorporated markers of informal internet speech (see Crystal 2001; Cook 2004), such as forgoing capitalization except for emphasis ("VIEL arbeiten," work a LOT) and appending emoticons to convey tone. As Jones and Schieffelin aver, the chat format contributed to reproducing oral talk. Sal, for example, initiated the conversation with a greeting, and we then took turns, using line returns to hold space for further utterances. Although we conversed in German, we drew on conventions of English-language internet speech, such as dropping pronouns. In one such instance, Sal wrote, "muss einen workshop vorbereiten," leaving the first-person singular *ich* (I) implied: "[I] must prepare for a workshop," as illustrated below:

Sal: guten tag übrigens :) gehts dir gut? [good day by the way :) how're you?]

Jordan: gut! was geht diese wochenende? [good! what's going on this weekend?]

Sal: oh, bei mir nicht soooooo viel. . . . muss einen workshop vorbereiten und VIEL arbeiten :S [oh, for me not soooooo much . . . must prepare for a workshop and work a LOT :S]

hast du pläne` [do you have plans`]

?

The emoticon ":S" here connoted frustration or worry; "soooooo" approximated the elongation of the spoken word for emphasis; and expressions later in the chat such as "hm" reproduced nonverbal sounds. Two emoticons (see below) were specific to Skype: (mm), standing for *mm-hmm*, or nodding agreement, and (doh), for the interjection *doh!*, popularized on the US TV program *The Simpsons*. In the course of the conversation, we conversed mainly in German but occasionally mixed in English ("excellent!"; "*einen* workshop *vorbereiten*"). Approximating talk rendered the conversation intimate and informal, while internet conventions situated the conversation online:

Jordan: super

klar. und morgen? halloween? [got it. and tomorrow? halloween?]

Sal: (doh)

klar . . . [gotcha . . .]

hm

sollte schon einiges gehen [should go to a few things already]

Jordan: ja, aber wohin? [yes, but where?]

Sal: das finde ich noch raus :) [that i still need to find out :)]

Jordan: excellent!

und wie geht's dir? [and how are you?]

Sal: arbeit arbeit arbeit :S . . . ist ein langes wochende (daher weiss ich auch noch nicht wieviel/ob ich feiern gehe) [work work work :S . . . it's a long weekend (so I don't know yet how much/whether I can go party)]

Jordan: :/

schade! [too bad!]

Sal: ja, mal sehen [yeah, will see]

vielleicht ja doch (mm) [maybe yes yet (mm)]

Sal, Alex, and their friends typically reserved this register of chat on Skype for conversing with close friends. As Alex explained, he maintained accounts on multiple platforms but restricted Skype to "the closest circle," those to whom he remained available at all times: "Skype is also, like, my main tool. And the thing is, that Skype is also . . . for example, a lot of people I have on ICQ or Facebook, I would never add on Skype. This is also [due to] a certain aspect of the technical functionalities of Skype [such as file sharing], but Skype is only getting like, the closest circle—the people who are allowed to see me online on Skype are the people I'm okay to talk at any time." He had adopted Skype so he could exchange music files easily, but it became the platform for close friends granted continual access to message him anytime (notably, replicating Jones and Schieffelin's finding [2009a], he referred to typewritten chat on Skype as "talk"). Choosing different platforms to manage relationships and closeness illustrates what Madianou and Miller (2013) term "polymedia," an integrated media environment in which media switching entails social, moral, and affective decisions. As financial and technical barriers to new technologies diminish, choosing between modes and platforms takes on greater social significance: "As a consequence the primary concern shifts from an emphasis on the constraints imposed by each medium (often cost-related, but also shaped by specific qualities) to an emphasis upon the social and emotional consequences of choosing between those different media" (170). Media switching becomes a component in social relations, in their terms, "re-socializing" media technologies.

Alex, for example, moved between browsing Facebook, a semipublic space for transnational and translocal connections; chatting with his closest friends (mostly in Berlin); and conversing on platforms he deemed less intimate, like ICQ or Facebook Messenger. The media preferences Alex and others articulated also call attention to the assumptions, often implicit, that informed their view of each platform's or channel's appropriate use, what Ilana Gershon (2010a) calls media ideologies. Expanding on the concept of language ideologies (Gal and Irvine 2000; Woolard 1998), Gershon details how understandings about different media platforms shape—and constitute—speech acts: "People were explicit about their media ideologies, which I take to be people's beliefs, attitudes and strategies about the media they use that function in ways parallel to how language ideologies function" (2010a, 391). She examines breakup conversations in particular as uncertain, unstable speech events that unfolded across media in contested ways. Her interlocutors often agonized over a romantic partner's choice of medium for effecting a breakup, in which media switching was often—but not always—highly significant. Media switching in these accounts further shows how platforms, particularly in an integrated media ecology, do not simply convey meaning but constitute it and cannot be interchanged.

Like internet speech, regional speech among the friend circle from Magdeburg could convey and incite intimacy. Jörg, Daniele, Katrine, and their close friends grew up speaking the regional *Ostfälisch* (Eastphalian) dialect at home, along with *Hochdeutsch* (standard or High German). This regional speech is comprehensible to Hochdeutsch speakers and shares features with the variations of German spoken nearby, including *Sachsen* (Saxon) and *Berlinerisch* (Berliner). These regional ways of speaking, unlike Hochdeutsch, connoted working-class, often rural origins, similar to those of the Norwegian dialects described by Karl Swinehart (2008). Swinehart analyzes the lyrics of a Norwegian folk-rock musician, Rotmo, who created a "chronotope," a social reality with spatial and temporal dimensions, through lyrics. Rotmo's music allowed listeners to align themselves with working-class personae and politics, to "occupy particular social spaces but inhabit them with particular ways of speaking" (298). As Jörg explained, he and his friends feared embarrassing themselves if they spoke Ostfälisch outside their close friend circle, especially with middle-class, urban, western Germans. But Daniele and Katrine often switched into regional speech at home or on the phone with family, softening the hard Hochdeutsch *g* in words like *gut* (good) to a soft *y* sound, represented in German by *j*. *Gut*, for example, became *jut*, and *genau* (exactly), *jenau*.

Like Alex, Eric, and others, Jörg often posted about music in English and even maintained an English-language music blog. Quoting song lyrics, on Facebook he one day posted—somewhat cryptically—"The music makes me sick. I stop to listen when you start to sing." Sabine and Daniele liked his post, although they typically wrote and commented in German. At other times, however, he posted updates about life in his neighborhood in German. One day in May, he wrote, "Grüner wird's nicht: Berlin . . . 5.24. Awesome" ("It doesn't get greener than this: Berlin . . . May 24. Awesome," mixing German and English), and included a photo of a tree-lined street and a small leafy park. Sabine posted to Facebook more rarely, and typically in German, one day wondering: "bleiben oder fahren?" (to stay or go?). But in chat, Jörg often mixed in more casual language and regional speech, substituting *kieken* for *gucken* (to look or watch). One afternoon, he messaged me over Facebook to invite me to a World Cup showing at a bar in nearby Kreuzberg:

Jörg: Hey Jordi! Was machsten? [Hey Jordi! Whatcha doin'?]

Jordan: workin'

Jordan: im Café [in a café]

Jordan: du? [you?]

Jörg: Booooring!

Jordan: aber notwendig! [but necessary!]

Jörg: Ich will gleich mit Dieter und Katrine und Daniele zur Bar24 fahren zum Fussball kieken! Da isses echt schön, sogar ohne Fussball. KOMM MIT!!
[I want to go soon with Dieter and Katrine and Daniele to Bar24 to watch football [soccer]! There's really good food there, even without football. COME WITH US!!]

Like Sal, Jörg approximated informal talk by adding vowels for emphasis (Booooring!), dropping pronouns, and using all caps for yelling, while mixing German and English. But he also incorporated regional vocabulary like *kieken*, otherwise reserved for intimate speech among close friends and family from Magdeburg. Language and platform switching here produced intimate spaces, allowing people to manage the audiences and publics through which they moved.

Language Mixing as Scalemaking

Language and media switching made it possible to move between—and manage—multiple publics and audiences in the same spaces, especially in text-based online contexts. While language choices often indexed and fostered degrees of intimacy, they equally entailed geographic dimensions, allowing users to move between—and generate—spatial levels. Communicating in global or Euro-English located conversations and encounters in transnational or translocal contexts, such as English-language conversations about electronic music. At the same time, informal, intimate registers brought local friendships and regional connections online, while switching into national languages could invoke national publics, in the sense of audiences of conationalists (I discuss other forms of online nationalism and affect in chapter 4). In some cases, people hailed a national public explicitly, while at other times, they began conversations in global English and then switched to a national language in an ensuing comment thread. Language alternation and mixing, I argue, invited people on social media to align themselves with worlds at multiple scales, such as translocal scenes and national publics, just as Norwegian folk music invited listeners to align themselves with a rural, working-class chronotope, in Swinehart's account. Language practices, combined with media switching, in this sense contributed to making and navigating spatial scales online.

Like many I interviewed, Alex preferred reading news online in German, mainly in national publications like *Der Spiegel* (see chapter 4). At the time of my fieldwork in 2009 and 2010, few people shared news stories on Facebook (see Kraemer 2017 for a discussion of the merger of social media and the news in 2013[4]). Most perceived Facebook as a site for peer relationships and leisure interests and visited news websites as part of their daily online activities. On occasion, however, Alex shared links to news articles. As he explained in an interview, he wrote in German to address a German-speaking audience he thought would be concerned with German news topics: "So I do post—if I, for example, relate to a German article—like yesterday, I read a really interesting article . . . and so I did the comment in German, because I knew that my American friends won't be interested in reading German articles." As I have described, he regularly discussed music in English, in both posts and comments. In one typical example, he shared a link to a YouTube video with the comment, "A day like this needs an appropriate soundtrack." The same day, a friend living in Berlin, a native English speaker, posted a video that Alex and Erik liked, and in the comments, the friend suggested another music project that might interest Alex. Alex replied in English, "Funny that you mentioned it!" and they discussed the two videos in English.

Other studies of young Europeans' language practices have similarly found that young people mix English and national languages, in multiple registers, in creative and consequential ways. Sirpa Leppänen (2007) analyzed different ways young people in Finland take up English online, mixing English and Finnish for different effects. For these young people, English increasingly became part of youth language, associated with transnational cultural practices, especially popular culture and media. Youth language, Leppänen argues, operates as a semiotic resource that produces youth as a cultural category, always flexible and contested (see Bucholtz 2002; Durham 2004). She views "youth language" as "a set of communicative and semiotic resources with which, within a normative social and cultural framework, youth identities, practices, and cultures are constructed and negotiated" (Leppänen 2007, 151), terming diverse youth semiotic worlds "youthscapes" (after Appadurai's [1996] "global ethnoscapes").

Finnish youth mixed English and Finnish in what Leppänen (2007, 152) considers an "interlingual space," especially in online contexts like blogs. Similar to event flyers and promotional materials in Berlin, Finnish hip-hop combines global English with Helsinki-specific regional slang, locating itself in a simultaneously urban and translocal context: "The Helsinki slang used in it anchors the lyrics within the cultural (metropolitan, urban) context of Finnish hip-hop" (2007, 160). In other instances, Finnish bloggers composed diary-like entries in English, despite using a Finnish blog platform with primarily Finnish readers. Including occasional Finnish words, however, "presupposes a Finnish audience who understands what they mean without any glosses" (166). Leppänen surmises that the usage online reflects a broader language shift in which many accept English as a common language for online media, as she explains: "English is needed in new forms of cultural expression on the web, as well in the establishment and negotiation of identity and a sense of belonging to a wider—local as well as translocal—community" (167).

Among my interlocutors in Berlin, connected to wider circles online, English was the language of media (compare to the "medialect" described by Akkaya [2014, 290]), especially of social media and electronic music. Many composed status updates in English, then switched to national languages in comment threads. This pattern recurred frequently, representing maybe half of such interactions I observed, if not more. In July 2010, for example, the studio artist Annika posted a humorous complaint in English in reference to a meme about the date of the "future" in the American film *Back to the Future*. The meme involves a digitally altered still photograph from the movie showing July 5, 2010, as a date the story's pivotal time machine is set to visit, leading Annika to ask why the imagined technologies are not yet available, as shown below:

Annika WHERE IS MY HOVERBOARD, damnit!?

vor 3 Stunden · Kommentieren · Gefällt mir

[**Friend 1**] 1 gefällt das.

Pascal http://vimeo.com/11968215

vor 2 Stunden · Gefällt mir

[**Friend 2**] Srsly.

vor 2 Stunden · Gefällt mir

[**Friend 1**] http://www.worldcorrespondents.com/july-5-2010-back-to-the
-future-destination-time-is-a-hoax/886926

geht schon, wir mussen aber noch 5 jahre warten :(

Pascal replied with a link to a video about an art project involving a hoverboard, while another friend wryly commented "srsly" (seriously), here sardonically. A friend who had liked the post added a link to an English-language article debunking the meme but added in German, "it's okay, we just have to wait another 5 years :(." In informal online speech, he dropped the predicate "es" (it) before "geht schon" and did not capitalize "Jahre" (years; nouns are capitalized in standard written German). Annika, who was a bilingual dual German-American citizen, explained in an interview that she maintained circles of "very local" friends she saw daily and close friends who lived far away, partly because she had lived in the United States for a number of years. Many of her friends were similarly "international kids" who moved often: "there's a lot of friends that just moved, like, all around the world within two years." Her audience was likely multilingual, as evidenced by the combination of English and German replies.

At other times, such conversations switched quickly into German or other national languages. As I have described, Alex typically shared music links in English but often switched to German when replying to comments. In the following example, he linked to the YouTube video for a song he wanted to share and then commented darkly in German, "I wasn't so sure about that. [That]'s why I drowned another nun."

> **Alex** A day like this needs an appropriate soundtrack:
> http://www.youtube.com/watch?v=Bggazfz9TfE&hd=1
>
> Crowbar 01 Conquering
>
> [www.youtube.com link]
>
> Conquering by Crowbar from their album Broken Glass
> http://www.myspace.com/crowbar
>
> Gestern um 20:24 · Kommentieren · Gefällt mir · Teilen
>
> **Alex** und [**Friend 1**] 1 gefällt das.
>
> **Alex** Da war ich mir nicht so sicher. Hab deswegen nochmal eine Nonne mit ertränkt. [I wasn't so sure about that. {That}'s why I drowned another nun.]
>
> vor 15 Stunden · Gefällt mir
>
> [**Friend 2**] immerhin consequent [at least consistent]
>
> vor 4 Stunden · Gefällt mir

Like Annika, Alex maintained a network of multilingual contacts on Facebook. In practice, however, his close friends who commented frequently were primarily German speakers. Alex's non-German EU friends in Berlin similarly addressed their Facebook contacts in English, then switched to their national language, such as French or Danish. David's audience, he recounted, comprised multilingual Europeans and others, and much of the time, people commented on his posts in English. Occasionally, however, the conversation switched to French:

> **David**: David mentions in this status update that you should listen to my guest DJ mix. It's below on this profile, or visit my website
>
> vor 7 Stunden · Kommentieren · Gefällt mir
>
> 6 Personen gefällt das.
>
> Alle 8 Kommentare anzeigen
>
> [**Friend 2**] oulah, vais devoir écouter le mix 5 fois avant de terminer ahahaha . . .
> Vor 6 Stunden
>
> **David** [Friend 1] The second track is not there for long. But well, it's there. :).
>
> [**Friend 2**] au boulot!

The second commenter, shown above, responded in informal online French, dropping the pronoun *Je* (I): "*oulah*, [I] will have to listen to the mix 5 times before finishing ahahaha." David had replied in English to a prior commenter, naming each commenter as he replied, then switched to informal French with the French speaker: "get to work!" The use of French here restricted part of the conversation to French speakers in this interlingual space.

English, as a shared language associated with online spaces, located these electronic music scenes in translocal and transnational circuits, linking together music fans in new spatial configurations. As Alex contended, some people posted in English despite having few non-German-speaking friends on Facebook. In these instances, English suggests instead that users imagined the worlds they participated in, or to which they aspired, as transnational and cosmopolitan. Like Finnish hip-hop artists in the Helsinki suburbs, for whom urban language articulated desires to live as city dwellers according to Leppänen (2007), these friend circles addressed transnational audiences on Facebook, articulating desires to live as cosmopolitan urban Germans or EU citizens and to inhabit such transnational scales online. Perhaps sometimes they composed Facebook comments quickly, switching to their primary language because it was easier, as Alex reported regarding the music store's newsletter. But the effect was to switch from a transnational, multilingual scale to a national one.

At other times, some preferred their national language to convey strong feelings and affective attachment. Alex described switching to German to discuss topics of national interest, and at other times, he wrote in German to express strong sentiment. After an especially successful music showcase Alex had spent many hours organizing, I took photographs backstage of him with some close friends. I shared the digital photos on Facebook, and he requested that I send them to him as well. Until then, he had promoted and discussed the event online entirely in English. He commented on each of the photos in internet English, with humorous captions, save one of himself and three friends, including his co-promoter, holding a bottle of vodka. He switched to German to write:

Lieblingsmenschen und Lieblingsgetränk mit mir in einem Bild! <3

[Favorite people and favorite drink with me in one picture! <3]

As he explained during an interview, he found German better suited to conveying certain ideas or experiences, particularly emotionally laden ones. German here, along with the "<3" (heart symbol, for love or affection), entails an affective register corresponding with the sentiment expressed in "favorite people and favorite drink," albeit humorously. Switching into German recalls other times that Germanness and German identity incited an affective sense of belonging, as I detail in the next chapter. Leppänen (2007) similarly found that Finnish youth often mix in Finnish words in English-language contexts when expressing strong feelings. One Finnish blogger who writes primarily in English included Finnish words in ways that suggest she envisions a Finnish-speaking public. In an especially emotional post memorializing her grandfather, she refers to him in Finnish by the familiar term *papa*. Leppänen reads the term as affectively charged, as she explains: "Switching to Finnish thus has an affective function in this context" (166).

For the young Germans and others in my research, as for Finnish bloggers, language mixing enabled movement between circles and connections at different geographic scales and degrees of intimacy. Yet these spatial scales, such as affective national publics, do not predate such linguistic practices. Instead, language mixing produces spatial scales as a means of organizing online spaces, a form of scalemaking. These practices rendered online spaces on social media as geographically multiple, where participants could move between—and generate—multiple spatial configurations by switching between, mixing, and otherwise deploying global and Euro-Englishes, European national languages, internet-specific registers, and affective modes. Just as English constituted a form of youth language that linked young, mobile Europeans to global and transnational worlds, it constituted those worlds as global or transnational. Similarly, by switching to national languages like German, young people on Facebook participated in and generated national publics in the same online spaces they associated with cosmopolitanism and multinationalism. Such spaces became multiscalar, reshaping experiences of place in everyday living.

Friend or *Freund*

As young Europeans on Facebook moved through multiple scales and circles, they typically perceived these sites as transnational or global (or not geographic at all). Most were aware of the US origins of social network sites like Facebook and Twitter (in contrast to national social network sites, news sites, and European-based services like Skype or Last.fm). If anything, the US, English-language origins of Facebook contributed to its appeal as a global social network platform, as Leppänen and others argue, yet "global" or "transnational" often entails linkages to US and English-language media. In contrast to this transnational or global appeal, Facebook's interface design and language categories reflect conceptions and metaphors of sociality specific to its coders and developers, particularly the computing culture of California's Silicon Valley (e.g., Agre 2002; English-Lueck 2002; Nafus 2003; Turner 2005).

During my fieldwork, Facebook was available in German and other national European languages, but these translations typically left untouched the site's interaction design—that is, the layout of buttons and menus, steps necessary to accomplish given tasks, possible interactions with others, and similar features.

The translations themselves often glossed over meaningful differences by using parallel terms, such as German *Freund* for English *friend* or *Gefällt mir* ("it pleases me") for *like*. As linguists and linguistic anthropologists have long shown, translation never seamlessly reproduces concepts from one language into another. Although German speakers often took such differences in stride, German *Freund* does not encompass the same category as Anglo-American *friend*. On the contrary, German speakers deployed numerous terms encompassed by the singular word in English, as I will detail. Despite the unevenness of this translation, many preferred Facebook to both US and German alternatives; its position as an English-language site located it in transnational and cosmopolitan worlds, constituting these users as modern, urban Germans.

Most of the young people in my research had joined Facebook within the past few years, typically when they moved to Berlin. Many maintained accounts on other social network sites like MySpace or the German university network, Studi.vz, as Jörg, the music journalist from Saxony-Anhalt, recounted: "I've only been on Facebook for about a month; I have a MySpace for bands but not personal friends." His friends Daniele and Karoline had used MySpace when living in Magdeburg, but they joined Facebook after moving to Berlin. Like Jörg, most associated MySpace with bands and music, something the site helped cultivate.

Others like Alex also kept an account on Studi.vz, a social network site limited to German university students. Alex derided the site, saying he preferred Facebook, but had not deleted his account entirely, as he explained: "I had a Studi.vz [account] from, like, the first day [of] university, but I don't use it at all anymore. I'm only in there to keep track of people I'm actually not interested in any more. . . . but I'm still curious about the possibility to look at what they are doing."[5]

Some, like Daniele, Karoline, and Alex, associated MySpace and Studi.vz with the past (as described in chapter 1) and with previous friend circles. In contrast, they viewed Facebook as hip and transnational, connecting them to cosmopolitan worlds online and in Berlin. This pattern emerged among other Europeans as well, including the circle of Dutch music fans who often visited Berlin. Marc described a "Dutch social networking [site] called Hives" as like "Facebook for Dutch people—Dutch only, but the same features. I hate it. All of Holland is on Hives, actually." He preferred Facebook as a more "international" space, where he could post in English to address a more "general" audience. He switched into Dutch to engage a smaller circle of Dutch friends, rather than moving between English- and Dutch-language platforms.

Despite Facebook's appeal as a transnational space, it encoded understandings of friendship that were often at odds with those of my interlocutors. At the time, most associated Facebook with peer relationships and leisure interests. For instance, many followed pages for music shows and bands or shared music links and videos, while few circulated political news (Kraemer 2017; see also chapter 4 on national news online). Yet many of the music fans, especially those working in music professionally, pursued their personal interests as part of their work life and were comfortable combining the two domains. Sabine, the music journalist and colleague of Jörg's, explained that she used Facebook to "keep in touch with people," mainly "friends and colleagues—that is, a few who are also friends." The only person I interviewed to separate his online activities into "work and play" had grown up in the United States. In contrast, these same people did perceive Facebook as a space for friends rather than family, with few exceptions (mainly for peers like siblings or cousins). Instead, they switched to Skype, email, or text messages to communicate with parents and grandparents. Marc from Amsterdam, who regularly visited Berlin, insisted: "No family [on Facebook]—I don't want family being on my social networks. I want to keep it separated. It's for friends."

Alex elaborated further on why he Skyped daily with his mother but would never add her on Facebook: "I would never friend—befriend—my dad or my mom on Facebook. My mom strangely has it, but she doesn't use it. Well, I think she joined it because a friend of hers told her, but she didn't do anything with it. But I know, for example, my mom is using, like, a business-related social network."

In practice, people like Marc often maintained close contact with their families, but not through Facebook, as he clarified: "If you need help, you go to your parents—your parents remain in very close relation, actually."

The English term *friend*, however, entails a different category than its German equivalent, *Freund*. Of course, many English speakers understand Facebook *friend* as distinct from other meanings of the word, as research on Facebook friends in contrast to "real" or "actual" friends demonstrates (boyd 2008; boyd and Ellison 2008; Ellison, Steinfield, and Lampe 2011). But *friend* on Facebook invokes a set of assumptions about sociality that reflect social media's origins in predominantly white, middle-class Western and US-based computing cultures. The image of "cyberspace," for example, took shape as a libertarian construct in which networked technologies flatten hierarchies and decentralize organization, destroying and replacing societal institutions in the process, as Phil Agre (2002) outlines. In Agre's account, the first generation of computer hackers were primarily engineers who were aligned with licit organizations like the military and helped build the first computers. Their successors, in contrast, adopted an antiestablishment stance as rebels and outlaws, a shift Agre links to new constructions of masculinity, specifically those of angry, wounded warriors in the wake of the Vietnam War: "The new hackers were located outside of institutions and rebelled against them. . . . The new hacker, by contrast, self-consciously styled himself an outlaw, with no clear line between the security-cracking adventurism that aimed to strengthen the integrity of the systems and the outright criminal activity that aimed to subvert them" (179). At the same time, Agre argues, computing increasingly became a feminized domain, as feminized clerical work (see also Hicks 2017; Light 1999; I analyze these themes of gender and computing in Berlin further in Kraemer 2021a, 2021b).[6]

While some social movements had viewed the internet as decadent, linked to materialism and secularity, others projected onto networked computing tropes of transcendentalism and communitarianism that continue to shape internet interfaces and communities, as Agre explains: "Other movements, however, do not associate the Internet with decadent institutions, but quite the contrary want to use the Internet to displace or destroy them. This, finally, is the origin of the ideology of cyberspace, with its elaborate claims to overturn hierarchies, decentralize society, eliminate intermediaries, and so on" (2002, 180).

Virtual communities and the digital infrastructure that enables them are similarly rooted in the 1960s counterculture of California and elsewhere (Turner 2005; see also Stone 1991). Fred Turner argues that the hypertext documents of the World Wide Web (that is, interlinked texts, whether card catalogs or websites) were predated by a print artifact, the Whole Earth Catalog. An earlier virtual community coalesced around what Turner considers the shared hypertext of the catalog. Many participants went on to join one of the first online communities, the WELL (Whole Earth 'Lectronic Link), which the catalog's founder, Stewart Brand, pioneered. The WELL, like the Whole Earth Catalog, reiterated the horizontal, nonhierarchical principles espoused by Brand and others, according to Turner: "a countercultural conception of community had already been built into the system" (2005, 498). These ideals shaped the network's design, as "virtual, as well as material, collectivity lived on in the software, management structures, and day-to-day rhetoric of the WELL" (498). Many features of the internet and digital platforms continue to reflect the countercultural principles underpinning the WELL: interactivity, integration into daily living, rapid dissemination of information, the mixing of social and economic activity, and peer-to-peer communication and infrastructure: "In the process, however, with the Whole Earth Catalog and its many imitators the movement developed a new relationship between information, technology, and community that would ultimately facilitate the integration of computing technology and associated work styles into the mainstream of American life" (511).

Facebook's broad (and singular) friend category exemplifies the predominance of Western, middle-class US understandings of friendship and sociality that often undergird social media. German *Freund*, in contrast, connotes a deep, enduring bond, approximating more closely the English qualification of close friend. As the music engineer Niels reflected, *Freundschaft* entailed definitive obligations: "Would you help them move? Let them stay over?" On the one hand, many recognized as stereotypes what David called "geographic clichés" of Americans as gregarious but superficial. But on the other hand, US constructions of sociality shaped Facebook's interaction design, leaving it often at odds with implicit expectations constituting German Freundschaft—and media's proper use. When I went a week without contacting Alex, for example, he messaged me via Skype to express his concern: "I was worried that I hadn't contacted you recently! :(." Sabine similarly chided me if she did not hear from me often enough. Freundschaft required frequent, sustained contact, whether over Facebook, chat, or copresent meeting. Facebook's architecture is built instead around what researchers often consider "lightweight interactions" (e.g., Ellison, Steinfield, and Lampe 2011) such as likes and comments—casual contact that supports both close ties and acquaintanceship. In many ways, it was this informal mode of sociality, along with the potential for transnational connection, that appealed to my interlocutors.

In other ways, the language of friendship on Facebook homogenized a great variety of German-language social distinctions. German speakers, for example, deployed a wide range of terms to distinguish Freunde (roughly, close friends) from other kinds of relations, variations that the category of friend failed to capture. All contacts on Facebook fall under the rubric friend, although Facebook had added subgroups such as "acquaintances" and the option to create customized ones (these options changed over time, as Facebook continually reorganizes its features). US English speakers typically modify *friend* to shade gradations of closeness or specificity (e.g., a "close friend" or a "friend from work"). But German speakers grade peer relations with great precision. Enumerating her contacts online during an interview, for example, Daniele listed "*Freunde, Bekannte, Arbeitskollegen*" (roughly comparable to close friends, friendly acquaintances, and work colleagues). *Bekannte*, literally those "known," was the most common term after *Freunde* to describe associates in the broader friend circle, but the word does not equate to *acquaintances*. US English *acquaintance* typically conveys social distance, precisely because an acquaintance is not a friend. Less frequently in interviews but commonly in everyday speech, I heard specialized or informal terms like *Kommilitone* (fellow student) or *Kumpel* (similar to British *mate*). In a Skype conversation, for example, Alex offered to share information about my project with "Kommilitonen." US English speakers might instead refer to "a friend from school," or simply "a friend of mine."

For German speakers, Facebook's fundamental organization elided careful enunciations of social distance, subsuming all peers under the category of friend/*Freund* (most Germans viewed Facebook in German but were aware of the English terminology *friend* or *like*). Yet these design features did not necessarily constrain German speakers; on the contrary, most preferred the site over

German Studi.vz precisely because it promised to expand their social worlds. As Niels phrased it, Facebook made possible *"Freundschaft erweiterung,"* extending friendship into online spaces, while supporting existing friend circles, what he called a "helper tool *für real Freundeskreis*" ("a 'helper tool' for the actual friend circle"). Facebook linked his closest or inner circle of friends to a "larger circle" online. Rather than foreground distinctions between "real" friends and Facebook ones, for Niels, social media expanded and sustained his circles.

Making Multiscalar Publics

For many mobile young people in my research, English situated social media in global and cosmopolitan circuits, allowing them to participate in online worlds as middle-class, urban cosmopolitans. Some forms of English online, such as Euro-English, were often specific to Berlin and other urban areas. English in Berlin did not erase geographic specificity but instead constituted a global English that allowed for alternative ways of being German—one not equally available to all urban Germans, especially those from former East Germany. On Facebook, many alternated between Euro-English and other idioms, including national languages and informal internet registers similar to Netspeak. Language switching articulated multiple publics and spatial scales in the same online spaces, allowing urban Germans to move between close friend circles, nationally imagined communities, translocal music scenes, and broader transnational circuits of popular culture. Some speech, such as affective registers and regional speech, produced more intimate publics in networked spaces, such as in Facebook conversations and instant messaging. In many instances, multiple publics and scales intersected online, yet language switching and mixing offered a means for urban Europeans to manage intimacy in their friend circles and (sometimes imagined) wider audiences, producing multiscalar publics.

This spatial multiplicity incorporated specific notions of sociality, such as implicitly US-based ones, that undergird computing interfaces and social media. The English-language Facebook friend, for example, entailed and effected normative understandings of sociality and community rooted in the computing cultures of Silicon Valley. Such constructions of sociality and of selfhood instantiate long-standing Western ideals for peer relationships, informing conceptions of what a social network, and by extension, a social network site, should be. Historical accounts of Western friendship, for example, ground such conceptions in eighteenth- and nineteenth-century thought on the nature of personhood and sociality, as formulated by Enlightenment thinkers like Adam Smith, David Hume, and Jean-Jacques Rousseau. The historian Allan Silver (1989) argues that modern friendship in their writings involved voluntary, intimate relations between non-fungible individuals who shared their "true" selves, paralleling modern relations like romantic marriage. Silver sums up this exchange as "a pure expression in the domain of personal relations of voluntary agency, as expressing individual agency and elective interpersonal affinities" (1989, 277–78). Adam Smith contrasted the personal sphere of private, elective affinities between peers—which Silver describes as "private, uncodified, informal, [and] idiosyncratic" (290)—with the instrumental relations of the market. Private friendship, purified of the exchange relations of the economic order, constitutes a shared moral order, which Scottish Enlightenment thinkers like Adam Ferguson viewed as a "private virtue and a public good" (Silver 1990, 1485).[7]

These notions of friendship, grounded in elective affinities among peers, surfaced in Facebook's architecture. Facebook friendship, for example, must be reciprocal, and Facebook user profiles foreground shared leisure interests such as tastes in popular media. These technical features never predetermine media practices or the forms of sociability they support; many examples abide of people reworking technical platforms to suit culturally specific practices (e.g., D. Miller et al. 2016). A typical profile page during my fieldwork included default categories like sex, city, birthday, hometown, relationship status, and religious views, followed by activities, interests, and favorite media (music, TV, movies, books). Few of these categories were required, however, and many people found creative means to resignify or subvert them. One person, for example, listed another music producer as his "parent" (Facebook allows family members to mutually identify one another according to predetermined roles like mother, father, cousin, etc.) and included "Pastafarianism," a parody religion devised by atheists, under "religious views." Social network sites like LinkedIn, a site for professional networking, share some of these features, such as reciprocal connections (unlike Twitter or some more recent platforms). LinkedIn also encourages connections up and down professional ladders and solicits detailed work histories but asks for little information about personal tastes and interests.

Beyond interface design, modern liberal notions of friendship permeate conceptions of peer social relations on social media, sometimes explicitly. The term *social* in social media referred initially to the potential to generate social capital (boyd and Ellison 2008; Donath 2007; Ellison, Steinfield, and Lampe 2006, 2007, 2011 Lenhart et al. 2007). The social here entails mutual linkages between peers, implementing a nonhierarchical peer-to-peer infrastructure. As Silver shows, Smith envisioned two parallel social systems, the market relations of the public sphere and the personal ties of the private sphere: "Self-interest in a market system increases the wealth of all; sociability sustains a universal morality from which all benefit" (1990, 1492). Smith's conception of sociability informed what sociologists later called "social solidarity" and influenced the sociology of "strong" versus "weak" ties, formulated by Mark Granovetter (1973), for example. Facebook purports to capitalize on these weak ties (e.g., Bakshy et al. 2012), operationalizing Granovetter's assertion that weak ties matter most for social capital. My interlocutors described these ties as their "larger circle" online, in contrast to their inner or close friend circle.

Facebook's normative sociality—peer relations grounded in mutual affinities—did not necessarily elide or substitute for other experiences of friendship and connection. As Daniel Miller and colleagues (2016) demonstrate in a multi-sited series of social media ethnographies, Facebook varies according to cultural context, in terms of what kind of social space it constitutes. They define social media not as platforms—Facebook, Twitter, Instagram—but as constellations of content, such as "the millions of tweets, the core genres, the regional differences and its social and emotional consequences for users" on Twitter (1). Geographically specific norms and practices have transformed social media, as new social spaces, as much as social media have transformed social life: "Content manifests and transforms local relationships and issues. Our study has thus turned out to be as much about how the world changed social media as about how social media changed the world" (1).

In fact, English and German speakers alike distinguished between the category of Facebook friend—or Freund—and vernacular conceptions of friendship. But Facebook's position as a US-based platform weights these constructions of sociality unevenly. Such interactional norms raise further questions about how liberal, Western ideals of friendship, selfhood, and peer sociality play out in other contexts. For these urban, mobile young people in Berlin and elsewhere, English on Facebook linked their social worlds to transnational circuits, allowing them to participate online as hip cosmopolitans. Although limited English proficiency at times created barriers for eastern Germans like Torsten or Katrine, these constraints rarely discouraged them. Instead, they and their friend circles navigated the multiplicity of worlds and scales online through language switching and mixing. These semiotic practices produced multiscalar publics structured by normative liberal sociality specific to the gendered, classed, and racial positioning of Facebook's creators. But such constructions of sociality, like normative mobility, were equally contested, opening up possibilities for other forms of sociality and connection.

NETWORKED NATIONAL FEELINGS

Friederike was typical of many of the young, middle-class Berlin residents in my fieldwork—born and raised in the American sector of West Berlin, she moved east to lively Kreuzberg after university. When I met her in 2009, she was working part-time at an art gallery while pursuing freelance photography. Like many in her close friend circle, she had recently joined Facebook to "stay in touch" with friends abroad. Facebook soon became widespread among her friends, superseding platforms like MySpace and the German Studi.vz, which many described as outdated and parochial (as described in chapter 1). And, like many of her peers, she spoke idiomatic US English, composed her web page and Facebook profile in English, and frequented English-language blogs. In conversations with me, she elaborated on her passions for photography, design, craft markets, and time spent with friends, and she recounted her "daily ritual" of checking Facebook, email, and art blogs, including *Spiegel Online* (Spiegel.de), the website of the popular national news magazine. This last activity surprised me because Friederike (who went by Rike) and her friends rarely discussed news stories on Facebook or elsewhere; instead, they described online spaces as cosmopolitan and transnational (or nongeographic) sites for friendship and shared interests. Yet in interviews, I found most considered checking national news sites daily as essential as social media—highly unusual in a European nation where relatively few had switched to online news.[1]

As anthropologists of media and transnationalism have noted for some time, media technologies, from the more static internet of the 1990s to interactive social and mobile media, can foster national communities in virtual spaces (e.g., Bernal

2006, 2014; Franklin 2010; Lee 2007). In contrast to expectations that global communication networks would engender global identities—or fracture national ones—national forms of selfhood, belonging, and identification inhere in online contexts. National selfhood—that is, selfhood linked to the territorial scale of the nation—endured among these mobile young Germans and other Europeans. For those who preferred transnational communities of interest to national virtual communities, unspoken feelings of national belonging surfaced through unremarkable activities such as reading news websites or preparing seasonal *Spargel* (white asparagus) meals. Although national identification has long been linked to ordinary practices (such as banal nationalism; Billig 1995), the networked, online context presented a new site for enacting identity and selfhood. As this book describes, emerging technologies, particularly social media, made it possible to alternate rapidly between audiences and communities, bringing together encounters at multiple geographic levels. This multiscalar quality of social media—and the affective cosmopolitan nationalism social media facilitated—requires rethinking the relationship between media, selfhood, and place.

In this chapter, I link media practices to ordinary ways of being and feeling German to illustrate two interrelated arguments on media and place: (1) modern national selfhood owes historically to scalemaking processes that linked selfhood to territorial organization, and (2) national publics can form through shared affect, which analyses of discursive representation do not fully address. I demonstrate how two seemingly unrelated practices—reading the news magazine *Spiegel Online* and sharing meals during *Spargelzeit*, the springtime season for white asparagus—entail unremarkable forms of national sentiment that took place in digital, networked contexts, fostering an emergent cosmopolitan nationalism. This approach offers insight more broadly into how emerging media reconfigure scales of selfhood and sociality among urban Europeans, as this book details, while focusing on enactments of nationalism, especially through affective means online.

Anthropologists have long attended to the cultural production of place, especially in the wake of increasing mobility, globalizing capital, and processes of deterritorialization and reterritorialization (Appadurai 1996; Clifford 1992; Gupta and Ferguson 1992, 1997; Hannerz 1996; see also Harvey 1989). Cultural geographers have called particular attention to the production of spatial scale—that is, the hierarchical ordering of social space from local to national and global (Brenner 1998, 2001; Lefebvre 1991; Marston 2000; N. Smith 1992). Capital's circulation tends, in Marx's terms, toward "annihilating space through time" yet requires spatial organization to accumulate, historically in the form of national regulation, policy, and infrastructure.[2] It is in this sense that I approach the national as a contested level of spatial ordering, produced through constellations of economic regulations, border policies, transit systems, and so forth in a larger system of nation-states and in dynamic relation to provisional levels like the local or the global, similar to what Anna Tsing (2005) describes as "scale-making" (see also Massey 1993).

Questions of scalemaking, as I argue in the introduction, remain central to understanding the supranational project of integrating Europe, whose cohesion has been in doubt since at least the sovereign debt crisis in 2010, and the tension intensified with the United Kingdom's 2016 Brexit vote to leave the European Union and 2020 departure. These concerns had deepened among many Germans in the 2010s with the arrival of refugees from Syria, Iraq, and elsewhere, after Syria's civil war and the rise of the Islamic State, which crystallized for some fears about Muslims and immigration. In some cases, these fears also kindled a resurgence in right-wing extremism, illustrated by the rise of anti-immigrant groups like PEGIDA in 2014.[3] Scale is equally key to thinking through the territorial or geographic entailments of emerging media for a shifting mobile middle class. Although some scholars once predicted that electronic media would destabilize national boundaries (e.g., Castells 1996; McLuhan [1964] 2003; Morley and Robins 1989), scholars have demonstrated that national affiliation did not disappear with the advent of globally circulating media. On the contrary, national communities reasserted themselves in novel ways. For the urban, transnational friend circles I studied, national news websites and communal Spargel meals alike offered means to enact—and generate—national sentiment that went unspoken, while linking them to worlds seen as connected and cosmopolitan.

National Scalemaking and Emerging Media

By 2009, Rike and some of her childhood friends had moved from more staid districts of former West Berlin to hip, gentrifying districts like Mitte, Prenzlauer Berg, and Friedrichshain (in the former East), or Kreuzberg and Neukölln (in the former West, once bordering the Wall, and the center of the Turkish German community). I met Rike through her friend circle, some of whom had grown up together in West Berlin while others, including non-German EU Europeans, had become acquainted through shared interests in art and experimental dance music like UK dubstep. Berlin also attracted young Germans from regions such as Saxony-Anhalt, including Karoline, who had grown up near Magdeburg in former East Germany and who managed a salon in Prenzlauer Berg. Karoline shared a flat in Friedrichshain with her close friend Anja, who worked in public relations for a small firm in West Berlin. Many in their close-knit friend circle from the same rural region lived nearby, working in service, retail, or semiprofessional fields.

FIGURE 11. The front facade of Kunsthaus (Art House) Tacheles, a multistory, graffiti-covered building with nightclubs, galleries, and more, along Oranienburger Strasse in Berlin in 2007. Photo by author.

As these young people moved within or to Berlin in the early 2000s, they adopted Facebook (and, to a lesser degree, Twitter and Tumblr), often abandoning platforms like MySpace or the German Studi.vz or place-based email lists (cf. boyd 2011b). Karoline, for example, used MySpace with friends in Magdeburg but joined Facebook to stay in touch with *Ausländer* (mainly EU Europeans and Americans) she met in Berlin. Facebook brought together friends from home and new acquaintances in Berlin, along with transnational networks of others with shared interests, especially music. Mobile technologies also provided new means to connect to close friends and family, including text messaging and video chat. After acquiring a home wireless network (WLAN), Karoline began spending more time on Facebook with Ausländer, coworkers, and friends from Magdeburg, while video chatting over Skype with family such as her *Oma* (grandmother). Yet, as she became more imbricated in life in Berlin—and, perhaps, able to "visit" family virtually—she curtailed monthly trips to her home village.

Social and mobile media can pull local, national, and transnational formations into the same spaces, from Facebook feeds to kitchen gatherings, generating new configurations of scale. Scholars have long contended with media and

FIGURE 12. Kunsthaus (Art House) Tacheles in 2007, from the back, showing extensive graffiti. Tacheles epitomized a post-1989 aesthetic of dereliction and abandonment and closed in 2012. Photo by author.

placemaking, from print capitalism and national imaginaries in the eighteenth and nineteenth centuries (Anderson [1983] 1991; Gellner 1983) to electronic media and globalization in the twentieth (Appadurai 1996; Morley and Robins 1989). These accounts, though often groundbreaking, pay less attention to the contingent ordering of social space—that is, the cultural production of scale. Cultural geographer Neil Brenner (1998, 2001), in contrast, analyzes how capital alternates between destabilizing territorial formations—such as medieval European city-states—and what he calls a "scalar fix" (1998, 462) that solidifies a new order, such as the nation-state system. These levels are always imbricated in others, such as the European Union, regional affiliations, or municipal governance.[4] Anna Tsing similarly considers the placemaking work of capital as scalemaking, in which "economic projects cannot limit themselves to conjuring at different scales—they must conjure the scales themselves" (2005, 57–58). Globalness or locality, regions or nations, do not precede the global circulation of capital but come into being through its "contingent articulations" (57–58). Scalemaking invokes cultural imaginaries to render certain orderings of space legible, though such claims remain multiple and divergent: "Those global worlds that most affect us are those that manage tentatively productive linkages with other scalemaking projects" (57–58). Digital, networked technologies are key to envisioning global imaginaries; yet, in my findings, emerging media produce contested experiences of place that are not always enunciated.

Approaching media and place in terms of scalemaking—how the spaces of the "local" or "national" are contingently ordered—offers purchase to rethink narratives in which national identities give way to global or postnational ones. As Thomas Eriksen (2007) argues, such narratives construe historical change in terms of increasing complexity and geographic scope, a teleology Brenner calls "scale-expanding" (1998, 477). According to Eriksen, "There is a widespread notion that increased complexity in social life creates larger and larger communities—not so many years ago, leading sociologists thus predicted the imminent rise of global identities, universal cosmopolitanism, and world governments" (2007, 5). From this perspective, media, especially digital media, would contribute to delinking identity—and selfhood—from place because, as Eriksen explains, "the deterri-torialized, supra-national character of the Internet would contribute to the frag-mentation of populations and the breakdown of stable national identities; some even foresaw the coming of an all-encompassing global identity" (6). Despite such predictions, anthropologists have found repeatedly that radio, television, and the internet provide new resources for fashioning national identity and belong-ing (Abu-Lughod 2005; Larkin 1997; Mankekar 1999; Mazzarella 2004; Spitulnik 1996; see also Appadurai 1996). Nationally based diasporic communities thrive on websites, discussion boards, and more recently, Facebook groups (Bernal 2006, 2014; Franklin 2010; Lee 2007), what Eriksen calls "virtual nationalism" (2007, 3). In fact, digital communications make it easier for mobile and diasporic people to maintain national ties transnationally (Vertovec 2004, 220; see also Madianou and Miller 2013).

National identities, of course, exist alongside—and in shifting relation to—local, regional, or transnational ones. But construing identity or selfhood in geographic terms—that is, as attached to a level of spatial ordering—means that such attachments can end, for example, through globally circulating media that appear to detach identity and selfhood from place. Historian Peter Sahlins (1989, 8), challenging the notion that national identities displaced local ones in early modern France, describes the history of nationalization as the "territorializa-tion of sovereignty," a process that fused dominant political formations with the bounded territory of the nation. This history illustrates how modern identity, or selfhood, in France became territorial, suggesting that nationalization depended on linking selfhood to the scale of the nascent nation—a shift in the nature of identity rather than in scope. Liisa Malkki (1992) similarly emphasizes how Western conceptions of the nation as a discrete territory naturalize relationships between people and place, culture and soil (primarily through arboreal metaphors of rootedness). I consider nationalization, in these Western contexts, a process in which the nascent liberal, individualized self formed concurrently with the incipient scale of the nation—a scalemaking project that was simultaneously a self-making project. From this perspective, the modern nation comprises the territorial facet of shifts in subjectivity from the eighteenth and nineteenth centuries, as Michel Foucault (1977, 1988, 1997), Judith Butler (1997), and others recount. Nations, as national communities, are not only imagined but enacted and felt in ways that unfold through ordinary media practices.

Reconceptualizing modern selfhood as part of nationalization calls attention to how the national scale structures subjectivity, offering insight into affective media practices that contrast with how those in my research represented themselves online. Few reported interest in virtual national communities, for example, preferring instead communities organized around shared interests, and when asked, many described themselves in post- or nonnational terms. For Rike and Karoline, Berlin—like Facebook—held the promise of cosmopolitan cultural belonging as part of a transnational, tech-based creative class. Aspiring to transnationalism, or consuming transnational media, was not new; on the contrary, East Germans had sought US and UK popular culture, such as rock music (which some link to the end of state socialism; see Hesse 1990; also Yurchak 2006 on Soviet youth). Yet, unlike on transnational social media, they rarely sought international or English-language news as part of their daily regimen. Instead, they visited national news sites that hailed them as fellow conationalists.

As an ordinary practice that few mentioned, reading national news online offered a site for enacting national selfhood in a cosmopolitan, networked context. Media theories of affect—as an embodied, sensory capacity—show how media can foster communities structured by shared feeling rather than discursive representation (Berlant 2008; Cvetkovich 2007; Muñoz 2000; K. Stewart 2007; see also Carlson and Stewart 2014; Anderson and Harrison 2010). In analyses of normative subjectivity and belonging, shared practices constitute collectives through moods and bodily sensing that exceed narrative experience or articulation. Normative affect structures acceptable, middle-class subjects as well as queer and minoritarian ones, offering resources for political participation and community formation through what Ann Cvetkovich calls "structures of feeling, sensibilities, everyday forms of cultural expression and affiliation that may not take the form of recognizable organizations or institutions" (2007, 461). This approach to acceptable subjectivity suggests how affective attachment to the nation, fostered through media, structures normative national selfhood, posing the further question of how German and European experiences of nationalism were transforming in relation to networked, multiscalar media.

Networked National Feelings

Among members of this emerging knowledge class, few embraced national symbols or representation or joined virtual national communities. Some explicitly refused nationalist identification, in the sense of discursive or semiotic performances of selfhood and belonging (e.g., Bucholtz and Hall 2004, 2005). This distancing, however, did not mean devaluing Germanness or things associated with it or denying German citizenship. It is not surprising that many Germans disavow nationalist identity, given how *Nationalismus* and expressions of German pride conjure images of the outlawed National Socialist Party and right-wing extremism.[5] But as one music fan who had grown up in a small East German town explained: "I never felt like 'I am a citizen of this country, and I am proud of it'; I just lived in a little small town and that was everything I needed to know." This claim was not particular to ethnic Germans or German citizens. A sound designer described himself simply as "European." His parents were Danish, but he was born in Luxembourg and attended an English-language school. These sentiments reflect the position of white Europeans for whom national citizenship was not at stake, unlike many diasporic groups or national minorities, who were invested in worlds they viewed as transnational and cosmopolitan. As in Michael Billig's (1995) assessment of "banal nationalism"—that is, unmarked forms of nationalist representation and practice that reproduce the nation ideologically— selfhood at the national scale asserted itself despite these disavowals or potential for deterritorialized identity. I approach Germanness not only as a discursive formation or imaginary but as a normative form of selfhood constituted at the scale of the nation.

The experiences of Anja, her roommate Karoline, and their friend circle illustrate how regional practices could structure Germanness, in the sense of feeling German, imbricating the regional scale in the national. Most had moved to Berlin in the early 2000s from near Magdeburg, the capital of Saxony-Anhalt (formerly in East Germany). In Berlin, they organized weekly kitchen meetups at their friend Jörg's apartment, inviting a core group of friends for informal drinks and conversation (primarily in German) around the kitchen table. Although kitchens were a common locus of get-togethers, this weekly practice was particular to Jörg, Karoline, and their friend circle. When I first moved in with their

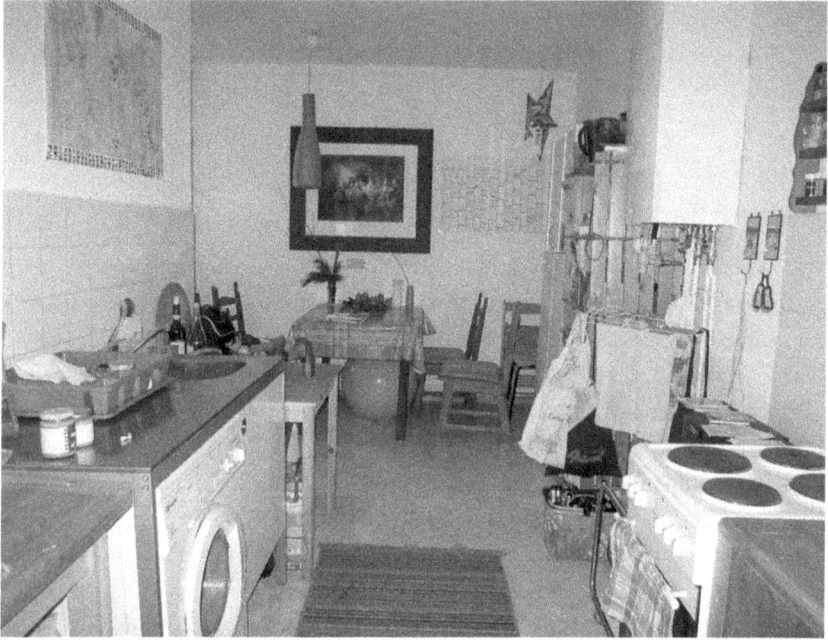

FIGURE 13.   Apartment kitchen in Friedrichshain, Berlin, 2009. Photo by author.

friend Daniele, she warned me one night that friends were coming over for their "weekly gathering," but I was not prepared for how many people began arriving around 9:00 p.m., crowding around the kitchen table: easily fifteen to twenty. Her friends arrived in a trickle, helping themselves to beer or ginger tea, adding extra folding chairs as needed. By 10:00 p.m., it was hard to get in or out of the kitchen, and people were engaged in lively conversation about everything from the winner of the latest election to favorite indie movies. By 11:00 p.m., many had returned home, though a few stayed later into the night. Because most of the crowd was from the same region, they often switched into regional speech (as detailed in chapter 3). Jörg explained later that they mostly avoided regional vocabulary and pronunciation except among close friends, for fear of appearing backward or rustic.[6]

Some aspects of their rural upbringing in former East Germany provoked anxiety or embarrassment in certain contexts, as I will discuss. Yet others, such as regional food, engendered warm memories of childhood and home. Notably, beloved foods like white asparagus (Spargel) were popular with most Germans but were prepared and served in regionally specific ways. Conflicting expressions of feeling German illustrate how national selfhood was structured by normative affect, refracted through regional identities. This relationship between national and regional German identity requires further explanation. While Anja, Karoline, and their friends grew up in East Germany (most were schoolchildren when the Berlin Wall came down), the regional borders have shifted over centuries of territorial reordering. Now one of the five *Neue Länder* (new federal states) since 1990, Saxony-Anhalt first unified in 1945 as a province of Prussia, then was later divided into the East German administrative districts of Magdeburg and Halle. The social and cultural divide between East and West is relatively recent; before the Cold War, the axis between North and South took greater prominence (Berghahn 1982; Breuilly and Speirs 2005; Staab 1998). In fact, many common stereotypes about German culture derive from regional southern traditions, such as Oktoberfest or lederhosen.

Berlin, like Saxony-Anhalt, is situated in the historically Protestant North, in what became East Germany. Regional histories and associations, of course, have since been refracted through forty-plus years of division between capitalist West and socialist East. After the Wende, for example, East Germans experienced widespread stigmatization by West Germans who portrayed them as backward, provincial, and intolerant of foreigners, blaming them for German ethnocentrism and extremism, as Dominic Boyer (2006b) has argued. Yet young eastern Germans I knew rarely articulated *Ostalgie*, nostalgia for the lost East German past and its signifiers, such as oft-denigrated but now beloved consumer products like the Trabi, a notoriously unreliable car (Berdahl 1999, 2000). Instead, they described things associated with the era as *"typische DDR"*[7] (typically East German) in apologetic or embarrassed tones, illustrating the legacy of the Cold War territorial division (what some call *die Mauer im Kopf*, the wall in the head or mind). These regional, rural, and eastern origins represent separate facets of identity and experience that combined to shade ways of feeling German.

The events of one evening illustrated awkward feelings associated with life in the German Democratic Republic (GDR), which Anja, Karoline, and others rarely discussed otherwise. Their friend Sabine invited us to watch *Boxhagener Platz* (2010), a film she had acquired through the music magazine where she worked. The film was named for a nearby square in Berlin ringed by hip bars, boutiques, and cafés, the site of a popular farmers' market and flea market, and depicted life there in 1968, when it looked quite different. Because of regional accents and terminology, I, a nonnative German speaker, had trouble following the dialogue and occasionally asked what was happening. "Ah," said Sabine, "you might have trouble with the dialogue because they are speaking in typical Berliner speech" (for example, in Berlinerisch *ich denke*, "I think," is pronounced *ik denk*), adding, "we also have to listen closely to understand it." At times, they seemed to find the film boring, chatting over the dialogue or laughing at moments that did not seem humorous. At multiple points, Sabine explained apologetically "This is a very typical GDR [*typische DDR*] story about typical German life," involving traditional foods, heavy drinking, strong family ties, and a close-knit neighborhood where everyone gossiped frequently.

Partway through the movie, Daniele shifted attention back to her new Apple laptop. She was borrowing a data surfstick from Sabine and asked again for the password. Sabine looked over, provided the password, and returned to watching the movie. Daniele then navigated to Facebook to browse her News Feed. Although she had added me as a Facebook friend earlier that day, I saw the request only then, so I grabbed my iPhone, logged on to Facebook, and accepted her friend request. I caught her eye as she received the notification, and we laughed. Facebook, unlike the film, was engaging and required no apologies. But Sabine's tone in describing the film reminded me of other times when she or her friends sounded embarrassed and even self-deprecating about their origins. On another evening, a friend of Daniele's was visiting from Magdeburg. I was leaving for an event at the nightclub Tacheles. When I asked her friend if he knew the spot, he shrugged, suddenly awkward, and demurred: "I'm just a country boy" ("*vom Land,*" the colloquial equivalent of "from the sticks"). He self-consciously attributed his unfamiliarity with the venue to his regional, rural origins. As Jörg had mentioned, he and his friends often avoided regional dialect and appearances for fear of being marginalized. This fear was linked specifically to class formations in which the regional idiom marked them as rural and uninformed, unlike the networked, cosmopolitan citizenship associated with both social media worlds and life in Berlin.

Knowing Spargel

Not everything associated with childhood in the GDR, however, provoked shame or inadequacy. Every spring, beginning in late April, white asparagus (Spargel) comes into season across northern Europe, and as anyone who visits Germany then can attest, it is exceptionally popular. I had eaten Spargel in restaurants, with hollandaise sauce or ham, but for Karoline, Daniele, and especially Jörg, *Spargelzeit* (literally "asparagus time") meant purchasing large quantities of fresh asparagus at the Boxhagener Platz market to cook and eat together. Many across Germany love Spargel, to be sure, and say it must be eaten fresh, ideally just after picking. Among those I knew, only the friend circle from Magdeburg organized regular Spargel group dinners. As a national German pastime, eating Spargel generated potent affective ties to home, in regionally inflected ways. Many anthropologists have analyzed food as a means for enacting and articulating shared belonging, implicated in the circulation of capital and the world-system (Appadurai 1981; Bordi 2006; Leitch 2003; Mintz 1985; Wilk 1999). I draw attention here, first, to embodied, affective ways of preparing and sharing Spargel; second, to warm feelings associated with regional identities (and facilitated by online media); and third, to how ordinary practices constituted participation in normative selfhood linked to the scale of the nation.

In early May, Jörg organized many Spargel meals, usually group dinners among his friend circle. One Wednesday, he invited me for lunch after a visit to the nearby farmers' market. When I arrived at his apartment, he proudly showed me a large box of *Beelitzer* Spargel. Beelitz is a nearby region of rural Branden-burg, and, as he explained, although freshness was key, so was regional prove-nance. Elsewhere in Europe, food quality is often framed in terms of naturalness, artisanal production, or authenticity (Heller 2007; Klumbytė 2010; Leitch 2003; Paxson 2010), but for Jörg, regional origin mattered—the more widely available Greek Spargel would not do. And while Spargel is eaten across Germany (and northern Europe), the accompaniments vary regionally. Jörg demonstrated prac-ticed proficiency wielding a dedicated Spargel peeler, which was dulled with use, to strip away the woody outer hull of white asparagus. It took me numerous tries to get the hang of it. He then boiled the Spargel while toasting breadcrumbs, *Semmelbrösel*, in butter, and steaming potatoes (*Dampfkartoffeln*). As he served the meal, he explained that the Semmelbrösel were supposed to crackle and siz-zle noisily when ladled over the asparagus, as his mother had shown him. He remained silent, however, about the unadorned potatoes, a dish too ordinary for comment. Spargelzeit appeared to incite this performance of regional identity in a way I had not previously observed.

After eating, we discussed food and food production. He borrowed my laptop to launch Google Maps in a browser. With the satellite image overlay selected, he navigated to his grandmother's house outside the city of Magdeburg. He zoomed in to point out the family farm, including a farmhouse dating back many gen-erations, which had since been sold off, and the land around the property. "My grandmother used to grow vegetables there when I was growing up," he explained. Unlike the *Boxhagener Platz* film, Spargelzeit appeared to evoke warm feelings associated with *Heimat* (home or homeland), specifically the regional land where he grew up and where his family had lived for generations. Networked geospatial media (or "geomedia"; DeNicola 2012) made possible a virtual visit from a flat in hip Friedrichshain to the regional place that produced these intimate ties—and his close friend circle.

Another Sunday that month, Jörg and his roommates organized a large group dinner and included other Ausländer, such as Nathan, a UK national on an intern-ship in Berlin. Unlike at weekly gatherings or casual lunches, the hosts laid out

FIGURE 14. Spargel dinner, with steamed potatoes and Maultaschen (dumplings), 2010. Photo by author.

the kitchen table more formally, setting out plates and silverware. Nathan, a third English-speaking guest, and I all marveled at the nearly eleven kilos of Spargel—more than two pounds per person. As we ate, Jörg, Nathan, and Dieter joked boisterously in German and English, teasing Jörg about his passion for indie music and making off-color remarks about the asparagus spears. One person proclaimed no love for Spargel but then ate large quantities, which Daniele captured in a digital photo that on Facebook garnered the humorous comment "*Spargelkönig!*" (asparagus king). Shared meals, unlike *Boxhagener Platz*, were a site for experiencing and enacting regional associations that did not provoke embarrassment or disavowals; on the contrary, these were occasions for inviting new acquaintances and sharing photos on Facebook. I link these practices to ways of feeling German because Spargelzeit connected memories of childhood and home to a sense of being German at the national scale—that is, with acceptable, national selfhood.

In this approach, I draw on the work of Lauren Berlant (2008), José Muñoz (2000), and Jennifer Carlson and Kathleen Stewart (2014), for whom shared affect incites acceptable subjectivity. Affect here indexes not individual emotional experience but a bodily response that exceeds awareness and self-narration, a capacity for affecting and being affected. Brian Massumi (1995, 89) considers affective responses to media as an "intensity" that is "irreducibly bodily and autonomic" in nature. Emotion, in contrast, represents "the socio-linguistic fixing of the quality of an experience," which becomes personal (88). Muñoz (2000, 68) locates affect in the production of ethnicity, arguing that US cultural citizenship, in the sense of political belonging, requires performing appropriate, dominant feelings and comportment—restrained, emotional neutrality that minoritizes queer and (in Munoz's terminology) Latino/a subjects who are stereotyped as excessively emotional. "Feeling brown," a minoritized structure of feeling, situates ethnicity in affective ways of being in the world, in contrast to normative affects prescribed for participation in a mainstream national public: "What unites and consolidates oppositional groups is not simply the fact of identity but the way in which they perform affect, especially in relation to an official 'national affect' that is aligned with a hegemonic class" (68). Berlant (2008) analyzes how mass media "women's literature" in the United States constitutes women as collective subjects of shared suffering. An aspirational structure of feeling (R. Williams 1977) here incites acceptable forms of subjectivity and national belonging, through attachments to the nation rarely articulated in words.

These accounts attend to marginalized subjects, detailing how acceptable or dominant forms of selfhood depend on normative belonging at the national level. My eastern German interlocutors inhabited an ambiguous or liminal position in this sense, marked as Other when they spoke their regional dialect outside intimate settings yet still white and aspiring to an emerging consumer middle class. Anja, Jörg, Karoline, and others never called themselves "*Ossis*" (a colloquial, sometimes derogatory term for East Germans) and rarely indexed themselves explicitly as easterners (though they implied such in other ways). More frequently, regional and eastern German identities unfolded through material and affective practice, what Carlson and Stewart (2014) call "mood work."

For the rural East Frisian housewives Carlson describes, in western Germany, ecologically minded consumption offered a means to sense out promised middle-class lifeworlds through shared activities and feelings: "More felt than spoken, these emergent forms compel modes of analysis that account for their lived materiality, their constituents and their impact. Mood work points to everyday ways of making life in a political moment that may one day be remembered in nostalgic tones, like cult consumer goods from a formerly divided Germany, or stories of post-war hardships" (Carlson and Stewart 2014, 125).

Eastern Germans in Berlin experienced—and sensed out—regional connection through Spargel meals and at informal weekly gatherings. One Sunday, Jörg attempted to correct the way Sabine was using the Spargel peeler. "That's not how you do it," he exclaimed. She rebuked him indignantly, insisting, "ich *kenne* Spargel"—"I *know* Spargel!" The verb *kennen* means to know, not in the abstract sense of *wissen*, of possessing knowledge, but as concrete, embodied know-how (what Pierre Bourdieu [1977] called habitus: acquired, class-specific competencies that appear natural). In her response, Sabine defended not only her Spargelpeeling technique but her (likely gendered) affective competence, derived from knowledge acquired informally at home, like regional speech. Shared ways of knowing and feeling about Spargel, and Heimat, constituted this circle as minoritized (and ethnologized) eastern German subjects. But unlike Ostalgie or the story in *Boxhagener Platz*, Spargelzeit connected them to warm, acceptable ways of feeling German. When they invited Ausländer acquaintances to join them and posted humorous photos of the Spargelkönig to Facebook, Spargel meals equally connected them to cosmopolitan life in hip, transnational Berlin.

Reading *Spiegel*

National belonging took shape through affective means, felt rather than spoken, as Carlson and Stewart (2014) detail. Approaching national selfhood as affective offers insight into online practices that contrasted with cosmopolitan or transnational self-representations. National affect calls further into question the link between territory and subjectivity—that is, how selfhood became linked to the emerging nation. As Malkki (1992) and others have shown, nationalist projects depend on naturalizing the relationship between people and national territory, as part of a system of nations. It remains less clear, however, what this naturalizing process means for selfhood and subjectivity. For many Germans and others in Berlin, social media in the late 2000s offered new sites for transnational connection (potentially, de- and reterritorializing identity), as I detail elsewhere (e.g., Kraemer 2014). Media circulated transnationally before the internet, of course, including among youth cultures and fan communities, from music magazines and satellite television (Hesse 1990; Kosnick 2000) to handmade zines and mixtapes (see also Yurchak 2006; Willis [1981] 1990).[8] But networked media accelerate such circulations, bringing together relationships at multiple scales rather than separating selfhood from place.

Erik, an acquaintance of Rike's (the photographer and electronic music fan), Alex (DJ, promoter, and grad student) and others, summed up the transnational appeal of social media, saying, "Things like Twitter—when you're following the people who share the same interests, you're learning so much about those people— it's worldwide, it's got so many possibilities. People from warzones can Twitter and write e-mails and everyone knows [about it]; the world gets a little smaller and I like it." Erik grew up in a rural town near Leipzig, "a small town in the middle of nowhere" in East Germany,[9] and moved to Hannover after attending *Gymnasium* (preparatory school, primarily for university). After taking the *Abitur* (the German university entrance exam), he spent time working before studying communications at a vocational school (*Berufsfachschule*). When we met, he was working for a public relations firm in Hannover, while his wife attended university. I met him in Berlin on a regular visit to see electronic music shows, shop for records and comic books, and spend time with friends like Rike and Alex. National identity or self-representation, he averred, was not meaningful to him (although of course it might matter differently under some circumstances), nor did he ground his identity territorially: "Nationality never really was my thing—I know I live in Germany; it's not important to me—I could live in France, or the States, or whatever." He enjoyed being online as a means of connectedness, saying: "I'm always online, almost always [*immer, fast immer*]. I have a laptop at work, next to my screen, so I can check my personal stuff 24/7. I like being connected, getting my e-mail, and Twitter. It feels good." On Facebook, he often posted about electronic music, sharing music videos and discussing new releases (in English, typically with close friends who were also German). His Twitter profile listed interests like "sound," "comics," and "robots" in English; his avatar was, accordingly, a comic book robot. He posted mostly (but not exclusively) in English, referring to shows in Hannover but not, that I observed, to national news.

Rike described the importance of Facebook for maintaining an extended circle of "very international friends" and similarly sought out transnational media, a potential resource for building identity detached from place. She downloaded American television shows (like many young people, she did not own a television), streamed music over Last.fm (partly because other services were blocked by international licensing agreements), and perused blogs. As she explained, "I feel more connected by reading blogs in the US and UK." Her friend Annika, a studio artist, echoed these sentiments and evinced similar heterogeneity in social media practices. On Facebook, she shared links to a British design magazine, bantered with Rike, and responded to events organized by Alex and others. Rike and Annika framed many of these activities in terms of "getting informed" and, as mentioned earlier, recounted a "daily ritual" of checking email, blogs, Facebook, and news (first in the morning, then in regular intervals throughout the day). Many repeated this language of "informing" (in English, or *sich informieren* in German) and performing a daily ritual (or routine) as practices with regular rhythms and quotidian temporality. These descriptions aligned with what I observed, as when Erik checked his phone or laptop throughout the day for email, Twitter, and Facebook updates; Alex messaged with me in the afternoons; or Daniele returned home in the evenings to browse Facebook and chat with friends.

Given the topics most people discussed on Facebook or in person, however, I did not expect news to take such prominence, a finding that emerged later when analyzing interviews. Some mentioned news or politics at kitchen gatherings, especially around an election, but typically they discussed music, films, or personal lives. And they rarely circulated news stories online—music videos or posts about daily life were more common (though this changed by 2015 if not earlier; sharing news became more frequent on Facebook by 2013;[10] see Kraemer 2017). What is more, I rarely saw print newspapers—the few that circulated were free city papers, such as the *Berliner Morgenpost*, or "city magazines" (*Stadtmagazine*) like *Tip Berlin* or the English-language *Ex-Berliner*, a popular arts-and-culture monthly. Anja, Karoline, Daniele, and other women accumulated back issues of fashion magazines like German *Vogue* or *Neon* to peruse on excursions to city parks and lake beaches. Glossy magazines and sometimes newspapers were a fixture at many Berlin cafés, neatly stacked in hanging racks, but I rarely saw anyone actually reading them.[11] And while television news covered national and international politics, I seldom observed anyone watching it (football, or soccer, matches were another matter; see chapter 6).[12]

Online, however, Karoline, Anja, Rike, Erik, and others reported reading news daily, specifically the same national publications, including *Spiegel Online* or FAZ.net (of the *Frankfurter Allgemeine Zeitung*) and, to a lesser degree, *Die Zeit*, a weekly paper.[13] Consistently, conationalists read the same national papers, despite the availability of international or European news, on the one hand, and regional publications, on the other. While not surprising, these practices contrast with other ways the divide persists between East and West ("die Mauer im Kopf"), including language competences—more of the music fans were fluent in both English and German, for example, than were the friends from Magdeburg. Rike, who grew up in West Berlin, read *Spiegel Online* daily, as did others in her friend circle, like Erik, who grew up in East Germany—and so did Karoline, Anja, and their close-knit circle from Saxony-Anhalt.

As Alex recounted, he frequently checked *Spiegel Online*, set as his browser's default website, although he was experimenting with making *Die Zeit* his "start page" (*Startseite*) instead: "The [site I visit] most is *Spiegel Online*, which is Germany's biggest news site, but since it's too biased with a certain political view, I actually switched my starting page to *Zeit*, which is a big newspaper. Unfortunately their site is not structured really well for real-time news, like *Spiegel* is. You can keep a bit of a better update on what's happening out there, because they are just updated more frequently. After *Spiegel*, it's Facebook. Facebook is, well . . . I'm really, really, really fascinated by the way my communication with my friends changed through Facebook."

Part of what fascinated Alex was how Facebook supported more dispersed forms of communication among his (often transnational) friends and acquaintances, what he called a more "efficient" way to stay informed and receive feedback;[14] news sites were for ordinary political news. A sound engineer, Niels, said he most often visited *Spiegel Online*, Facebook, and Google but preferred Google as his *Startseite*. Though he and others read Facebook, Twitter, and blogs in English and German, most Germans read news in German.

Alex explained this preference in detail, even though at other times he went to lengths to consume media, such as US movies, in English: "I sometimes go on to the *New York Times*, sometimes *BBC*, [when] I get sent news articles from the *BBC*. But I feel like the news coverage in German is quite sufficient for what I want to know. Everything in German, like, German topics, I read in German because this is the best way to get the information. But if I'm interested in American news, then I get them from American newspapers, like, mostly the *New York Times* and sometimes the *Financial Times* because I'm interested in financial news."

Alex's friend Sal described checking email and news in the morning, initially saying: "I read a lot of newspapers, mostly German, and British. *Spiegel*. *Frankfurter Allgemeine*. And *BBC Worldnews*. Mostly, that I do right after reading my email." But he qualified: "I'm more drawn to blog stuff, to blog kind of news, because I'm really tired in the morning, I don't want to read that much. I want to have everything distilled. So certain blogs are much more important. *The Onion*, of course [US satirical news]. And that's that. I'm not very versatile in that regard." But, as a skilled electronic music producer, bilingual in German and English, Sal was highly versatile in other media practices, from managing a professional profile on social media to following underground music trends on web forums. Sabine similarly reported reading news in German, primarily *Spiegel*, though as an avid fan of indie music (and music journalist), she read music blogs, such as concert reviews, in English and German and occasionally posted to Facebook in English. Daniele spoke limited English and preferred national German news, "*Spiegel* or *Zeit Online*, all in German, but everything else is not necessarily German," and posted to Facebook in German but sometimes chatted over Facebook Messenger in English—with the help of Google Translate—and spoke some English with clients at work.

Like eating Spargel, reading *Spiegel* incited an ordinary, felt sense of Germanness that few put into words. Massumi (2002, 24) describes the affective response in media reception as a "gap between *content* and *effect*"—that is, a bodily capacity not fully captured by constructed narratives of emotion. For Berlant, media texts generate affective "intimate" publics that "[foreground] affective and emotional attachments located in fantasies of the common, the everyday, and a sense of ordinariness" (2008, 10). Sites like *Spiegel* hail an audience of conationalists, as Anderson argued ([1983] 1991, 46), whether or not they explicitly identify as such. But participating in a national reading public also unfolds through shared affect, a felt rather than discursive connection that may not register as emotion.

Certainly, as Alex articulated, German-based news covers topics relevant to life in Germany, in the Habermasian sense of topics "of national interest" (Rasmussen 2013, 99), which partly explains why non-German residents consistently read news sites from their home countries. French-born David, for example, owned a small record label, spoke English and German, and rarely mentioned his family or French origins. But online, he read French newspapers *Le Monde* and *Libération*, alongside German- and English-language ones. Conversely, German-American Pascal made *Spiegel Online* his start page when he lived in the United States for a few months; he explained: "That's how I'd catch up on my German news." He added: "I must say, I've gotten so hooked on NPR since I was in the States, that I have no clue about German politics." In this way, he expressed attachment to national news, in the form of US public radio. The sound engineer with Danish parents, Viktor, described his nationality as "European" and visited English- and Danish-language sites, primarily Danish ones for news, "good Swedish and Danish news sites, like Politiken.se, etc." He also participated in an online forum for a close group of male Danish-speaking friends with similar hobbies and interests—a rare example of a nationally based online community in my research.

As Eriksen (2007) points out, networked media facilitate rather than undermine national identity, but this capacity cannot account for why my interlocutors preferred national news (online), on the one hand, but *transnational* (often US-based) social media, on the other. On the contrary, most rejected national social network sites. Many recounted leaving the German site Studi.vz for German university students. Alex migrated to Facebook when he moved to Berlin but had used Studi.vz as a student: "I had a Studi.vz [account] from, like, the first day of university, but I don't use it at all anymore. I'm only in there to keep track of people I'm actually not interested in any more." Alex rarely associated social media with negative or unpleasant feelings, but here, he maintained his account only to monitor former friends. Daniele similarly linked Facebook with moving to Berlin and meeting Ausländer: "Everyone had been using Studi.vz, MySpace, etc., before, but then I began to use Facebook with foreigners [Ausländer] in Berlin, because it was easier to stay in touch with them."

National news reflects the role of the nation-state in shaping topics of concern, but the classic model of the bourgeois public sphere does not account for those who disavowed national belonging; read little or no local, regional, or supranational news online; and spurned national social network sites. One person I interviewed—one of the few not connected to the friend circles—did mention regional news when recounting his daily online activities. A freelance journalist originally from Austria, Jan had grown up in Hamburg and read regional news sites: "For 20 minutes [a day] I read news—*Der Spiegel*, daily papers, *Berliner Zeitung* subscription, and Hamburg regional news." But this was partly because, as a journalist, it was his "24-hour job to stay informed," and he sometimes wrote for regional papers. No others in my research mentioned reading local papers. Networked social media, more so than other mass media, make it possible to participate simultaneously in—or at least rapidly switch between—national, regional, and other geographically based communities. To address this multiplicity, Terje Rasmussen (2013, 100) reworks Habermas's view of a unified public sphere, describing the heterogeneity of online media as a "networked community" that combines both public and private forms of communication, while Jim McGuigan (2005) proposes a "cultural public sphere" that accounts for affective engagement with media.[15]

Given the multiplicity of media platforms and channels, decisions about which media to use matter. Terming this multiplicity "polymedia," Mirca Madianou and Daniel Miller (2013, 170) contend that, when media choices are not constrained by technological and social barriers, they entail social, emotional, or even moral decisions.[16] Reading *Spiegel Online* while rejecting Studi.vz entailed an affective choice that constituted social worlds. There were practical reasons, certainly, for reading German (or French or Danish) news. But the ordinariness—and predominance—of the same national news sites, as important to daily living as social media, testifies to the tenacity of national projects in the absence of discursive articulation. Like print news, national news websites hailed audiences as part of a nationally imagined community, with similar temporal rhythms of reading, yet, unlike fashion magazines, newspapers were rarely in evidence. This silence around news reading suggests that participating in a national public was, like steamed potatoes, too ordinary to warrant comment.

Multiscalar Nationalism

In Benedict Anderson's classic formulation, print capitalism fostered national sentiment by addressing readers as an imagined community of anonymous conationalists: "These fellow-readers, to whom they were connected through print, formed, in their secular, particular, visible invisibility, the embryo of the nationally imagined community" ([1983] 1991, 46). This fellowship resulted in part from the homogenized, daily rhythms of newspaper circulation. It seems no coincidence that my interlocutors read the news according to daily rhythms, despite the "always-on" availability of online news. And national papers online still address audiences as conationalists, fostering a reading public at the national scale. These national publics, however, were shifting in relation to globally circulating media, especially on social media, which reconfigure local, regional, and transnational connections. A deeply felt sense of national selfhood endured for young Germans who preferred transnational cultural circuits yet enacted national belonging through ordinary practices such as consuming German foods and German (or other national) news. Mobile young Berlin residents I studied, in contrast to a majority of Germans, participated in implicitly national publics online, engendering a connected, cosmopolitan Germanness I consider multiscalar.

In rethinking the relationship between media and place, I have turned, first, to the analytic of scale to denaturalize territorialization as a process conjoining sovereignty, culture, and place in scalar progression. I have proposed, second, an affective approach to media and subjectivity to illustrate how shared feelings and practices constitute national selfhood alongside (or in contrast to) semiotic representations for young people who desire to be connected and cosmopolitan. Together, these accounts of scalemaking and affect offer insight into cosmopolitan experiences of national selfhood that do not necessarily correspond to the expanding scope of territorial organization or concomitant circulation of media.

In his reflections on Ernst Gellner and nationalism after the internet, Eriksen sums up the conventional view that geographically based identities expand in scope as media enable new imaginings: "Global cultural history of the Big Ditch kind favoured by Gellner—the movement from bands and tribes to cities and states—can fruitfully be seen as a movement from the concrete to the abstract. . . . In relation to the Internet, McLuhan's (1964) cliché of the global village is often invoked to argue that since the web of communication is now global rather than national, the community with which individuals identify can also, for the first time in human history, encompass the globe" (2007, 5–6).

I reproduce this quote at length to elucidate a view of media, territory, and identity that invokes a teleology of scale. I advocate instead breaking down territorial ordering into components—policies, infrastructures, media practices, and so forth—to understand the geographic entailments of capital. Reconceptualizing the nation as a contingent, albeit dominant, ordering of social space recasts place online as a multiplicity of practices (Graham 2013; see also Marston, Jones, and Woodward 2005), beyond the binary of local versus global. This approach entails rethinking nationalization—that is, considering how territorializing the nation gave rise to new experiences of identity and selfhood. This transformation included cultivating (and naturalizing) affective ties to the imagined national territory in a system of nation-states. Modern selfhood entailed, historically, a new relationship between subject and place, in which cultural and political belonging requires—and incites—acceptable ways of being and feeling. From this perspective, national belonging is more than imagined; it is felt and embodied, entwining subjectivity with the territorial ordering of the nation.

Nationalization as scalemaking project incites national subjects and structures online activities such as news reading (the more recent interweaving of news on social media may be reshaping national publics further; e.g., Kraemer 2017). National selfhood—and national publics—are shifting in relation to other geographic formations. According to one person, the 2006 World Cup championship held in Germany was "one of the few times Germans can sing the national anthem, display the flag, and so forth, without feeling the stigma of the past—it's okay in part because everyone else is doing it too," perceiving Germany as part of a supranational or transnational system. Despite the appeal of transnational connection, however, few Europeans identify with the level of integrated Europe or the European Union (Rasmussen 2013; Tarrow 2001). The Germans (and other Europeans) I studied participated in national communities in ordinary, unspoken ways, whether reading *Spiegel* or eating Spargel, precisely because accessing middle-class lifeworlds depends on normative subjectivity at the national scale. Yet feeling German online or in Berlin enmeshed national selfhood in cosmopolitan, transnational circuits. Like Sidney Tarrow's (2001) "rooted cosmopolitans,"[17] they pursued transnational connection while maintaining affective ties to place.[18]

A further ethnographic encounter limns the contours of this networked, multiscalar nationalism: watching the Quentin Tarantino film *Inglourious Basterds* (2009).[19] One January evening in 2010, Alex and his roommate invited me to their Neukölln apartment for dessert and a movie. It quickly became clear that the film departed from my expectations. I was afraid it would be awkward to watch, especially as an American Jew, until I saw how the film reimagines the ending of World War II (which I will not give away here). It became evident that my hosts, fans of cult and indie films, had watched the film numerous times (in English, never dubbed; cf. Boellstorff 2003) and considered it a favorite. They delightedly dissected the performances of the German-speaking actors, especially Austrian-born Christoph Waltz, who won numerous awards for the role. "He used to be on television," Alex explained to me, "but he wasn't the best actor." Another actor, likely Michael Fassbender, they claimed was among the best German performers in American cinema, which seemed to please them. They commented on the German-speaking actors' lines and accents (Saxon, Austrian, and so forth) and laughed at some characters' names ("I cracked up in the theater for many minutes after hearing that one!"). Relatively few Hollywood films take place in Germany with German actors and dialogue—in fact, an American character's accent speaking German is pivotal to one scene. The film allowed Alex and his roommate to participate *as Germans* in precisely the kinds of transnational cultural circuits opened up by Facebook and online media. They brought German cultural competencies to analyze the film in a way I could not as an Ausländer. In this sense, emerging media contributed to a networked cosmopolitan nationalism, allowing them to be and feel German as affective national subjects, while connecting them to a multiscalar world-in-the-making.

SCALING MEDIA INFRASTRUCTURES

In April 2009, millions of internet users in Germany were disappointed to discover that music videos on the media-sharing site YouTube were suddenly no longer available. The videos were not removed entirely, only blocked in Germany, and viewers there encountered a legal notice: *"Dieses Video ist in deinem Land nicht verfügbar"* (This video is not available in your country). This policy change was the result of failed negotiations between Google, YouTube's parent company, and a German copyright society, GEMA, after their previous agreement had expired. By German law, the distribution of intellectual property like music videos must involve a copyright collection society such as GEMA to negotiate licensing, as opposed to a one-time payment. GEMA maintained that Google should compensate them (and ostensibly, their members—musicians, composers, and other copyright holders) each time a YouTube user viewed a rights-protected music video, for one euro cent, amounting to 1.6 million euros annually at the time.[1] When GEMA and Google could not come to a new agreement, YouTube viewers in Germany swiftly found themselves denied access—on the basis of geography, or least their IP addresses—to the site's huge catalog of music videos.

International licensing agreements such as these reveal—and require—an extensive material and regulatory system that belies the image of a deterritorialized, ephemeral digital world superimposed upon the "real" world of brute matter (e.g., Graham 2013; Sandvig 2013). Challenging this description is a vibrant literature on the materiality of digital worlds, including Katherine Hayles's (2004) "media specific analysis" that treats code and print as equally, yet differentially, material (see also Hayles 1999); Jean-François Blanchette's (2011) history of the constraints of bits and wires; and Sarah Pink, Elisenda Ardévol, and Débora Lanzeni's (2016) processual approach to materialization in digital and design anthropology. Such questions extend concerns articulated, in different registers, in conversations on new materialisms and feminist technology studies (e.g., Barad 2003; Haraway 1991); the material semiotics of John Law, Annemarie Mol, and others (e.g., Law 2010; Law and Mol 1995); affect theory (e.g., Clough et al. 2007; Massumi 2002) in media studies; and nonrepresentational theories in human geography (e.g., Anderson and Harrison 2010). In different ways, these literatures share an animating principle concerning how meaning—including language, semiotics, and signification—can appear to detach from matter as a firm, often unyielding substrate. These critiques reassess Cartesian dualism in its epistemic and ontological entailments, particularly Saussurian poststructuralist approaches that separate signifier from signified.

In this context, media (digital and otherwise) occupy a double position, perhaps uniquely so, as both medium and mode of signification, a conveyor whose specificity shapes its meaning. If media are understood only as the material substrate of communications, then meanings should circulate through digital networks and analog texts alike, floating and unmoored à Jean Baudrillard. I take media instead to be lively agents in sense making whose material and physical capacities (called affordances in some literature; see discussion in chapter 1) shape the cultural circuits they comprise. In this, I share Tim Ingold's (2007) critique of materiality in which he advocates a processual approach to materials in flux, attending to their specific qualities rather than construing them as stable objects imbued with agency. The material, technical, and regulatory systems (that is, infrastructures) that enable digital communications shape digital worlds through their conjoined signifying and physical properties—and are shaped in turn by existing histories, practices, and understandings. In this chapter, I consider the role of the communications infrastructure in Europe, primarily in Berlin, in generating spatial formations at different scales, such as the local or national, in conversation with a growing literature on infrastructure in anthropology (e.g., Anand 2011; Larkin 2004, 2013) and in internet studies broadly (Sandvig 2013; Dourish and Bell 2007).

By the mid-2000s in Germany, mobile networking and other information technologies had spread rapidly. Mobile phone subscriptions had reached over 100 percent of the population by 2007. Mobile broadband—that is, high-speed data—had been nonexistent in 2002; 26.2 percent of inhabitants had subscriptions by 2010; nearly three-quarters (71.2%) had them by 2015; the number peaked at 94.7 percent in 2022. Similarly, home internet was available to fewer than half

(46.1%) of residents in 2002, and by 2015, the number reached 90.3 percent, with broadband (high-speed) access jumping from single-digit percentages to over a third of the population.[2] While these changes reflect adoption rates across Europe, they must be considered in light of the broader infrastructural shifts that characterized Germany, primarily Berlin and eastern Germany, in the years after the *Wende*, or Change, in 1989 that led to the merging of the Federal Republic of Germany (West Germany) and the German Democratic Republic (East Germany) in 1990. By 1989, the telecommunications system in West Germany had already been at the brink of a major reorganization. The *Wende* triggered extensive restructuring to link up two national infrastructures, including communications, transit, and public space.

For the circles of mobile young people in my research, many were getting online and acquiring their first laptops and wireless networks in the early 2000s, a time that coincided with their arrival in central Berlin, as this book has detailed. Most had joined social media sites like Facebook for the first time, often abandoning platforms like MySpace or the German Studi.vz (for university students), as described in chapters 1 and 4. These practices converged as mobile technologies provided more opportunities for engaging with social media, as many have described (Baym 2010; boyd 2014, Madianou and Miller 2013, D. Miller et al. 2016). Although in Germany and other European nations, high-speed internet connectivity is available to most residents, the process of connecting in Berlin was rarely seamless.

In this chapter, I consider the material and regulatory components—the infrastructure—of social and mobile media practices to investigate ad hoc means of managing this unevenness, including cost, technical competence, and alternative forms of sociality that shaped online activities. I analyze creative ways of getting around licensing laws and expensive services as forms of tactical consumption, alongside what I call *logistical labor*, the domestic flip side of managerial labor, required for navigating consumer technology and media infrastructure. I locate these practices in broader histories of getting by in Berlin and East Germany, to understand how they generated feelings of mutuality, sometimes linked to collective means of managing life in the former GDR. This approach addresses the co-constitution of socio-technical systems, from material components to regulatory regimes and technical expertise. But attention to infrastructure also requires reconsidering what is material about digital materiality. Rather than viewing the world as bisected by a meaning/matter divide, in which materiality is construed as hard, durable, and constraining, I show how the communications infrastructure—and engagements with it—remade the space of the city or experiences of the nation for these friend circles. Getting online, downloading restricted media, or using mobile phones while abroad required interfacing with infrastructural systems at multiple scales, materializing and reconfiguring levels like the national and supranational as a form of scalemaking.

Getting Online in Two Cities

During my fieldwork from 2009 to 2010, I lived in a room-share (Wohngemein-schaft, or WG, literally a housing community) in the former East Berlin district Friedrichshain, in a spacious Altbau (prewar building) with a number of young women from Saxony-Anhalt. Friedrichshain bordered trendy, gentrified Pren-zlauer Berg on its north and Kreuzberg, the center of the Turkish German com-munity and a district historically popular with artists, anarchists, and the like, on the west across the river Spree. By 2009, Friedrichshain was undergoing the kind of transition taking place across many parts of Berlin, as young people, cafés, and boutiques moved in, transforming it from the more somber Kiez (neighborhood) of the 1970s and 1980s, as depicted in films, to a lively, creative, "Weltoffen" (cos-mopolitan) place. Although this transformation recalled processes of reurban-ization in many places, Berlin's bifurcated infrastructure shaped daily living and media practices with consequences for who could get online and how.

Two of my roommates, Katrine and Daniele, both in their late twenties, came from the same rural village in Saxony-Anhalt, one of Germany's "new federal states" (*neuen Bundesländer*). Katrine worked in an art gallery, and Daniele managed a boutique in neighboring Prenzlauer Berg, which had gentrified in the early 2000s and was popular with young, predominantly white families and professionals. When I first moved in, I asked Daniele for the wireless network (WLAN) name and passcode, having been assured that the rent included wireless internet access. Daniele jotted down the information for me but then explained that they were sharing the connection with a neighbor to split the cost of service. Initially, I assumed this neighbor lived in the same building, perhaps in an apart-ment above or below. But I soon realized the connection only worked in certain rooms. Katrine and Daniele were sharing an older laptop typically left out in the living room, one of the few spaces with connectivity. Katrine recommended I sit close to the windows for the best signal strength. "We're borrowing a neighbor's WLAN," she explained, "and it only works in parts of the apartment—not the kitchen."

Later, I discovered that the neighbor, their close friend Jörg, lived two flights up—and across the street. This explained the erratic signal strength and the logistical contortions required to use it. I proposed ordering our own service, but Daniele demurred at first, saying we would have to choose from one of many providers. The process of installing new service in Berlin was reputed to be involved and time consuming, often taking weeks for a technician to arrive (something I had heard from others as well). Eventually, I ordered service from a provider Daniele had seen advertised locally. Despite these concerns, the service was installed and working, excepting a few minor glitches, within a few weeks, after the modem and wireless router arrived in the mail and a technician came to install it. Daniele's reservations seemed to be more about the process of navigating providers and installation rather than the price, which was relatively affordable. A few months later, Katrine voiced similar frustrations when she needed a new phone, daunted by choosing between various providers and plans, saying, "I have no patience for the fine print" (of different service contracts). Choosing data plans or home broadband entailed wading through service plans with highly technical specifications—upload speeds, download speeds—and required a landline, which many young people did not use.

In contrast to my roommates, most people I interviewed did have their own WLAN at home, and many regaled me with its technical specifications. Alex, the DJ and promoter, volunteered, "I have at the moment a 16 Mbits, no, 1.2 Mbit upstream, but this would be 16,000 kB per second. . . . Yeah, Mbps, no, Mbps is Mbit." Another music producer similarly described his DSL connection: "6000 DSL (actually 2000 in Neukölln [a neighborhood]), not even cable TV, WLAN." Though a few people lived alone, most lived in room-shares. Pascal, an art student who lived with two roommates, explained, "We share DSL, 1mb/s, WLAN, for 20 euros a month. I had dial-up, then ISDN, now DSL. There's WLAN at school but it requires Cisco to connect." Most described their service in terms of the wires—DSL, for example—and data speeds, but some, such as Viktor, a sound designer, also mentioned the provider: "I have a 14MB connection, through O2, it's DSL with WLAN." Studio artist Annika described problems she had with the connection in her live/work art studio, where she was supposed to have speeds of "50 up/20 down—no wait, other way"; because the service was not working properly, she was using a surfstick instead.

Detailing the specifics of getting online articulated technical competence and know-how and was common among those who identified as technologically savvy. Such competence was also typically gendered: men in my fieldwork tended to describe themselves as knowledgeable about tech and were more likely than women in the same friend circles to volunteer to be interviewed (on the gendering of such technologies in Berlin, see Kraemer 2021a, 2021b). Such enthusiasm for precisely enumerating data speeds often correlated with interest in music production: the most technologically inclined were (predominantly male) music producers and sound engineers. Among my interlocutors, self-described music nerds, especially (but not exclusively) those among the circle of electronic music fans, devoted themselves to arranging in-home recording studios, production equipment, and personal stereo systems. Among the friend circle of eastern Germans, fewer recited the precise bit rate of their internet service, but some, like Jörg and Sabine, were eager to show me their devices and described blogging, emailing colleagues, and similar practices in detail.

The history of telecommunications infrastructure in Berlin contributed to differences in how young people got online, between friend circles and between places. These media and communications systems had been deeply implicated in—and constitutive of—the changes that led to reunification in 1990 and to broader processes of Europeanization. In West Germany (as elsewhere) in the 1980s and 1990s, electronic media proliferated, including cable and satellite television, cassettes, video games, and personal computers. The popularity of electronic media among young people has often triggered widespread anxieties about youth, morality, and accelerating consumerism and globalization (e.g., Bonfadelli 1993). In contrast, ethnographic research, since at least the work of Paul Willis ([1981] 1990; see also boyd 2014; Buckingham 2008; Durham 2008), has repeatedly shown that youth engage with electronic media in creative, often counterhegemonic ways. In the same period, it was difficult for Western researchers to learn about media in East Germany, where print and broadcast were managed by the socialist state (Hesse 1990). In the early decades of the Cold War, media outlets primarily served as state propaganda, but the formal political borders were permeable to broadcast signals (Hesse 1990; Kilborn 1993). The American soap opera *Dallas*, for example (subject of Ien Ang's foundational 1985 media reception study, in part because of its international viewership), was quite popular, as it was among Ang's Dutch viewers, mainly women. Pressured by access to Western television, news, and music, the East German government tried, unsuccessfully, to compete. Consuming West German media, according to Kurt Hesse (1990), temporarily eased dissatisfaction in East Germany but ultimately furnished alternate "dreamworlds" that motivated eventual political upheaval. Efforts to create more "youth-oriented" programming came too late (Kilborn 1993, 456).

In late-1980s West Germany, networked computing systems and mobile communications were well underway, especially compared with the data networks and infrastructure in East Germany. While most households had landlines in West Germany, for example, over a million households were still awaiting them in East Germany by 1989 (Schnöring and Szafran 1994). The limited number of extant data networks was fragmentary, consisting of incompatible private systems for bureaucratic elites, with no public infrastructure. West Germany, meanwhile, was integrating increasingly into the western European communications sphere and the incipient European Union, including through regulatory bodies like the European Commission. The European Commission in the 1980s supported the implementation of the Global System for Mobile Communications (GSM) protocol as an open, interoperable standard. Mobile communication expanded rapidly throughout western Europe in the 1990s, with a surge in text messaging (1994). GSM assured interoperability within Europe, providing a foundation for communication at the supranational level (and helping produce that level as a spatial scale). Mobile phone service in the former East Germany, in contrast, was hampered by the Russian military's continued use of the 900 MHz band specified in the GSM standard.

The *Wende* came just as seismic shifts were occurring in communication technologies. West Germany had already initiated a plan to privatize and partly deregulate its central telecommunications bureau, Telekom, and to liberalize nascent mobile and satellite markets. The fall of the Berlin Wall triggered a rush to "modernize" and "update" East Germany's telecommunications system, seen by some as backward and underdeveloped (Schnöring and Szafran 1994, 464). This included rapid improvements to the communications infrastructure, and thousands of network connections were installed, with the explicit goal of facilitating cross-border communication and, especially, the inflow of Western capital. The East German media system more broadly, including print and broadcast networks, was taken over by West German authorities in what some have described as another *Anschluss,* or annexation (see Borneman 1992; Kilborn 1993; Schnöring and Szafran 1994). This critique has been leveled more generally at the process of reunification, which at the time was not seen as the inevitable outcome of the 1989 uprising. Although the eastern German communications system was revamped in a short time frame, this overhaul involved importing the western German system—including its policy framework and infrastructure design—wholesale, similar to processes for redeveloping urban spaces and public transit (see Peters 2010; Weszkalnys 2010).

Most young people in these friend circles, who had typically moved to central Berlin in the early 2000s, had home wireless networks and mobile phones, though many had recently acquired their first laptop and only a few had high-speed-enabled smartphones. Germany, unlike Sweden or the Netherlands, was never at the forefront of network connectivity in Europe but was comparable to other wealthy industrial nations. By the time of my fieldwork in 2010, there were more mobile phone subscriptions than people, 85.7 percent of inhabitants had home computers, and 82.5 percent had home internet. Although internet access and mobile phones were common by the late 1990s, high-speed broadband access jumped notably starting in the middle of the next decade.[3] Home broadband (e.g., cable, ISDN, or DSL service) surged from percentages in the low single digits in the early 2000s to over a third of the population in 2015, while high-speed mobile data subscriptions (e.g., 3G service and up) became available in the middle of the decade, reaching 71.2 percent in 2015, and peaking at 94.7 percent in 2022. These numbers illustrate the rapid pace of technological change from 2000 to 2015, in terms of high-speed internet access, but also illuminate the unevenness in this process, as mobile networking took off much faster than home internet service.

Statistics, of course, do not tell the complex story of how this process unfolded or what differences continue to shape experiences between eastern and western Germany. Daniele and Katrine, for example, had the means to acquire a home wireless network and new mobile phones—what impeded them were the labor and competences needed to navigate the fine print of service contracts and to troubleshoot technical glitches. As I discuss in the next section, I term these forms of work *logistical labor*, a counterpart to the increased bureaucratization and managerialism of professional middle-class labor. Sharing wireless service, even if inadequate, recalled practices from the GDR era to manage a highly unequal telecommunications system. Many East Germans had shared phone lines with neighbors, taking messages for one another, to offset the inequities of this inadequate infrastructure (Schnöring and Szafran 1994, 462). Sharing service also paralleled practices, such as exchanging mobile phone handsets as in chapter 3, that diverged from technology's implicit design (i.e., mobile handsets are designed for individuals; home wireless network configurations usually presume a single household). But sharing WLAN connected close friends and neighbors who visited one another often, outlining a mutual sociality that outweighed the sometimes poor quality of the network connection.

Logistical Labor, Tactical Consumption

Getting online—for social media, email, news, media sharing, and so forth—is never an all-or-nothing process, as many scholars writing against the "digital divide" argue. Beyond technical means, such as the availability of broadband or computing hardware, it involves learned competences to navigate new interfaces, evaluate service options, and decide what hardware to use. Devices and interfaces have become more user friendly since the early days of text-based operating systems, starting with the graphical interfaces of the 1990s and moving to the more recent advent of "user-centered design," usability testing, and the rise of "user experience" as a central concern for tech companies. Despite initial visions of technological "convergence" (Jenkins 2006), services and devices on the market multiplied, converging in some senses (devices like phones, tablets, personal computers, televisions, and gaming consoles bring together multiple services, platforms, and media channels, from video chat to streaming and messaging) but diverging in others, as types of devices and media platforms proliferated. Such proliferation entails more work on the part of user-consumers: managing digital music libraries, social media privacy settings and accounts, and endless end-user license agreements and performing other devolving, unpaid logistical labor.

By *logistical labor*, I mean the individualized work of managing technical and bureaucratic systems, from sifting through the fine print of service contracts to filling out endless customer-satisfaction surveys. One of the hallmarks of "Web 2.0," the second-generation internet technologies that developed in the early 2000s, was its "user-centered" focus, specifically on unpaid user-generated content that provides value for for-profit tech companies (see Wesch 2007; Fuchs 2010). These new platforms and services were described at the time as more interactive and social, defined by user-created content such as media sharing (e.g., Flickr, YouTube), social bookmarking (e.g., Del.ico.us), and blogging. This terminology atrophied in the mid-2000s with the ascent of "social" media, the umbrella term for social network sites organized around interlinked user profiles (boyd and Ellison 2008). These platforms typically depend on profits from users' uncompensated labor, whether restaurant recommendations (Yelp, Qype), streaming video preferences (Netflix), or content on image-based sites like Pinterest and Instagram. Like affective labor, with which it overlaps, logistical labor involves managing settings, personal profiles, and friend lists for an ever-expanding roster of decentralized services. Logistical labor characterizes home life in late modernity more broadly, as the flip side of workplace managerialism. In this sense, it is closely entwined with "audit culture," as described by Marilyn Strathern (2000) and others—that is, constant self-assessment, evaluation, and quantification in the corporatized university and elsewhere. Logistical labor and managerialism likely trace to the restructuring of the professional middle classes around bureaucratic labor in the wake of capitalism's post–Cold War victory; this shift, as David Graeber argues, "has led to both a continual inflation of what are often purely make-work managerial and administrative positions—'bullshit jobs'—and an endless bureaucratization of daily life, driven, in large part, by the Internet" (2014, 77).

I am less inclined to see this shift as driven by the internet; rather, I propose the question, How do digital technologies intersect with managerial regimes of labor and living? Here I draw on Chandra Mukerji's (2009) analysis of material objects that challenged the agency of human actors like engineers. In her history of the seventeenth-century French Canal du Midi, a monumental engineering (and infrastructural) undertaking, Mukerji documents how the material force of water challenged the limits of engineering expertise and modes of political governance. The water's agency, in this sense, exceeded individual human will or authority to shape the development of the canal. She terms this counteragency of objects "logistical power," the significance of ordering and mobilizing natural things as "a form of dominion or regulation of the natural order" (215), in contrast to strategic forms of political domination. Logistical power marks the ways infrastructure's material qualities shape socio-technical systems and practices as much as human intent does. Getting online, similarly, entails navigating logistical, technical, material, and bureaucratic systems at the conjuncture of infrastructure (including its material qualities) and increasingly technocratic management.[4]

The challenges of logistical labor in internet and computing access became evident in my fieldwork when Daniele decided to purchase a new laptop. She had been sharing an older PC with Katrine, but after making new friends in Berlin, especially EU-Ausländer (foreigners), she began using Facebook more frequently, which was difficult for her during work hours. She managed a small boutique in Prenzlauer Berg but could not use the store's computer for personal use. Like many eastern Germans I knew, Daniele did not have a computer at home as a child; the Wall came down when she was still in primary school. Her first time using a computer by herself, she told me, was at work when she was twenty, though she had played computer games with a cousin before that. She had taken a computer course at school, but it was not "*hilfreich*" (helpful). She had begun accessing the internet a few years before in 2004, when a roommate set up DSL service. She did have an iPod music player, which may have contributed to her choice of an Apple laptop.

The only Apple Store in Germany at the time was located in the wealthier western German port city of Hamburg.[5] Although Berlin has been the seat of reunified Germany's federal government since 1999, it remains one of Europe's poorest metropolises. Daniele headed instead to a consumer electronics superstore, Mediamarkt, in the Alexa mall at Alexanderplatz and brought along me and Katrine. Alexanderplatz, a capacious commercial and transit hub in Mitte, comprises a large, open concrete plaza dominated by the iconic Soviet *Fernsehturm* (television tower). The tower, which looms over much of the eastern half of the city, is situated over a nexus of rail train, subway, and tram lines alongside shopping strips, apartment towers, a mall, and department stores. The plaza's redevelopment was the subject of much contention among residents and urban planners in the early 2000s, as described by Weszkalnys (2010), and it sits in stark contrast to the narrow cobblestone streets of adjacent Prenzlauer Berg, with sidewalk cafés, small boutiques, and old churches, or the grand monumental architecture of imperial Mitte.

On the top floor of Mediamarkt, one section simulated the look and feel of an Apple Store—uncluttered rectangular white tables, hardwood floors, streamlined displays of Apple MacBook computers and iPod music players. Mediamarkt had a special offer on the purchase of an entry-level white MacBook, but Daniele was unsure of what to get. Apple products and other consumer electronics were expensive compared to subsidized necessities like food, making the purchase that much more significant.[6] We spent nearly an hour browsing and waiting for Daniele to decide. In the meantime, I noticed a large flat-screen display, an iMac computer, showing a picture of a white student on an exchange program—to Germany. Consuming Apple products in an ersatz Apple store in Berlin enabled participation in global consumption but also positioned German consumers as outsiders, as had accessing US music videos on YouTube.

Daniele solicited our input and finally settled on the latest MacBook model. The new purchase triggered further work to set up the computer. She brought her laptop to the house of another friend, Nina, who had invited us over, and asked me for assistance. Initial setup required an internet connection, but Nina lived alone and used a mobile surfstick. The stick was branded with the logo for O2, a UK-based mobile service provider with a German subsidiary, popular for their monthly contract data plans. The surfstick allowed Nina to purchase monthly service without committing to a long contract or activating a landline. She hoped to order DSL service with WLAN, but the surfstick provided on-the-road internet access, which was especially useful in her work as a film production assistant.

As Michel de Certeau (1984) has articulated, informal means of consumption can constitute decentralized resistance to dominant, institutional modes of power. Building on Foucault's formulation of power as diffuse and capillary—operating through the regularization of space and place and of bodies and gestures, as well as through the proliferation of discourse—de Certeau theorizes diffuse means of resistance. He identifies power with the monopoly over official places and discourses, whether institutional buildings or maps. Ordinary practices of consumption and use in his account can constitute opposition to these dominant regimes, through ways of getting by and "making do," such as devoting company time to personal pursuits (29–30). Ways of making do occupy, in de Certeau's words, "no proper space," always borrowing from formal spaces and asserting agency through "practices of use" (xix), such as reading practices or ways of moving through space. Tactics of resistance are in this sense continually unfolding, as subordinated subjects react to conditions that they cannot determine. Where hegemonic, strategic forms of power inhabit formal, institutional spaces (and ways of organizing space), tactics are by definition without place: "A tactic is a calculated action determined by the absence of a proper locus. No delimitation of an exteriority, then, provides it with the condition necessary for autonomy. The space of a tactic is the space of other" (37–38).

After de Certeau, I read many of my interlocutors' technology practices as ways of managing a variegated, uneven communications infrastructure. The early 2000s were a period of rapid change for Berlin and its built environment and for networked communications broadly. Relative to internet access in many places, the German system was well developed and affordable, but Berlin was poorer than other German cities. Services like broadband—necessary for content like streaming video—were just taking off. Combined with divergent histories of internet access and competences, this rapid shift engendered unevenness in getting online, as illustrated by the experiences of young people in service and knowledge sectors. One graphic design freelancer I interviewed, for example, depended on tethering his laptop to the internet through his iPhone or worked from internet cafés for higher speeds, as he did not have WLAN at home: "I have no Internet access at home. Just the iPhone. I connect over Bluetooth—I use the Bluetooth connection in the iPhone, and I often work in Internet cafés." Although tethering was possible with a special data plan, it was illicit otherwise. To communicate with clients, he relied on his relatively fast, current iPhone, in contrast to his older, slower laptop, which he could not afford to replace.

Using surfsticks, tethering, or working from cafés (otherwise an atypical practice in Berlin; see Kraemer 2022) constituted tactical forms of internet access, ways of responding to formal systems of mobile networking and WLAN from no proper place. Nina could use her surfstick at home as well as from her car, circumventing the need to install service at home; cafés provided internet access (and office space) to mobile, sometimes contingent knowledge workers. Even once these users got online, connecting to the internet from a German IP address limited the content they could view. This limitation stemmed not from expense or the technical capacity of the system but from formal telecommunications policy, like international licensing agreements. Purchasing computers and service plans entailed new forms of logistical labor, further bureaucratizing home life and thrusting managerial work onto consumers. Yet young people in this emerging middle class found ways to manage infrastructural unevenness and respond to dominant orderings of space through informal tactics that often enabled participation in cosmopolitan worlds.

From Surfsticks to File Sharing

By the late aughts, television series and movies were increasingly available to stream on demand online, from Netflix in the United States to Zattoo in Germany. Numerous factors contributed to the rise of streaming video, such as high-speed internet connections and more powerful mobile devices. But US copyright law requires that distributors secure licensing from the relevant copyright holder (or a licensing agency), an increasingly expensive proposition as streaming services expanded their catalogs. Although Netflix since offers service *in* Germany—that is, to German viewers—at the time, US-based subscribers could not view videos on their Netflix accounts *from* Germany. While German network television was freely available online, such as through Zattoo, few people in these friend circles watched it. Many did not own a television set at all.

But, as with other media, most people were interested in shows and movies from the United States (and elsewhere, like the United Kingdom). Some US titles were available through cable or satellite, but few people subscribed (with the exception of the music fans in Amsterdam, as I will describe). Myriad semi-licit services, however, had sprouted online, usually on domains in countries with few regulations, like Tonga (.to), popular with torrent sites (file-sharing sites often used for pirating).[7] These included Kino.to and MegaUpload/MegaVideo (both since taken down, and the owner of MegaUpload arrested[8]). While setting up Daniele's laptop, we discussed the possibility of watching US shows, and Nina jumped in to ask, "Could I do that? To watch American shows?" I had looked into ways to watch US shows that I otherwise would have viewed on Netflix, and I offered to demonstrate: "Sure, what would you want to watch?"[9] "*Grey's Anatomy*" she suggested. The German-language search results on her laptop, however, differed from what Google returned on mine—even when connecting from the same place. When Nina realized these services were quasi-legal streaming sites, however, she quickly objected, "But that's illegal!" She reported hearing stories of Germans who ran into legal trouble downloading pirated music. While she was enthusiastic about watching shows like *Grey's Anatomy*, she was more concerned about potential legal risks.

Others evinced fewer compunctions, however, and many turned to torrents, ad-supported streaming services, or other means to acquire unlicensed content. Another acquaintance of Daniele's, Karoline, recounted watching American comedies such as *Scrubs* and *Friends* on Kino.to, which streamed episodes uploaded by other users at no cost but limited how many minutes each user could watch per day. Among the electronic music fans, many devoted considerable time to configuring their home electronics, including network setups to share files, primarily audio. Alex, Sal, Viktor, and others, like many music enthusiasts, consumed music voraciously through multiple channels, including purchasing actual records and sharing digital files. File sharing offered them a means to access hard-to-find music like rare albums and imports, more than to avoid legal purchase, as the music industry often contends.

One music promoter described how his computer connected to the internet to upload and download files in the background: "I would say that my computer is running about 12 to 16 hours a day. Even if I'm not home or I'm sleeping, then it might be uploading torrents, or downloading torrents, or uploading stuff to my server, because I do have a server, where I share music with friends. A lot of my work is computer-based, so I have to spend a lot of time in front of the computer and since I don't watch TV or have money for newspapers, most of my information, like news-related information, comes also through the computer."

He mentioned an exclusive torrent site for sharing files, a "private tracker . . . which is like a gated community for sharing music." Such services were seen as affording protection by vetting participants, in contrast to public sites like the Pirate Bay, widely panned for users' lack of sophistication. One music producer explained that he preferred Skype over other messaging services because of its file-sharing capabilities, which allowed him to share music both with friends and for professional collaborations. Others, such as a music fan who found that file sharing made watching television a "more active process," described torrenting through invite-only sites.

The circle of Dutch music fans (connected through events and festivals like Musikfest, described in chapter 1) reported similar activities. Marc and his friends Sophie and Matthew, who often visited their friends in Berlin, paid for cable television and owned large flat-screen TVs. But the many TV channels available in Amsterdam often did not include the hit US or UK shows they were most interested in watching, which they downloaded online instead. As Marc explained: "I have a ton of movies and TV series in my watch list, most hit shows of course. *Lost, Dexter, Justified, Breaking Bad*. All American shows, exclusively. Some Brit shows I watch too."

Even when such shows were available, they were broadcast sooner in the United States, making Dutch viewers wait to access them: "I have a TV, and a I have a projector, but it's not hooked up now. I have my total package of all channels available, but I actually don't watch that much TV anymore, because I download most of my TV shows. I can record on my cable box, [but] the torrents are earlier on the Internet than they would broadcast them here in Holland. On-demand here is ridiculously expensive."

Marc, Sophie, and others in their circle were employed in technical and creative fields, like IT, research, and journalism, and were more able to afford television sets or cable service than many of their friends in Berlin. They turned to torrenting and file sharing not because of the cost but because licensing agreements meant that international programming aired later in the Netherlands, positioning them as outsiders to these cosmopolitan media worlds. In contrast, torrents, disseminated through a peer-to-peer protocol, could be available near instantaneously, once a show aired and was recorded and shared (typically illicitly).[10] Downloading and sharing torrents was popular not to avoid paying for content but to participate in transnational circuits of popular culture, circuits in which licensing structures rendered them secondary. Place, specifically the scale of the nation, reasserted itself in these media practices through national (and international) regulatory regimes. Like surfsticks, file sharing made it possible to circumvent infrastructural unevenness, eliciting tactical forms of consumption for those with the right tech competences. Yet such tactics were the purview of those whose location, both geographic and social, required managing these place-based regimes, in some ways reinstating their own peripheralness.

Managing Mobile Borders: Mobile Tariffs "im Ausland"

These ways of evading international regulatory regimes were often about participating in cosmopolitan, transnational cultural circuits, yet in other instances, the national scale reasserted itself. Media infrastructures such as mobile networking could reinstate borders that EU policies had attenuated, as travelers found when crossing them. This infrastructure also generated experiences of (and resulted from) rural areas as technologically underdeveloped and temporally lagging. Many people perceived mobile networking as enabling global or transnational connections, such as through mobile social media. In practice, mobile service depended on national, regional, or sometimes municipal service providers, regulated by national agencies (often coordinated at the supranational level by the European Union; Schnöring and Szafran 1994). Popular multinational providers at the time, like UK-based O2, operated separate subsidiaries in various European nations, including Germany. Siloing service along national lines meant that O2 subscribers in Germany could not use their regular service plans out of the country, even elsewhere in the European Union where O2 operated. Instead, subscribers found themselves subject to higher fees for high-speed data, voice calls, and text messages (SMS) when abroad. The national organization of mobile service was not always evident in daily practice in populous urban areas like Berlin. People in my fieldwork encountered the limits of national service providers in two primary places: rural regions and national borders. As they did with other tactics of scalemaking, my interlocutors managed these borders in creative, ad hoc ways that shaped their experience of space and place.

Outside urban centers, as in rural Saxony-Anhalt where Daniele, Katrine, Jörg, and others were from, about an hour by train from Berlin, mobile service became intermittent and uneven. On a weekend I accompanied Daniele and others to visit her home village for a birthday party, service became spotty as we drove from the train station to the cluster of small towns and villages where they had grown up. High-speed data in particular became scarce, making it difficult to use navigation or access social media. This pattern is common outside urban areas in many places, largely because of the expense of maintaining cellular towers in sparsely populated places. Daniele had framed this reduced access in temporal rather than spatial terms, describing her home village as like *"früher"* (earlier) technologically. Her parents connected to the internet through dial-up service (via a modem and phone line) because high-speed broadband was not yet available. Such uneven access was exacerbated by differing histories of communications infrastructure in West Germany and East Germany. Many of those who had grown up in western Germany after the Wende had computers and internet service in their homes by the middle to late 1990s, whereas in eastern Germany, internet and mobile telephony were typically implemented later on.[11] Issues of access thus linked rural places to temporal "backwardness," echoing ways those from rural regions, like Daniele and her friends, described themselves (see also Schnöring and Szafran 1994, 465–66). As recounted in chapter 4, for example, a friend of Daniele's had deprecatingly called himself just a boy "von dem Land"— that is, from the country. Similarly, Daniele contrasted how she and her friends in Berlin had moved on to Facebook, which was hip and transnational, with how her friends in Magdeburg continued to use MySpace, which she found outdated, associating it with the past. As Daniele began spending more time on Facebook, she found visiting her parents increasingly frustrating as she could not keep up with her friends in Berlin and their activities online.

Uneven infrastructure in rural areas contributed to these feelings that rural regions lagged behind city life. This unevenness further perpetuated historical divides between eastern and western Germans, sedimenting differing histories of place into the built environment. The connection between spatial organization and the communications infrastructure became even more evident when crossing national borders. The national regulation of mobile networking belied common images of a global, borderless online world—and contrasted with increasing European integration through border policies. Since the Schengen Agreements in 1985 and 1990, German citizens have been able to travel to many other European nations without border controls or visas (Leitner 1997), including all contiguous nations, most EU countries, and a few others, like Switzerland.

But the telecommunications networks are still administered at the national level, albeit coordinated supranationally. Sweden, for example, developed mobile phone standards in the 1950s, and in the 1980s, GSM (Global System for Mobile Communications) was adopted as a uniform, interoperable standard protocol (Dunnewijk and Hultén 2007). At the time, the European Commission (and later the European Union) supported the supranational implementation of GSM, unifying the mobile telecommunication system to some degree. While such standardization recalls nineteenth-century efforts to standardize and homogenize national languages, facilitating nationalization, mobile networking service is divided into national providers. In 2007, when mobile adoption was first expanding in Europe, national regulatory authorities (NRAs) were responsible for retail markets, although wholesale markets were regulated by the European Commission (2007). Numerous international mobile service providers in Europe operate independent national subsidiaries, alongside partly privatized federal services like Deutsche Telekom (also Germany's main internet provider). Deutsche Telekom formed when the West German telephone provider (and postal service) Deutsche Bundespost was privatized in 1996. Deutsche Bundespost had been slated for reform in 1990, but the reform was delayed by the Wende in 1989 and 1990. Afterward, East German communication services were restructured according to West German standards and policies, favoring liberalization and privatization. The telecommunications system was standardized across Germany as part of the process of reunification, yet the eastern "new states" (Neues Länder) were often characterized as "backwards" (Schnöring and Szafran 1994, 465–66), echoing many eastern Germans' own language and imaginings.

These European border policies contributed to building a space of supranational mobility, at least for acceptable middle-class subjects (as detailed in chapter 2). But the national scale reasserted itself at national borders, precisely through these seemingly placeless mobile networks. I experienced this digital, networked border firsthand when taking a train from Berlin to Amsterdam to visit a circle of music fans including Marc, Sophie, and Matthew, whom I had met in October 2009 at Musikfest in western Germany, and who were connected to the circle of music fans in Berlin. As the high-speed train approached the border between Germany and the Netherlands, it began to slow down. We were still within the Schengen area, and no one asked for my passport. But the transit infrastructure across the border was not identical, and the tracks changed over, requiring the train to move more slowly (such transitions happen frequently, sometimes requiring entirely different train equipment, as when traveling east from Germany to the Czech Republic). As the train slowed, my smartphone buzzed twice in quick succession with two text messages warning me about the increased cost of voice calls and high-speed data while "*im Ausland*" (abroad). My phone cast about for a Dutch network to connect to in lieu of German O2. The telecommunication network, like the rail lines, changed over when crossing the border—despite the interoperability of the GSM standard.

Once in the Netherlands, I was able to use my phone on a Dutch network, but voice and data service became much more expensive (text messages, while no longer free, cost less than voice or data). The ostensible mobility my device afforded became considerably reduced, as I could no longer navigate with mapping apps or communicate seamlessly across platforms. Instead, I relied on the singular channel of text messages (SMS) to coordinate with my hosts and find my way to their home. Leaving Germany effectively rendered my mobile device, a multipurpose smartphone, much less indispensable. When the Dutch music fans visited Berlin, they experienced similar limitations. Marc and a few of his friends visited on a number of weekends during my fieldwork, often renting a short-term furnished apartment. At home in Amsterdam, they often contacted one another over voice, text, and social media, but in Berlin, they coordinated plans entirely over text messages. Although their apartment rental included wireless internet (WLAN), their unit was on an upper floor where the router signal did not reach. Instead, Marc showed me a 3G surfstick the management had provided.

As mobile devices and high-speed data service became integrated into daily life, the national ordering of telecommunications networks reiterated—and instantiated—the national scale. Nations were not all on equal footing, however. According to the roaming-fee chart I consulted on the O2 website, prices depended on which country a user's account was based in and where they were traveling. From a German provider like O2, mobile service abroad cost less in other European nations than in most other parts of the world. At the time of my fieldwork, most carriers still locked their handsets (that is, restricted them to one carrier), especially full-featured smartphones, to prevent consumers from easily switching providers. Early on in my fieldwork, I attempted to unlock a US phone I had brought with me. First, I brought it to a small mobile phone shop, where an associate offered to try but returned it to me after a number of days without success. It was not until I looked up online how to do so illicitly—voiding my phone's warranty in the process—that I was able to download hacking software to circumvent Apple's protections.[12] One of the music fans, in contrast, purchased an unlocked phone from Italy, paying its full retail value (hundreds of euros). In Germany, he could only purchase the same phone locked, with a two-year service plan. These national regulatory systems reasserted, and generated, national borders through technologies often perceived as global or placeless. National regulations and infrastructure shaped experiences of travel, mobility, and space for young people in these friend circles, at a time when supranational European border policies had reduced other barriers, such as visas or passport control.

Infrastructure as Placemaking

In Brian Larkin's (2013) annual review of the anthropology of infrastructure, he writes: "Infrastructures are matter that enable the movement of other matter. Their peculiar ontology lies in the facts that they are things and also the relation between things" (329). Media infrastructures, like networked communication systems, raise the question of what kind of matter digital media entail, or rather, what the qualities of digital things are. In Hayles's 2004 account of digital materiality, digital texts are no more or less material than print media, but their materiality differs. Code, for example, is layered and dynamic, though largely invisible, enabling different interactions and practices. Materiality here does not index inert matter or physical properties alone but "a dynamic quality that *emerges* from the interplay between the text as a physical artifact, its conceptual content, and the interpretive activities of readers and writers" (72, emphasis in original). Media, in my analysis, are notable for commingling material qualities with signifying or interpretive practices. In attending to the dynamic, meaningful materiality of the communications infrastructure, from wireless networks to file sharing, I make two arguments: (1) media infrastructures shape experiences of place, challenging perceptions of digital technologies as placeless and deterritorialized, and (2) place-based histories and practices, from Berlin's bifurcated infrastructure to international regulatory systems, continue to position these emerging middle-class Europeans as outside the cosmopolitan worlds they often associate with digital connection.

The turn to infrastructure studies, cutting across anthropology, science and technology studies, media studies, and other literatures, offers what Christian Sandvig (2013) describes as a turn to "the spatialization of formerly placeless media-related practices" (101). Sandvig identifies shared concerns with rethinking meaning/matter divides both in science and technology studies (e.g., Star 1999), which call attention to the importance of social ties in technical and engineering systems, and in new materialist turns in media theory that locate cultural processes in physical ecologies of dirt and wires, electrical capacities and resistance, rare earths mining and electronic waste (e.g., Blanchette 2011; Rosner et al. 2012). Mediating such concerns may seem self-evident to anthropological projects that have long situated culture in material practice.

In early 2000s Berlin, the communications infrastructure was transforming rapidly with the advent of digital technologies like mobile networking and social media. This process paralleled, and cannot be separated from, shifts in the reorganization of the city post-reunification, such as linking divergent transit systems or redeveloping neighborhoods and public spaces, often highly contested undertakings. Infrastructure includes not only wires and cellular towers but also national and international regulatory bodies that coordinate communications standards like GSM, regulate internet providers, and enforce licensing agreements and copyright policy, the "arrangements of practices" constituted by "tacit labor," according to Sandvig (2013, 97). In this sense, systems that enable digital communication equally reinstantiate geographic scales like the national or supranational. Constellated practices, channels, and technical systems respatialize online practices through scalemaking—that is, by producing multiple, interpenetrating levels of spatial organization. Accessing Facebook, for instance, involved acquiring a personal computer at a local retailer; setting up internet service, often administered at the municipal or national level; and navigating to a US-based site with servers in both the United States and Europe. Facebook detects users' locations (through their IP address) and offers a "localized" interface—that is, one translated into German. Media like YouTube videos further entangle users in a complex of international licensing laws and distribution agreements, which repositioned German and other viewers outside the supposedly placeless (or global) sphere of internet discourse. Place, in this sense, exists online, in ways that emerging media reconfigure.

Conversely, place-based histories shaped ways people approach and interact with digital technologies. As I have described, longtime ways of getting by and making do characterized daily living in Berlin for these young, sometimes precarious members of a rapidly changing middle class. Some practices, like sharing phones, predate the Wende, a means of managing the unequal communications system in the GDR. Other activities, described in chapter 6, recall practices that took shape after, such as makeshift, illicit dance parties that prefigure invite-only message boards and improvised film showings. As with friends interchanging mobile phones, circumventing the rules of an uneven communications system could generate shared feelings of mutuality. Other practices, like surfsticks and file sharing, constitute tactical modes of consumption comparable to de Certeau's informal, displaced, and contingent ways subjects use and consume in late capitalist regimes. Proliferating digital technologies, combined with the neoliberal bureaucratizing of everyday life, contribute further to what I term logistical labor. This kind of busy work is the flip side of managerial labor in the knowledge economy—setting up user profiles, configuring networks, choosing service plans, responding to customer-satisfaction surveys, and so on. Lack of technical expertise, or just mental fatigue, can form a barrier to engaging with digital and mobile media, despite the availability of such technologies.

Even as digital and mobile media enabled multiscalar, cosmopolitan forms of connection, the infrastructure of mobile networking depended on national regulation and licensing. While the project of European integration had removed border controls in the Schengen area, communications and transit infrastructure reinstated the national scale of territorial ordering. Geographically mobile Europeans and travelers had to contend with expensive data and voice calls when abroad, which reduced their mobile phones to basic functions like text messaging. My interlocutors in Berlin, Amsterdam, and elsewhere found ways to manage these digital borders, such as through 3G (broadband) surfsticks. Yet doing so belied the image of online connection as seamless or global. In rural places, limited access to high-speed data service contributed to perceptions that rural regions were more "backward," delayed in their implicitly teleological development. Berlin, in contrast, became a space of the present or near future, where mobile, cosmopolitan Germans and Ausländer found friendships through night-life, socialized on transnational social media like Facebook, and enjoyed high-speed data connections at home and in public. In contrast to claims of global connection, Berlin's media infrastructures elucidate multiple configurations of space and place that took shape on and through emerging media.

PUBLIC MEDIA IN URBAN SPACE

Managing media infrastructures often recapitulated longtime tactical ways of getting by and making do in Berlin, as the preceding chapter explored. Getting online could be an uneven process, shaped by Berlin's bisected infrastructure and history. These tactical media practices extended to visual media like television viewing in ways that produced new experiences of urban space and fostered cosmopolitan nationalism. In this chapter, I examine illicit, makeshift, and ad hoc engagements with public media and mobile networks that engendered feelings of mutuality and reshaped the scales of the city, the nation, and at times, the continent. These practices included an unofficial, semi-licit film viewing in a warehouse in Prenzlauer Berg, recalling the underground parties of the 1990s; improvisational setups for viewing the FIFA World Cup football (or soccer) series in 2010; and nightlife tactics that generated fleeting but shared sentiments. In many of these instances, Berlin's underground dance cultures provided a framework or idiom for consuming or sharing public media in informal or ad hoc ways that generated unspoken feelings of mutuality, what I elsewhere call "public media mutuality" (Kraemer 2022). Setups more typical for an underground nightclub appeared during the World Cup to view matches in communal spaces from cafés to clubs and the literal public street.

Unlike Berlin's prior art communes and parties in abandoned spaces, communal World Cup viewings—like social media (chapter 1), Euro-English (chapter 3), or online news (chapter 4)—offered spaces to enact shared participation in an emergent cosmopolitan nationalism, especially as Germany's team progressed to the playoffs. The series, in fact, was the only time during my fieldwork when the national flag hung from nearby apartment buildings or cars or when football fans wore clothes and face paint in Germany's national colors. According to one of my interlocutors, the World Cup games represented one of the few times Germans felt comfortable articulating national identity or pride, particularly because fans from other nations (including many non-German Europeans in Berlin) did the same. For the friend circles in my fieldwork, the urban context, such as countercultural and underground spaces, rendered national sensibilities hip, cosmopolitan, and acceptable. At the same time, the broader supranational context remade national identity into a component of a larger, complementary system of nation-states, offering a way to participate in communal urban life as European and global citizens, in the same way others celebrated their national teams.

Nationalism, in the sense of national selfhood and belonging, took shape in the context of an increasingly integrated Europe—that is, as part of a system of nation-states. Historians John Breuilly and Ronald Speirs (2005), for example, contrast Germany's reunification in 1990, which took place in the context of a politically integrated Europe, with Otto von Bismarck's nineteenth-century nationalization project. Although Breuilly and Speirs frame Germany's twentieth-century reunification as reconnecting a singular "divided nation" (2), they note the "dense network of supra-state relations" that reworks what contemporary nationalism means (3). Sabine Mannitz (2006) similarly argues that the European state system, including the European Union, has tempered German nationalism: national German identity has come to constitute one among many, part of a broader multinational system. For some cosmopolitan young Germans, expressing national pride in public was acceptable—and in fact, constituted being hip and urban—when participating in a multinational, television-viewing public.

In the following sections, I describe scenes of ad hoc and improvisational ways of engaging with public media that fostered mutual sentiments and reconfigured experiences of urban space. The experimental and DIY (do-it-yourself) spaces of Berlin's underground club cultures situated many of these practices in the city's history of sheltering perceived outsiders and countercultural movements, including artists, activists, and queer communities. The nightlife practice of "guest-listing" (getting friends and acquaintances into music events for free), for example, fostered forms of mutuality that took shape in nightlife and underground music scenes, a fluid, shifting connectedness Luis-Manuel Garcia (2013a) calls "liquidarity." Similarly makeshift viewings of World Cup matches remade everyday public spaces, from cafés to parks, as multiscalar sites of hip urban nationalism, while situating contemporary Germanness in a multinational network of nations and nationalisms. These diverse scenes of communal media practices show how tactical modes of interacting with visual and mobile media produced multiple, divergent, and multiscalar experiences of urban space.

Warehouse Publics

On a drizzly evening in March 2010, I perched on an overturned bucket in a drafty corrugated metal warehouse in Prenzlauer Berg, a largely gentrified, hip district of former East Berlin. The warehouse had been staged as an impromptu movie theater, with a large projection screen at one end. A friend and frequent interlocutor, the DJ and graduate student Alex, had invited me via a Facebook event page, and I had followed instructions to meet near the Senefelderplatz U-Bahn (metro) station at 9:00 p.m.—directions that had much in common with those for an underground dance party. Organizers of the heady raves of the post-Wende 1990s, for example, had taken advantage of Berlin's many abandoned buildings, staging all-night techno parties that required special knowledge to locate (Sark 2019; see also Borneman and Senders 2000; MacDougall 2011; Nye 2013; Partridge 2008). On this evening, I emerged from the train station to find a crowd of approximately one hundred people gathered on the sidewalk in front of a discount grocery store. I texted with Alex to find where he, Pascal, and two other American friends were located in the crowd.

The organizers collected a small entrance fee, then led attendees through a doorway into a cobblestone courtyard typical of neighborhood buildings. Pascal joked nervously about whether we had just been scammed. As we walked, we met up with another friend, Niels, then followed the throng across a weedy parking lot, over a low wall, and onto a muddy strip of grass. Ahead lay the warehouse, its wide doors open. Inside, we found stacked crates of beer and rows of folding seats—or in some cases, overturned buckets—beyond. In the center of one row was a projector connected to a DVD player, likely through a laptop. As at many music shows and dance parties, the entrance fee included a complimentary beer, so we each helped ourselves to a bottle from the crates and then took seats, just as the organizers began the film.

The covert location and directions, the appropriated warehouse space, and even the complimentary beers evoked underground, quasi-licit, often makeshift or DIY (a practice and aesthetic closely associated with punk and squatter scenes) dance parties of the post-Wende 1990s. By the 2000s, while still embracing a gritty, derelict sensibility that recalled the earlier era, most dance parties took place in more above-board venues, from Tacheles in Mitte to smaller venues in Kreuzberg or Friedrichshain. The audience comprised young, mostly white Germans and EU-Europeans speaking German or Euro English (see chapter 3). The film, *White Lightnin'*, an independent 2009 UK release, offers a fictional biopic of the famed West Virginian mountain dancer Jesco White, shown with German subtitles (big-budget foreign releases in Germany, in contrast, are typically dubbed). Alex and his friends had mentioned in other instances that they preferred English-language films with subtitles (as described in chapters 3 and 4). But with the uneven sound system, frequently shifting volume, Appalachian accents and speech, and quiet chatter among the audience, it was difficult for me—even as a native US English speaker—to follow the dialogue. I often relied on the German subtitles to confirm what I had heard.

Although the makeshift setting was similar to that of many music and art events in Berlin, the showing contrasted with more typical settings where my interlocutors watched films with friends, such as living rooms or cinemas. The world of the film—grainy, violent, bleak, and increasingly fevered and psychedelic—also seemed distant from my interlocutors' lives in Berlin, where extreme poverty is relatively rare and basic needs like housing and health care are met (for citizens) by the state. The film depicted rural Appalachia in the 1970s and 1980s, a dilapidated world of drugs, violence, and bare life where charismatic Protestantism shapes people's inner, psychic lives. Many of the plot points hinged on aspects of life in the United States that surprised my German and European friends, such as persistent white poverty. The score further intensified the film's surreal narrative, with ambient, droning sounds overlaid with frenzied laughter and singing. Toward the film's increasingly dissociative denouement, however, the playback began stuttering, and the organizers took an unplanned intermission to fix the problem.

After the showing, Alex and Pascal convened outside with other friends who had attended. One friend in particular had spent extended time in North Carolina with family, and the film's story was closer to her family's experiences than I had thought. She reflected on her connection to cousins living near Appalachia and debated whether the story was true (Jesco White, the film's subject, is real, but the events of the story veer sharply from his actual life, according to what Alex and I later read on Wikipedia). Then she and Pascal announced they were heading to Watergate, a popular house music nightclub, and Alex invited me to join him at a bar where a friend of his was working. Later, on the U-Bahn, I asked Alex how he thought others in the audience would respond to the film and its depiction of white rural poverty. He explained that "most Germans have heard about [this side of the United States] but don't really believe it's real" and that people in Germany "can't understand how such poverty can exist in a great, mighty country like the US, since in Germany, such poverty doesn't exist, except voluntarily," such as among "crusty punks or squatters." This contention paralleled conversations during the 2009 debates over President Barack Obama's Affordable Care Act, which some of my interlocutors followed with bewilderment. They struggled to square their view of the United States as a postindustrial superpower with the reality of its expensive, often inaccessible health care system, in contrast to Germany's dual public/private system, which most viewed positively.

Despite the audience's enthusiastic engagement with the film, viewing via official channels appears to have been difficult. An independent film produced in the United Kingdom, it had been released the previous year (2009) at the Sundance film festival and was shown later that year at a film festival in Berlin.[1] The organizers, however, appear to have pursued less licit channels, acquiring a DVD for the unofficial showing. The DVD itself was probably a licensed version (it was possible to purchase the authorized DVD online; pirating was more typical for digital files, although in theory pirated files could be burned to DVD). In these ways, the showing overlapped with the digital piracy practices like file sharing or semi-licit TV streaming described in chapter 5—less a means to avoid paying and more a way to manage uneven licensing restrictions across national borders.

Like illicit file sharing, this unofficial film screening served not to undermine corporate purveyors but to work around a patchwork system of international licensing agreements, distribution chains, and communications infrastructure that belie the seamless, global facade of digital media. As a tactic of managing infrastructural unevenness, the viewing harked back to the ways of getting by typical of post-Wende youth culture in Berlin, especially underground nightlife. Even in the years preceding the Wende, young people had organized underground and clandestine events. West Berlin, a Cold War–era refuge for queer people, artists, squatters, and activists, had long hosted spaces for subcultural nightlife and parties (e.g., Sark 2019; MacDougall 2011). In East Germany, interest in Western popular and underground music, such as punk, new wave, and industrial rock, grew throughout the 1980s; allegedly, a small number of East German young people in Potsdam had tried to organize a goth rock meetup in 1988, which was broken up by state police. The festival returned in 1992 in Leipzig as a massively popular event called Wave Gotik Treffen, which continues to attract thousands of attendees yearly.[2] The aesthetics of these events lived on in the otherwise licit parties of the early 2000s, epitomized in the dingy, graffiti-covered concrete of destinations like Tacheles or Berghain, in a massive repurposed electrical substation. Like underground parties—and in contrast to file-sharing practices, mostly conducted in private—the warehouse screening fostered a shared public, a sense of commonality or mutuality that took shape through illicit media viewing.

Nightlife Tactics: "Liquidarity"

Unofficial or unpermitted events are not unique to Berlin's nightlife or underground culture. But ways of getting by and making do, after de Certeau 1984, characterized many aspects of the subcultural music scenes in which my interlocutors participated. De Certeau, as discussed in chapter 5, distinguished between formal strategies of institutional and regulatory power situated in proper places and informal tactics of getting by that resist or evade dominant power through the reappropriation of time and space: "Strategies pin their hopes on the resistance that the establishment of a place offers to the erosion of time; tactics on a clever utilization of time, of the opportunities it presents and also of the play that it introduces into the foundations of power" (38–39). Such informal tactics structured spaces like music events and dance parties, engendering feelings of mutual, often unspoken connection and producing intimate publics that reworked relations among strangers (see Garcia 2013a, 2013b).

The aesthetics of repurposed club spaces like Tacheles or Berghain were rooted in the derelict and abandoned buildings of East Berlin after the Wende.[3] Tacheles, the art commune and nightclub, occupied an early twentieth-century former shopping arcade, while Berghain, Berlin's most notorious techno club (and the second incarnation of famed late-1990s club Ostgut) inhabited a cavernous former power station. These spacious venues were often left unfinished, the raw concrete adorned with graffiti, recalling the squats and communes of West (and later, former East) Berlin (MacDougall 2011; Boym 2008). As Svetlana Boym wrote in 2008: "Tacheles is an inhabited ruin that is already aestheticized, estranged, reimagined. . . . Tacheles is nostalgic for the bohemian island Berlin and for the time when the East dreamed of the West, which in turn was dreaming of the East" (208). Reappropriating such spaces constituted a tactic in de Certeau's sense, contributing to a shared perception of what made Berlin Berlin—evoking not *Ostalgie* (nostalgia for the lost East German past) but nostalgia for the vanished possibilities of the 1990s, as a transitional space and time (*Zwischennutzung*; Ward 2019, 114)—and of the creativeness and openness associated with the city's post-Wende "voids" (Huyssen 1997).

In the course of Alex's work as a music promoter and DJ, he made friends and contacts at numerous venues by organizing, promoting, and attending shows and parties. One evening, I accompanied him and another friend to Berghain, a hulking edifice situated in an otherwise desolate lot near the river Spree. Along with infamous techno and house music clubs like Tresor, Berghain traces its roots to the 1990s, when old factories and warehouses were appropriated as illicit club venues. Berghain opened at its most recent location in 1999, in a former power plant with vaulted ceilings and multiple levels, where soaring windows were blacked out by louvered covers. But, perhaps owing to its outsize reputation, gaining entrance was notoriously tricky. The head doorman—a heavily tattooed photographer who had gained a degree of celebrity for his literal gatekeeping—decided who could enter, while a lengthening queue snaked down a long gravel drive. That evening, as I waited next to Alex, two Irish men in their twenties complained loudly after the doorman rejected them. "What? Is it because we don't speak German?" one of them exclaimed before leaving in a huff. When Alex and I eventually reached the front of the line, he said quickly, "I'm on the guest list, and they're with me." We entered immediately, with no further vetting.

Nightlife practices like guest-listing were common among the electronic music fans, many of whom were themselves musicians, producers, or sound engineers, and nightlife, especially electronic music shows, constituted a key site of leisure and peer sociality. Nightlife, more typically indie rock and electro events, played a less central but still significant role among the friend circle from Saxony-Anhalt as well. Tobias, a radio DJ, often played at nearby clubs, spinning indie electro (a genre of indie rock with electronic instrumentation, vocals, and a danceable four-four beat) and regularly attended live shows with friends. Occasionally, his friends Clara and Agathe visited all-night techno parties at clubs like Watergate or Tresor, which were popular with Berlin's "clubbing tourists" (Rapp 2010; on Berlin's "techno-tourists," see also Garcia 2016). These weekend or short-term visitors hailed from places like Dublin, Amsterdam, or Barcelona or farther afield, and such events became a primary venue for this friend circle to meet Ausländer friends (as described in chapter 1).

Among both friend circles, going out quickly became expensive. Generally, the cost of living in Berlin (famously Europe's poorest capital) was lower than in other European metropolises or German cities like Hamburg or Munich. Low rents made it feasible for artists and musicians to support themselves with part-time and gig work (although this was rapidly changing). But live shows and nightclubs typically cost fifteen to twenty euros or more for entrance, plus transportation, additional drinks, coat check, and other costs. This amount was rarely prohibitive on any given night, but the cumulative outlay required most people to prioritize which events to attend and how often. Even as a grant-funded researcher, I encountered limits to how often I could accompany friends and interlocutors when invited, a problem Garcia (2013b, 7) outlines in his assessment of fieldwork methodologies for nightlife research. One weekend, for example, I declined an invitation to a concert that, at twenty euros, cost more than most. In comparison, a respectable bottle of lager at the local *Spätkauf* (convenience store) ran about 1.50 euros, a one-way ride on the U-Bahn in the central zones about 2.50 euros, pizza at a popular local spot 7 to 8 euros, wine 2 to 5 euros, and a liter of milk less than a euro at the supermarket nearest my apartment.[4]

For those with the right connections, however, the guest list offered the possibility of gratis entry. Social capital, accumulated by going out and building ties within a given music scene, furnished a workaround. Typically, performers, organizers, and staff were allowed one or more guest-list spots for a given event, and most clubs maintained a running list of people regularly granted free entry. These spots, which many referred to as their "plus one," constituted part of a performer or organizer's compensation, especially at small events that might net little profit. Organizers and club managers often extended reciprocal guest-list spots to other promoters and producers, fostering ties within and across small music scenes. These free spots also boosted attendance, another form of currency that helped venues, organizers, or event series become established by attracting a reliable insider crowd.

The same evening I had declined one invitation because of the cost, a recently met acquaintance messaged me on Facebook to propose other plans. I suggested a venue popular with Alex and his friend circle, but he demurred: "[I'm] kind of broke so lets see . . ." and then added, "but waiting for news for g[uest] list spot at WMF tonight . . . will definitely keep you posted." Others similarly determined which events to attend on the basis of the styles of music, the performers or DJs booked, the friends who might be there, and the kind of crowd they expected (in terms of both size and types of people, such as "tourists" versus scene regulars).

Shoring up such connections in turn generated further opportunities to meet new managers, promoters, and agents—and to gain new guest-list spots. Beyond the financial expedience of generating social capital, being guest-listed conferred subcultural legitimacy, crystallizing networks of mutual recognition and credibility, comparable to Sarah Thornton's (1996) account of subcultural capital in 1990s UK club cultures (see also Bourdieu 1984). Thornton takes up Bourdieu's formulation of cultural capital—that is, internalized cultural knowledge and competence acquired implicitly, according to class position—to explain how taste operates in youth subcultures. In club cultures organized around electronic dance music (both licit nightclubs and illicit raves), the right subcultural tastes and knowledges allowed scene insiders to position themselves against "poseurs," or dilettantes, as well as against "mainstream" music, in ways that simultaneously reproduced class distinctions (Thornton 1996, 101). Earning guest-list spots required not only social connections but the right subcultural knowledge, including affective and embodied competences, which demonstrated discriminating taste in electronic music and enacted belonging in these underground scenes.

On another evening that illustrated these dynamics, Alex invited me to an event at Tacheles, the art commune in a repurposed shopping arcade in Mitte. Mitte (literally "middle") occupies Berlin's center and encompasses some of Berlin's grandest architecture from its imperial era—the Brandenburg Gate, the Pergamon Museum, and the Berliner Dom cathedral, as well as embassies, Humboldt University, and the like. After World War II, Mitte became part of East Berlin, bordering the Wall, which divided it from Kreuzberg in West Berlin (as made famous by Checkpoint Charlie). In 1990, not long after the Wall fell in November 1989, Kunsthaus Tacheles, as described in the introduction, had opened near the Neue Synagogue in what had once been Berlin's Jewish quarter and slum. The name Tacheles itself was reputed to be Yiddish for "straight talking," according to an interview with one of its founders.[5] Twenty years on, Tacheles had preserved its unrenovated postwar aesthetic—raw concrete layered with graffiti and grime, residual war damage, dim lighting, an adjacent unruly weed-choked lot—yet operated as a lively and vibrant space with a cinema, art studios, and other attractions.

The surrounding corner of Mitte, in contrast, had gentrified rapidly since the Wende, especially when the reunited German government returned to Berlin from Bonn. Even as the streets around it became an upscale shopping and tourism district, Tacheles conserved its early 1990s sensibilities inside and out. Alex professed that by the early 2000s, Tacheles's dance clubs mainly attracted tourists, to his dismay: "It doesn't get the best crowd. Most are tourists because of the location." But we attended to support his friend Viktor, who was performing in an attic-like space on the top floor, under sloped ceilings. After ascending a central staircase bedecked with a riot of spray-painted tags and images, we approached the door staff. Alex asked whether he was on the guest list, and in affirmation, the staff ushered us both inside. Beyond, we found ourselves in a poorly heated, shadowy space with bare furnishings, unlike some plusher, newer clubs. In one room, a folding table made for a makeshift bar. As Alex had anticipated, few people had come, mostly small groups of young men.

After Viktor's set, Alex went to greet him. His main reason for attending was to support his friend by being present—but not by paying at the door. Beyond serving as a means to assert social position, guest-listing fostered connectedness within these small music worlds. Where Bourdieu's (1984) cultural capital recapitulates class status through ingrained tastes and judgments, Thornton's (1996) subcultural capital operates inside but necessarily in accordance with the dominant field of cultural production. Thornton interpolates a notion of youth subcultures into Bourdieu's framework, grounded in the Birmingham School's approach to youth culture (e.g., Stuart and Hall [1975] 1993; Hebdige 1979; McRobbie 1993; Willis [1981] 1990). For Stuart and Hall ([1975] 1993), working-class youth resisted their class position through style, from mods to Teddy Boys, skinheads, and Rastafarians. For these non-elite youth, subcultural credibility among their peers did not necessarily translate into broader social standing or leverage. In contrast, many youth subcultures of the 1990s and 2000s, like Ethan Watters's "urban tribes" (2003), increasingly comprised middle- and upper-middle-class youth, forging ties based on shared interests in creative pursuits (which Stuart and Hall might have considered a middle-class counterculture instead).

For an emerging creative class in Berlin, subcultural knowledge could be converted to dominant forms of capital—prominent DJ residencies, successful music labels, in-the-know music journalism.

Despite this potential, subcultural capital often circulated within the limited field of small-scale, overlapping music scenes. In this segment of Berlin's nightlife, value lay in fostering shared connection and mutuality among circles of fans, promoters, producers, and DJs, especially for those who entwined their professional lives with their leisure interests. In this context, guest-listing practices supported a fluid connectivity that extended beyond what my interlocutors termed their inner friend circles, interlinking with extended, cosmopolitan networks of acquaintances and fellow enthusiasts. Garcia describes the fleeting communal sentiments that coalesced on the Berghain dance floor as "liquidarity," an embodied sense of belonging located in shared affect (Garcia 2013a, 248). Like media, this embodied, fleeting form of social cohesion inhabits the interstices between the material and the meaningful, reconfiguring the divide between them. In Hayles's (1999) account of virtual materiality, she defines the virtual as matter interlaced with information and argues for recognizing the materiality of digital media (see also Kraemer 2021a).[6] In nightclubs, or through practices like guest-listing, shared sentiment temporarily materialized, generating fluid social bonds. Garcia's formulation here builds on Berlant's (2008) work on stranger sociability and intimate publics, to theorize how tacit norms materialize through vague perceptions of common feeling. For Berlant, shared affect can ground media publics and social belonging: "A public is intimate when it foregrounds affective and emotional attachments located in fantasies of the common, the everyday, and a sense of ordinariness" (2008, 10). In Garcia's account, strangers dancing to the meandering beat of techno developed ways of interacting and communicating that produced feelings of mutuality, such as through gestures and articulations of care rather than spoken discourse. Pinning down the details—or limits—of such effervescent bonds risked dissolving them.

The contingent, transient quality of dance-floor solidarity illustrates Garcia's liquidarity as a viscous imbrication like the sliding bonds between fluid molecules. Like virtuality, liquidarity reconfigures boundaries between embodiment and sociality, matter and signification. As an embodied sense of belonging and cohesion, it was rarely articulated by its subjects, yet it could temporarily produce an intimate public: "The sense of fluid solidarity arises from the embodied improvisation of an intimate public" (Garcia 2013a, 247). This fleeting mutuality also belied numerous exclusions. Alex's tourists were, for example, there for the "'wrong' reasons," as Garcia puts it (2013a, 238; on "hipster tourists," see also Garcia 2015, 2016). As a tactic of getting by, guest-listing generated cohesion across diffuse, porous music scenes, a form of social capital that equally fostered undefined, unspoken connection beyond immediate friend circles to incite translocal assemblages. Similarly, illicit and unpermitted events served less to evade formal regulations or forms of power (most club nights in the 2000s were licit, despite the bare-bones aesthetics) than to create ways of using shared space that engendered mutual connection. These informal, improvisational, and sometimes illicit means of using space produced affective publics constituted through public media practices, reworking boundaries between materiality and meaning and reconfiguring the scales of the local and translocal.

Television Tactics in Public: The World Cup

From the illicit film screening to liquid sociality in nightlife, repurposing space created tenuous, fleeting experiences of mutuality and connection. In the spring of 2010, another way of using public space unfolded unlike what I had observed to that point. That June, the FIFA World Cup football (soccer in the US) championship, which happens every four years, took place in Johannesburg, South Africa, and the games were broadcast widely. With the warming weather, the district of Friedrichshain near my room-share came alive, especially the blocks around Simon-Dach Strasse, an area known as Simon-Dach Kiez (*Kiez* literally means "corner"). Cafés and restaurants moved tables outdoors, my roommates began organizing Sunday park gatherings, and neighborhood residents spent evenings strolling outside, beers in hand. Winters in Berlin can be long, dark, dreary affairs, even when punctuated by cheery Christmas markets and holiday lights. The lengthening days lured out residents across Berlin, to areas such as the popular Landwerk Kanal in Kreuzberg, across the river Spree. That year, the arrival of spring was followed by a further transformation in public space to view World Cup matches. Restaurants installed capacious flat-screen televisions suspended over outdoor tables or devoted entire walls to floor-to-ceiling projection screens. Over the course of the championship games, public viewings remade the spaces of parks, cafés, and city streets into new sites for articulating cosmopolitan nationalism.

Some of my interlocutors were regular football fans, like Tobias, who occasionally came over to watch Bundesliga (Germany's national football league) matches on Daniele's small television, over the airwaves. But the widespread, communal showings to watch the matches had little precedent in media practices I had previously observed. Daniele occasionally watched a movie or TV show if friends were visiting, typically while they browsed on laptops or lounged. I rarely saw her watch TV by herself, although she reported streaming shows on her laptop. Tobias, Jörg, and a few others followed the Bundesliga matches during the regular season and organized occasional group viewings at a friend's house or sports bar, but these did not typically include his entire friend circle (unlike the weekly kitchen gatherings in chapter 4). I had also glimpsed football matches on smaller TVs in cafés and corner stores (*Spätis*), where usually employees were the main audience.

During the 2010 World Cup, the friend circle from Saxony-Anhalt, the circle of music fans, and many of their extended friends and contacts in places like Amsterdam gathered frequently to watch the matches with noted fervor. The championship's popularity extended across diverse Berlin neighborhoods, from trendy Simon-Dach Kiez, known for its Ausländer "hipster tourists," to predominantly Turkish German districts like Neukölln, south of Kreuzberg. One evening, for example, on the way to visit friends at their Neukölln flat, I passed multiple cafés and Spätkaufs where patrons gathered to watch the games on large screens.

From June through early July, until the final match, I viewed what felt like countless games across multiple friend circles, including in Berlin and in Amsterdam, with the circle of electronic music fans. Such enthusiasm was not universal; I also visited with music fans in Copenhagen, where we attended a show in the autonomous squat Christiana, and joined another friend in Hamburg, none of whom evinced interest in the games, although Hamburg devoted a large central park to public viewings. In Berlin, friends, neighbors, and acquaintances demonstrated increasing investment in the tournament as Germany's team moved to the final rounds. Unlike video downloads or streams—the way most people in my fieldwork watched television—these World Cup viewings took place in communal, public settings. Like other tactics of using shared space in Berlin, these showings relied on ad hoc, temporary, and provisional setups to stream and display the games.

Three scenes exemplify the improvisational arrangements and contexts of viewing World Cup matches that season. More formal public viewings took place as well, often simulating the experience of attending the live games in Johannesburg. Germany had hosted the prior championship, four years before, so many Berliners had been able to attend a game. In Hamburg, my host Konrad showed me an outdoor stadium where the city was hosting large-scale public viewings, projecting the game onto a cinema-sized screen. Berlin also has its share of sports bars that play Bundesliga games, usually on smaller screens. Few people I knew frequented sports bars, however, and the cafés and restaurants of Simon-Dach Kiez did not typically screen football matches at other times. Even the corner café on a small, sleepy park near my room-share devoted an entire wall to a projection screen for the games. One evening in early June, I met out-of-town US friends at a Sri Lankan restaurant between Simon-Dach Strasse and Boxhagener Platz, the main square and site of popular farmer and flea markets, and the night the games began. Nearly every café, bar, and restaurant around the square and adjoining streets had sprouted capacious flat-screen TVs that seemed out of proportion with the size of the establishments. At the restaurant, we walked between crowded sidewalk tables where people were drinking beer elbow-to-elbow and eyeing the game overhead. The inside, however, was quiet and nearly empty.

I saw this tableau repeated down side streets and along Simon-Dach Strasse, where residents and tourists crowded the sidewalks, meandering from bar to bar while checking on the opening match. Often, the matches seemed inescapable. One Sunday, trying to work on my laptop in a small park, I heard shouts and cheering coming from the café on the corner. After the match, football fans strolled through the park blowing on the noisy vuvuzelas, shrill horns popular that year in Berlin and elsewhere. Another afternoon, Jörg messaged me, exhorting me to meet him and some friends at "Bar24," a venue I did not recognize.

> **Jörg**: I want to go soon with Dieter and Katrine and Daniele to Bar24 to watch football [soccer]! There's really good food there, even without football. COME WITH US!! [*Ich will gleich mit Dieter und Katrine und Daniele zur Bar24 fahren zum Fussball kieken! Da isses echt schön, sogar ohne Fussball. KOMM MIT!!*]
>
> **Jordan**: Bar 24 or 25? [*Ba[r]24 oder 25?*]
>
> **Jordan**: but you're eating there? [*aber ihr isst da?*]
>
> **Jörg**: 24! It's actually called (Johannis)Burg24. Directly next to the Bar. We are there. [*24! Also eigentlich heisst das (Johannis)Burg24. Direkt neben der Bar. Wir sind da.*]
>
> **Jörg**: Not yet, but soon. [*Noch nich, aber gleich.*]
>
> **Jörg**: cool [*kool*]
>
> **Jordan**: sounds good [*klingt gut*]
>
> **Jörg**: Super! Don't wear so much black ;). I'm heading over now. [*Super! Zieh nich soviel schwarz an ;) Ich hau jetzt los.*]

After chatting back and forth, Jörg explained that Bar24 was "actually called (Johannis)Burg24, directly next to the Bar"—that is, Bar 25, another notorious nightclub and radical commune infamous for its freewheeling after-hours parties. Although I had never been to Bar 25, I had heard stories about multiday, psychedelic adventures in what one person described as a playground for adults. Unlike the dim and cavernous spaces of Berghain or Tacheles, Bar 25 comprised a sprawling outdoor complex on the banks of the river Spree. It was founded as a semi-anarchic collective, and many of the staff lived there full-time. When I arrived at the address, however, I realized that Johannisburg24, or just Bar24, was not a separate location but an appropriation of the complex's outdoor amphitheater. After entering the gate, I walked past food stands, a large tiki bar fabricated from salvaged junk, a swimming pool, a skating half-pipe, and a beach volleyball court.

FIGURE 15.   The tiki-themed outdoor bar at Bar25, during the 2010 World Cup. Photo by author.

Past a tiki bar and food stands selling grilled sausage and roast corn, I walked through another gate that led to the amphitheater, where a large LCD screen stood at one end and the river flowed past, behind scrubby vegetation. Like much of the venue, the amphitheater seemed haphazardly constructed. A large semicircle of metal and wood bleachers faced the screen, with partial sunshades strung up above. On the bleachers, I found Jörg, Daniele, Katrine, and Dieter drinking beer and eating plates of grilled *würst* and roasted corn on the cob while waiting for the next match (Brazil against Chile) to begin. The bleachers were not crowded, but many seats were taken, and above and behind us rose rickety private viewing boxes, decorated like a theater stage with dark red drapery.

As with the warehouse film screening at the beginning of the chapter, the setting fused the ad hoc, improvisational arrangements of Berlin's illicit nightclubs with norms of communal, public media viewing. The game began to play on the large LCD screen, and at first, Jörg, Daniele, and their friends watched quietly. Eventually, however, they began chatting and discussing the gameplay. Dieter, for example, asked me which team I was "for" (*für jemand zu sein*) and explained that because most others were rooting for Brazil, he was rooting for Chile as the underdog. By halftime, it became increasingly evident that Brazil would win, and Jörg leaned over to explain that historically Brazil had scored many more goals than Chile. At the halftime break, many people filed out to refresh drinks or use the restrooms. Jörg and Katrine turned to their smartphones, checking email and Facebook. From my own Facebook feed, however, I saw no evidence that they had posted about the game specifically, suggesting that they were catching up on their News Feeds instead.

These communal viewings took place among this friend circle beyond Berlin as well, as on one weekend when Daniele, Katrine, Tobias, and many of their friends went to stay with their families while celebrating a friend's birthday. Most were from small towns and villages near Magdeburg, the regional capital, where many had gone to university. Daniele and Tobias had coordinated with a friend living in Magdeburg who worked at a café there. When we arrived, the café was not yet open and was occupied only by staff. A large group of around ten to fifteen friends— almost entirely from Daniele and Tobias's friend circle in Berlin—gathered to watch the afternoon's match (Ghana versus Australia) on a large projector screen in the spacious front room, closely packing the café's chairs in semicircular rows.

Most rooted for Australia, which in part reflected the ties many had there (racism or Eurocentrism may have played a role, but if so, it was tacit). Katrine had spent six months traveling and living in Australia, while her close friend Kirsten was currently living there. One of their Ausländer friends in Berlin, Emily, was Australian, from an originally South Asian family. As at Bar24, however, people's attention began drifting away from the match as the afternoon wore on. Tobias's father and brother arrived, as did more friends from both Berlin and Magdeburg. Some ordered food or moved to sit farther from the screen to chat quietly. Eventually, the game stalled to a tie, and the gathered audience began to dissipate. Tobias left to visit his family, while others left in small groups, reconvening later that evening at the birthday party. As in Berlin, the café transformed into a temporary site of communal viewing, remaking a public or semipublic place into an unofficial venue for the World Cup.

Although weekly kitchen meetups were the norm for Daniele, Katrine, and their friend circle, the World Cup matches incited larger-scale, communal viewings, often multiple times in a week. The circle of electronic music fans met up less consistently the rest of the year—not necessarily less often but more disparately, assembling in small clusters before going out on the weekend or organizing small group dinners. Among both circles, however, these larger, semipublic showings were common during the series, becoming increasingly difficult to miss as the matches neared their conclusion. Germany's team made it to the semifinal rounds and had only to beat Spain to advance to the ultimate championship match. A final scene illustrates how World Cup showings appropriated not only spaces like cafés, parks, and quasi-licit nightclubs but a fundamental locus of urban publics, the literal street. On a side street in Kreuzberg's hip Wrangelkiez, bordering the

Spree and home to renowned techno clubs like Watergate, I observed this emergent cosmopolitan European nationalism finding its expression.

Pascal, an art and design student close with many of the music fans, invited me to watch the semifinal game between Germany and Spain with friends in Kreuzberg. The evening was warm, and the sidewalks of Wrangelkiez, normally buzzing in the summer, were clotted with strolling pedestrians and occasional cyclists (mostly on the bike paths) eddying around the district's cafés and bars. Pascal and I walked our bikes down a quieter, leafy side street, where a large screen had been erected on the sidewalk. A projector and a laptop were stacked up not far from the curb on a precarious arrangement of occasional tables. A tangle of wires coiled out from the stack, snaking into a concrete apartment building that fronted the stretch of sidewalk.

Around the projector, folding seats faced the screen, pooling across the sidewalk and spilling into an otherwise quiet residential side street. Pascal explained that the viewing had been organized by a group of architecture student friends, who had raised an awning of some kind to shade the projector screen fixed to

FIGURE 16. Projecting the 2010 World Cup final match on the sidewalk in Kreuzberg. Photo by author.

one of the building's balconies, to make the projection visible in the late-evening summer light. A few people were gathering around, while the screen displayed the TV channel that would be broadcasting the game. Pascal directed me to find seats while he ducked into a nearby Spätkauf for beers. As at the illicit film screening, ad hoc arrangements made it possible to watch the semifinal match communally, sharing access to the TV broadcast in literal public space. Unlike watching a foreign independent film, an experience that articulated possibilities for transnational connection and sensibilities, seeing the World Cup match instead invoked national sentiments, in quite visible ways.

Excitement had been building across the city as Germany's team approached the final games. Football fans telegraphed their enthusiasm through national symbols. Many hung flags from apartment balconies or waved them from cars; some even wore capes in red, black, and gold or painted their faces (although such expressions were muted compared to the riot of orange that had overtaken Amsterdam during my visit a few weeks before). From the students' makeshift awning, a German flag was hanging, and next to the projector, someone had strung a plastic garland of red, black, and yellow flowers. More people arrived and found seats, and a few wore the flag's colors. One young woman displayed the German flag painted on her face with the word *Spielerfrau*, which connotes "football player's girlfriend" or wife;[7] another young woman wore a red blouse, black skirt, and yellow tights.

By the time the game began, all of the seats were occupied, and additional people stood behind them in the street. Few cars passed by, and those that did drove slowly. Initially, the crowd was hushed and tense, but increasingly, as the game progressed, they began cheering and talking excitedly, mainly in English and German. By halftime, neither team had scored, and the excitement began souring to frustration. Pascal and two other friends who had arrived later allowed their attention to wander, discussing school, future plans, and so forth. One friend who had arrived late admitted, "I like watching the big games, but I don't actually care who wins, you know?" By the time Spain's team finally scored a single, decisive goal, much of the anticipation and energy had dissipated. Behind us, a small crowd cheered—in Spanish. Pascal's other friend sat next to us in stunned silence, barely responding when we all said our goodbyes.

Pascal and his friends, like many in the crowd, seemed dejected as they gathered their belongings and began to leave. But no one complained or directed any criticism toward the opposing team's fans. As I described in chapter 4, according to one interlocuter, many Germans found it acceptable to express national feelings during the World Cup—sentiments that were otherwise taboo or uncomfortable—in large part because others were doing the same. As with other articulations of national sentiment in Berlin, waving the German flag took place in the context of the hip, cosmopolitan, multinational city—here, in the actual public street. As with the warehouse screenings, dance-floor liquidarity, and communal football viewings at Bar24, the informal, makeshift setting helped foster a temporary, often fleeting sense of mutuality and cohesion, here coalescing around national feelings and excitement for the German team. But as a way of making public space, this national sentiment reflected the cosmopolitan ties this emerging middle class forged in Berlin, remaking nationalism as hip and urban, comparable to the cosmopolitan nationalism of speaking Euro-English in chapter 3. Watching the World Cup in the streets of Kreuzberg with other young, mobile, middle-class Europeans constituted a cosmopolitan, multiscalar site for enacting national feeling.

Tactics of Scalemaking

As this chapter details, these public media practices repurposed space in tactical ways, engendering communal sentiments and temporary cohesions at multiple, imbricated spatial scales. From an illicit warehouse film screening to embodied, liquid mutuality in Berlin's underground nightlife and to public football viewings, improvisational uses of space fostered local and translocal music scenes, on the one hand, and an emerging cosmopolitan nationalism, on the other. In these examples, ad hoc spatial arrangements recalled the spirit of openness and creativity of Berlin's lost "voids" after the Wende, when young people appropriated abandoned or neglected buildings for dance clubs, art studios, and communal living. In this vein, screening a foreign film in a vacant warehouse offered a tactical means to circumvent international licensing agreements. But unlike the illicit downloading practices described in chapter 5, viewing the film in a semipublic, semi-licit space contributed to feelings of commonality and connection, bringing a cosmopolitan urban public into being. Similarly, tactical ways of getting by in Berlin's underground nightlife, such as gaining free entrance to clubs through guest-listing, fostered mutual connection and subcultural capital across small music scenes.

These illicit and semi-licit practices also generated the fleeting dance-floor solidarity Garcia (2013a) describes as liquidarity, a fluid, shared affect more embodied than spoken. Liquidarity wove tenuous bonds across close-knit circles of music fans, beyond the immediate "inner friends circle" my interlocutors described. In Berlin, such connections rendered these electronic nightlife spaces as simultaneously local, grounded in histories and practices specific to Berlin, and translocal, linked to music scenes and networks of fans across Europe and elsewhere. In contrast to nightlife tactics, public viewings of 2010 World Cup matches offered sites to enact an emerging cosmopolitan nationalism. Communal football viewings typically involved the same kinds of improvisational media setups to stream the matches, either over live television or via web streaming. Despite the urban, multinational makeup of World Cup fans, the series invoked nationalist sentiment and identification that was otherwise rare, as viewers and fans rooted for their national teams and displayed national colors and emblems. For Germans in Berlin, these expressions of nationalism became acceptable precisely because of the multinational, cosmopolitan context.

Such tactical, everyday means of managing media and space recalled creative ways of repurposing abandoned spaces after the Wende, but they also recalled ways people in East Germany had navigated the inadequate infrastructure of the GDR. East Germans, for example, managed to share their fixed (landline) telephones—by taking messages for one another, for example—because the East German government had never finished connecting all households (Schnöring and Szafran 1994, 462). Negotiating and managing public media technologies in these ways generated spatial connections at multiple, interpenetrating scales, reworking understandings of the local or urban, the nation or global, and the multiple, shifting connections between them. These improvisational means of managing media and space fostered connections that were often fleeting, tenuous, embodied, and affective, coalescing only temporarily. The spatial scales that formed through such tactical practices similarly cohered only temporarily, as new connections, identities, practices, and technologies took shape. These shifts became evident when I returned to Berlin in 2015, as I recount in the epilogue.

Epilogue

ILLIBERAL SPACES

If the 1990s and 2000s were characterized by capital's globalization, an emerging information-based network society, and the urbanization of the "creative class," the 2010s saw the breakdown of many twentieth-century liberal institutions and the rise of a new precariat. In Europe, the 2009 sovereign debt crisis had provoked concerns about the breakdown of the euro zone, the shared currency zone of sixteen EU nations and the symbol of Europe's successful integration in the twenty-first century (Peebles 2011). By 2010, Germany was bailing out Greece to prevent it from leaving the euro zone and further destabilizing the euro.[1] Chancellor Angela Merkel framed the threat to the euro not just in monetary terms but as a threat to the unity and integrity of the European Union: "If the euro fails, Europe will fail."[2] In the teleology of late capitalist scalemaking, scale-expanding projects like Europeanization should move forward; the potential decline of the European Union threatened assumptions that capital's expansion would bring about lasting peace and stability. Germany and other EU nations responded to the debt crisis and the global recession of 2008 with austerity measures, dismantling or undermining the social welfare system in the United Kingdom, Greece, Spain, and elsewhere.[3]

A number of popular movements took shape in response to the economic crises of 2008–9. In the United States, the revanchist right-wing Tea Party, sometimes accused of being an artificial "astroturf" rather than genuine grassroots movement, made use of Twitter and other social media in new ways (e.g., C. Pearson 2013), and a decentralized, left-wing anticapitalist movement, Occupy Wallstreet, followed in the fall of 2011 (e.g., Juris 2012; Collins 2012). The previous year, 2010, had seen a string of antiauthoritarian uprisings across North

Africa and the Middle East, particularly in Tunisia and Egypt, collectively termed the Arab Spring (Tufekci 2014, 2017; but c.f. Abu-Lughod 2012). Like the Tea Party, and later the Occupy movements, pro-democracy activists and protestors organized mass demonstrations in part through social media like Twitter and Facebook, demonstrating social media's potential to enable new forms of resistance and political organizing. In southern Europe, Spain's pro-democracy Los Indignados movement had similarly formed in response to the 2008 housing crisis and skyrocketing unemployment, incorporating social media and horizontal organization such as public encampments, assemblies, and consensus-based decision-making (Postill 2014). Decentralized, networked media seemed poised to transform democracy and enable resistance against growing inequality.

Three years later, however, such visions of radical social change had failed to materialize. In Europe, an economic slowdown combined with growing numbers of war refugees and asylum seekers from Syria, North Africa, Iraq, and elsewhere—fleeing civil war and the post–Iraq War emergence of ISIL or ISIS—provoked reactionary anti-immigrant sentiment among many (see S. Holmes and Castañeda 2016; Treitler 2016). Far-right nationalist parties like Geert Wilders's in the Netherlands and Marine Le Pen's in France gained steam, often pitting liberal European ideals of secularism, feminism, and gay rights against the imagined Other of supposedly antifeminist, homophobic Muslims (see Boyer 2005; Bunzl 2005). Anthropologists of Europe like Dominic Boyer and Matti Bunzl had remarked in the mid-2000s that Islam was taking shape as Europe's predominant Other, in which the coherence of shared European identity depended on viewing the Muslim world as monolithic and threatening. Far-right German movements like PEGIDA (Patriotic Europeans against the Islamization of the West), for example, demonstrated en masse in Dresden and elsewhere in 2014, replacing the 1989 anti-Wall slogan "Wir sind ein Volk" (We are one people) with banners proclaiming "Wir sind das Volk" (We are *the* people).[4] The protests triggered a backlash, the #NoPEGIDA counterprotest and Twitter hashtag campaign, which linked together public spaces across Europe in new ways, similar to the 2015 #JeSuisCharlie hashtag, in the wake of the mass shooting at the French satire magazine *Charlie Hebdo* (Kraemer 2017). These social media movements articulated both nationalist and liberal cosmopolitan European sentiments.

In Berlin, the potential fracturing of Europe reverberated in numerous ways. In the lives of the young people in my fieldwork, the most intimate scales were breaking apart as well. I returned to Berlin in 2015, for the first time in nearly five years. Much had changed in the intervening time, from the technological (touchscreen smartphones had replaced candy-bar and flip phone models as the dominant types available) to the personal (most of my research participants' lives had changed as they transitioned out of their twenties and thirties). Many of these personal changes pertained to moving from one stage of life to another—completing schooling, making career changes, having children, spending less time in clubs and bars. The broader social, political, and economic context figured in as well, as previously inexpensive central districts of Berlin had become unaffordable for many residents, while some benefited from the rise of "sharing economy" services like Airbnb. The nature of social media and the prevailing political conditions had changed as well; news media had become more integrated into social media like Facebook, partly through changes to Facebook's News Feed algorithm (Kraemer 2017, 2018). Many of my interlocutors, who rarely expressed political sentiments online, became involved in protest movements, volunteered with refugees, or sought to address questions of racial and gender inequality in music scenes. These changes meant that, in many instances, the most intimate friend circles— the "inner" or "close" circle so many had valued—had come apart.

Rise and Fall of the Berlin Hipster

By 2015, much had changed for those imagined as the "creative class"—that is, designers, artists, music producers, and tech professionals sought after by advertisers as "trendsetters" (see Slobodian and Sterling 2013). Informal practices like subletting had taken place on free online classified sites, mainly US-based Craigslist.org or WG-Gesuchte (room-share search, a German-language site). By 2015, US tech start-up Airbnb was rapidly replacing these services, as part of the "sharing economy" that sought to "disrupt" industries like hospitality, largely through the casualization of labor, allowing hosts to rent directly to guests through an online platform (a type of work known as platform labor). Airbnb transformed the online experience of short-term rentals as well, substituting a minimalist interface with airy images of rentals that was much sleeker than the text-based interfaces of more DIY sites. Airbnb has been shown to exacerbate inequality in other European cities, such as Barcelona, where travelers could increasingly stay in previously residential neighborhoods (Cócola Gant 2016; Cansoy and Schor 2017). Although Airbnb claims that their service expands financial opportunities, researchers have found that most revenue accrues to a small number of investors (Cansoy and Schor 2017).

Airbnb's rise coincided with—and likely contributed to—rising rents in Berlin. One of my first reunions was with Annika, the studio artist. She no longer lived in the same space as her art studio but was renting out the room instead, and she had broken up with her boyfriend. For her and her family, Airbnb made it possible to rent out an apartment her father owned in Berlin: "It would just be empty if we didn't, and that wouldn't make sense." The host of an Airbnb studio apartment where I stayed articulated further the contradictions of high rents in the city. He worked out of another unit in the same building, a few floors above, with the same layout as the rental. The Airbnb studio, however, had been renovated to be airy and light, with an open floor plan; sparse, Ikea-style furnishings, like a low platform bed; new appliances; and high-tech amenities like a smartphone speaker unit. His office, in contrast, was more cramped, with a galley kitchen and aging appliances, numerous desks and chairs, a large worktable, two computer monitors, and what appeared to be years of accumulated stuff—old electronics, office supplies, books, and the like. He contended that the rising rents had resulted in part because of the debt crisis, specifically because wealthy people from Greece, Italy, and Spain had invested in new luxury condos in upscale Mitte, as a safe way to park their wealth. He claimed that rents had doubled in the past few years, making it difficult for residents to move to a new apartment in the same area. Neukölln—still a largely Turkish German neighborhood during my fieldwork—had gentrified as it became popular with middle-class, mainly white Germans and Ausländer, and many people he knew (who moved there when rents were cheaper) had moved out as costs rose. The latest secretly cool neighborhood was no longer in East Berlin or multicultural districts like Neukölln, in his view, but staid, bougie Charlottenburg in the former West.

My friend and interlocutor Jörg reiterated my host's comments. These changes in the price and makeup of neighborhoods coincided for him and his friend circle with personal changes in their lives. Their friend circle had begun fraying as friends grew apart, moved in with romantic partners, or focused on their careers. Jörg was still living in his old apartment, but his roommate had moved out. I met up with him and Sabine at a café near his apartment in Friedrichshain. We coordinated over iMessage—Sabine had eventually replaced her Blackberry with an Apple device, as she had hoped. When I arrived, she was checking in with Jörg over the messaging platform WhatsApp (later bought by Facebook). She told me more about how their friend circle, once linked by shared origins in Saxony-Anhalt, had begun breaking up. Daniele had moved out of her room-share with Katrine, and they had some kind of falling out—they "disagreed about something and haven't talked since." Sabine and Daniele drifted apart as well, not talking to or seeing each other as often, "since she [Daniele] got a boyfriend." Jörg's life had changed even more dramatically. He met a woman in New Zealand, the sister of another neighbor in his building, also from Saxony-Anhalt. When they returned to Berlin, she was pregnant with their first baby, and they moved in together: "And Dieter [Jörg's roommate] moved out and she moved in."

While waiting for Jörg, I noted Sabine's iPhone, by then an older model. "Oh, this is my second one," she responded. "What happened to your old Blackberry?" I asked. She seemed surprised, recollecting. "I had an iPhone, didn't I? You remember that? I loved my Blackberry." When I asked if she had ever bought the Mac-

Book she wanted, she initially thought she had already had it at the time, until I reminded her about her old PC laptop. "Yes, I have a MacBook now." Jörg soon arrived with his partner and their new baby, but Sabine did not stay long. Jörg and I reminisced about the past, and I mentioned writing about *Spargel* in my dissertation (see Kraemer 2018). Turning to his partner, he described the "Spargel feasts" they used to organize. "We did this one year as well at a shabby loft in Kreuzberg/Neukölln, and fried a whole lot of meat, but there were like twenty people, and it was hard to pull off actually." Jörg expanded on the changes my Airbnb host had described, referencing a recent law that allowed landlords to make renovations and increase rents for leaseholders, forcing some families to move out; he added, "Some Turkish families in Neukölln, for example." He went on to explain: "You could rent a place for 700, 800 [euros], now it's 1,300." The couple was considering moving across the city to Schöneberg, a leafy neighborhood of former West Berlin; once known for its thriving gay and lesbian nightlife, it was now a respectable upper-middle-class neighborhood (and still a center of gay life). It would be closer to his new job, and, in his view, it had stronger schools: "It's very multikulti, but the parents are more academic," especially compared to schools in Neukölln with what he viewed as many undereducated "refugee families."

While many in Jörg and Sabine's friend circle had moved in with partners, others like Daniele began going out more often to Berlin's all-night clubs. I met up later that week with Katrine and with Daniele, separately. Katrine reported that Daniele was no longer spending much time with their friend circle and was single, unlike Katrine and Kirsten, who had met long-term partners. Daniele had begun frequenting Berlin's numerous techno clubs, something she had engaged in only occasionally before, gravitating away from her friends who had new partners or had started families. Instead, she had become more versed in the music and DJs performing at Berlin clubs, explaining, "I go to Berghain, but only if I like the DJs." Rising rents pushed an earlier wave of young, creative middle-class residents, like my Airbnb host or studio artist Annika, out of the areas they helped gentrify. For the friend circle from Saxony-Anhalt, many were shifting from one stage of life to another, leaving room-shares and setting up new, nuclear households. For Daniele, Berlin's clubs were increasingly overrun with nightlife tourists who weren't serious about the music: "There are too many hipsters now; they aren't real techno fans."

Two Million Likes

For the friend circle from Saxony-Anhalt, their lives were changing along with the city—they were often focusing more on careers and starting families, while navigating the rising cost of living and the changing demographics of the city. Similar changes were taking place among the electronic music fans. During my longer fieldwork visit, from 2009 to 2010, I was in frequent, often daily contact with close interlocutors like Alex, Sal, and Pascal, primarily on Skype, on Facebook, and over text messages. After I had returned to the United States, though, we stayed in touch intermittently, even though these channels were still available to us. I initially attributed this attenuation to our lack of shared, everyday context and proximity, such as getting together or going out frequently, as well as the time difference. But when I visited Berlin in 2015, it was surprisingly difficult to reconnect with everyone in the friend circle. I had sent out an email inquiry in advance, to which few people responded. I could not reactivate my previous SIM card and mobile number easily, nor did I get a new local number until after I arrived and purchased a prepaid SIM card, which meant that I did not have people's numbers saved in my phone. I posted to Facebook, but the algorithms that determine each person's News Feed make it difficult to ensure that those I knew in Berlin saw my update, without tagging them explicitly (which I opted against for confidentiality).[5]

Even once I arrived, setting up a prepaid phone card was tricky and confusing. It was no longer difficult to unlock one's phone, because of US regulations that required manufacturers to allow users to do so. But my previous service provider, O2, no longer sold prepaid cards, and a retail associate directed me instead to a nearby *Spätkauf* (convenience store). Activating the card required registering online, with a German address, and uploading funds onto it. One friend in Berlin recommended using WhatsApp instead, which had since become popular as an alternative to text messages, by sending messages over mobile data service instead (typically flat rate, in contrast to text messages at the time). But none of my research participants mentioned WhatsApp, so instead, I headed for venues where I knew they might be. Alex was working part-time at a new bar, and a number of Dutch fans were visiting to attend a music showcase at a venue in a former East German train repair facility in Friedrichshain.

On my way from the Warschauer Strasse train station, I observed another way the city had changed: the more visible presence of asylum seekers, war refugees, and other migrants, whose mobility was often framed as threatening. A line of young men, mostly African, were hawking party drugs from the side of the bridge over the train lines, presumably to the many clubgoers. I had been told that there were drug dealers selling marijuana in Görlitzer Park in Kreuzberg but never encountered any myself.

The music producer Sal told me later that drug dealing had increased there as well, by people he thought were likely refugees or asylum seekers. He and his friend circle had rarely expressed anti-immigrant sentiments—on the contrary, many had been activated politically in response to anti-immigrant organizing by far-right groups such as PEGIDA. But Sal and others perceived that public spaces in Berlin were changing as a result of increased immigration, linked to broader shifts that were also unfolding online (evident, for example, during the #JeSuis-Charlie campaign, after the 2015 *Charlie Hebdo* mass shooting, which took place during this fieldwork visit; see Kraemer 2017).

Finally, I managed to meet up with a few of the electronic music fans, to learn that what had seemed like a very tight-knit circle had similarly unraveled. Viktor, a Danish musician, described for me many of the group's changes over dinner together. One friend had a new girlfriend and rarely went out anymore: "I've seen my friend, what, twice in the past four years?" Max had a new girlfriend as well but went out more frequently because he had become a successful music promoter ("You walk with him at one of his events and everyone comes up to him, all these famous DJs, and it's like, wow, Max, everyone knows you. But then they ask him if he can book them, and you realize, they just want something from him"). Viktor had shifted his focus away from producing music to music management, taking numerous work-related trips to Asia and elsewhere. His girlfriend had not found the situation tenable, however, and their relationship ended. Max's success owed in part to a series of multicity online video parties ("Video Room") that took place simultaneously in clubs and on social media. His increased visibility had garnered him both fame and derision online, sometimes making him the target of derogatory nicknames calling him a hipster. David, the record label and shop owner, and his business partner had closed the record store when business slowed down even as rents increased. According to Viktor, it had been affordable to run the store "maybe back when rents were cheap." David's business partner had become more withdrawn as the business became unsustainable, and both went out less.

Viktor felt that for many music producers and others, it could be difficult to know when to stop trying for a certain kind of success, especially as they grew older. The longer people lingered without getting a break, the less likely he thought success would be: "[People] in their forties, still trying to make music, like hey man, I just need to make that one loop, that one track. . . . Man, it's not going to happen [if it hasn't happened by now], you'd already be making music." When it became difficult to maintain a high level of output, he decided to focus on management instead of making music: "To make a living, you really have to grind it out." In his current job, his inside knowledge of the industry was a benefit. Later in the week, I met with his friend Sal, who framed these changes differently. As a successful but introverted sound designer, he remained intently focused on his professional work. He had collaborated with some of his friends on various music-related projects, but they parted ways when their expectations around work differed. He told me, "We have a different work ethic." He confided that he had not yet met Max's new girlfriend; the last time they had talked, Max had just recently met her and asked Sal for advice. They had agreed to get together in a week but never did. Although Sal acknowledged that everything had changed with their friend circle, he averred that now "[he was] in multiple friend circles, circles for different things."

Along with these changes—rising rents, ongoing gentrification, the arrival of new migrants and refugees, growing far-right extremism, and the dissolution of old friendships—the role of social media and other digital technologies had shifted as well. Most notably, news-reading practices had fused with social media in a novel way, as I document elsewhere (Kraemer 2017, 2018). Many had viewed social media like Facebook positively but were now increasingly skeptical. Sal felt that Facebook's News Feed, which had become much more complex algorithmically, made the world seem much worse than it was: "Everything is shit, it's all shit. Is it really like that?" Political sentiments and commentary also became much more common, whereas previously social media were primarily sites to discuss music and pursue friendships. These shifts to reading news articles on Facebook and Twitter and expressing political sentiments became especially evident halfway through my visit, when there was a mass shooting at the offices of the satirical, controversial magazine *Charlie Hebdo* in Paris. News of the shooting reverberated across Facebook and Twitter, particularly among those with ties to France. One woman, Annette, with many friends and family in France, wrote, "Sorry for the sad & political post. Anyone with an interest in the French political press know who these two persons are (were, sadly)," with a link to the Twitter status of the French *LePoint*, showing photos of two murdered cartoonists. Daniel, in Cologne, wrote: "The comments by PEGIDA regarding Charlie Hebdo make me sick, sad, angry. I'm . . . speechless." Max shared an update saying, "I'm concerned. Frightened and speechless. Now is time to become a political person." In a matter of hours, memorial vigils had been organized in cities across Europe, and French-speaking residents in Berlin shared them with one another in French and German. Meanwhile, the hashtag #JeSuisCharlie took off as a collective campaign that quickly crossed from social media to signs in public places like Pariser Platz, in front of the Brandenburg Gate and the French Consulate in Berlin.

By 2015, social media had become a site where news stories unfolded in real time, corresponding with two major updates to the News Feed in 2013 (Kraemer 2017a, 2017b). That January, Facebook launched a feature called Instant Articles, which loaded external news links directly into Facebook's mobile app, in an attempt to capitalize on the popularity of reading news articles shared on Facebook rather than going directly to news sites, as my interlocutors had done in 2009 and 2010. Major US news publications like the *New York Times* and *Washington*

Post initially embraced this feature, although ultimately, many abandoned it a few years later, when their traffic referrals from Facebook plummeted in 2017.[6] Later that year, in August, the company announced changes to the News Feed algorithm, which determines the content each user sees and the order they see it in, particularly regarding their Pages feature. This update prioritized "high quality content" which Facebook defined as "timely," "relevant," and "from a source you would trust."[7] Their goal was explicitly to increase "interactions" (sometimes called engagement) such as likes, comments, and shares, which correlate with greater ad revenue. In practice, this update meant users saw more news stories and articles from established outlets and less "clickbait" and meme posts from viral content providers aiming to "game News Feed distribution." As more people in the United States and elsewhere began reading news articles through Facebook, the site—and specifically the News Feed—gained greater influence over what stories people saw. Site engagement and ad revenue increased for Facebook but decreased for media outlets and other content providers.[8] Together, these changes to the News Feed contributed to (and reflected) new ways of integrating and interacting with news stories online.

Along with reading and sharing news stories on social media—which had been quite separate during my prior research (Kraemer 2018)—many of the music fans began addressing overtly political topics on social media and engaging in other forms of political action. Max, for example, became involved with efforts to redress gender inequality and sexism in electronic music. In the ensuing years, he had frequently faced backlash and criticism for taking strong stances on this topic, even though he had a long history of political activity (primarily anti-fascist), which had primarily taken place offline. After the 2016 US election and Brexit, he began participating more frequently in anti-fascist and antiracist protests and demonstrations in Berlin and elsewhere (when I tried to see him on a personal visit in 2017, he was unavailable: "There's a Nazi demo in my neighborhood which I have to protest"). In 2017, a mutual friend recounted that Annette had "disappeared" from the music scene altogether and had instead "dedicated herself to helping refugees." I observed fewer overtly political posts and commentary from the friends from Saxony-Anhalt, but on a subsequent visit with Jörg in 2017, he described how on Facebook, people he knew now expressed sentiments that they once reserved for spaces like pubs, such as unpopular or offensive political views.

When I finally saw Max in 2015, he recounted his success with one of his online events, called Video Room.[9] Video Room began in London as an underground party recorded and streamed live over Facebook. Max had brought Video Room to Berlin, where it began attracting famous DJs. Where previously, he owned a secondhand iPhone, more recently he was able to afford a full-price unlocked iPhone 6, then the latest model, which he could expense "because I had some money I had to spend before the end of the year." Video Room, which started with a few thousand fans online, exploded in popularity: "We had like, 5000 likes, now we have two million." Facebook in its earlier iteration had integrated local rhythms and translocal connections into everyday living, but through events like Video Room, it became a place where people participated directly in translocal music scenes. New social media platforms like Instagram, combined with smartphones, further intensified possibilities for fame in what some scholars call "the attention economy" (e.g., Marwick 2015). Even as translocal living unfolded online, the precarious economy of gig and platform labor, like Uber and Airbnb, and the casualization of labor more broadly were transforming life in Berlin in new ways, in many cases fracturing the scalemaking projects described in this book.

From Scalemaking to Scale Breaking

The eventual coming apart of my interlocutors' close friend circles reflects life changes as they moved from being young adults, living with roommates and going out frequently, to focusing more on careers and family life. As one person put it, many of his friends were moving into a different "stage of life" where they saw friends less often and spent less time going out to music shows and parties. What is clear in retrospect is that scalemaking processes are never inevitable or determined by technologies independently of social context. The media practices in this book emerged in the context of the urbanization of an emerging knowledge class tied to broader social and economic processes, including influxes of investment capital and the "new" economy. Rather than world peace through McLuhan's ([1964] 2003, 31) "global village" of online connection and homogeneity, much of the world has experienced intensifying inequality and political retrenchment in nationalist, nativist policies. What this book illustrates, I hope, is that the space- and placemaking capacities of new technologies do not inhere in fixed, a priori technological features, such as the Facebook News Feed or smartphones with mobile broadband, but instead coalesce through prevailing conditions and contexts, such as urbanization and precarity.

In this book, I have charted the diversity and complexity of placemaking practices on and through emerging media among circles of urban, middle-class cosmopolitans in the 2000s in Berlin. When these young people moved to Berlin, many encountered Facebook and other platforms for the first time. Facebook, like Berlin, represented for them the promise of cosmopolitan connectedness, such as participation in translocal music scenes or transnational cultural circuits. Like life in Berlin, Facebook offered ways of being German or European through which they could enact hip, urban forms of national selfhood alongside identities at other scales, including an emergent sense of supranational Euro-peanness (Kraemer 2017). Social media in this sense reworked experiences of Berlin by generating national, regional, and transnational connections and bringing them into new configurations. Similarly, mobile media, such as smart-phones and mobile networking, reworked everyday experiences of urban space, in class-specific ways. Smartphones and locative media could enable acceptable, middle-class forms of movement—and selfhood—but at other times facilitated alternative, collective forms of sociality and mutuality. Like Facebook, mobile phones signaled, and embodied, class aspirations to move through urban space as hip cosmopolitans, extending some forms of sociality while excluding or fore-closing others, as articulated through prosthetic imaginaries.

In online spaces, language practices were key to managing audiences and pub-lics at different scales (and to generating those scales). My interlocutors preferred Facebook to other social network sites, as a space for cosmopolitan and transna-tional connection, yet primarily interacted with their most intimate friend circles. They had to negotiate implicitly US middle-class norms around friendship and sociality, as exemplified by differences between the US term *friend* and its Ger-man cognate *Freund*. The multiplicity of language practices among Europeans on Facebook—switching between and mixing national idioms, standard speech, and internet-specific registers, which are often affectively charged—produced multiscalar spaces online, while European variants of English located certain practices, such as those associated with electronic music, in spaces of Berlin. The national scale, in this context, took shape particularly in relation to news-reading practices. Although speaking English—like using Facebook—could index young Germans in my fieldwork as urban and cosmopolitan, reading German-language news online entailed an unspoken, affective way of being and feeling German. Reading the national news site *Spiegel.de* in Berlin—like other practices described as typically German—brought national forms of selfhood and identity into the multiscalar spaces of life in hip, cosmopolitan Berlin.

The forms of scalemaking that took place on and through emerging media required, and invoked, extensive media infrastructures and multinational regula-tory regimes. For many, getting online was not seamless and was shaped by Berlin's bifurcated history and infrastructure. Ways of accessing online and mobile media often entailed tactical and geographically specific practices such as illicitly shar-ing files, sharing wireless networks, or creatively evading international licensing regulations. Examining infrastructure in terms of placemaking calls attention to the situated, contingent nature of digital materiality, as a lively interplay of matter and meaning making that shaped the scales of the local, national, and transnational. Similarly, tactical ways of engaging with media in Berlin reflected long-standing ways of getting by that produced diverse experiences of public space. The improvisational and ad hoc arrangements associated with Berlin's underground nightlife (both before and after reunification in 1990) reappeared in multiple contexts, from a semi-licit film showing to communal World Cup matches on TV. These communal media practices, some underground and others more publicly visible, reworked everyday spaces in Berlin in ways that facilitated fluid, unspoken feelings of connection and mutuality at multiple scales.

Together, these reworkings of space, place, and scale held possibilities for forms of sociality and mutual connection that were often felt more than spoken. As the supranational scale of the European Union, like the intimate scales of their close friend circles, began to break apart in the ensuing years, these forms of sociality provided means to articulate a shared sense of Europeanness. This often-unspoken sensibility became evident during the 2015 #JeSuisCharlie campaign, which linked together social media and urban spaces in new configurations, as protests unfurled across Paris, Twitter, Berlin, and elsewhere. These practices cannot be divorced from the social and economic conditions in which they unfolded and were enmeshed—the urbanization of an emerging middle-class in Berlin, the city's policies pursuing certain kinds of capital, and ultimately, the increasingly contingent, precarious nature of work. Services like Airbnb and the ridesharing platform Uber were just taking off when I returned in 2015 but have since become widespread, engendering new inequalities and bifurcations. Nor can such an analysis ignore the exclusions on which many scalemaking practices were predicated: of class, as this book has detailed, but also of race, gender, sexuality, and disability, among others; in Europe, these exclusions entailed imagining Muslims, whether Moroccans in the Netherlands or Turkish Germans in Berlin, as monolithic and non-European and refugees as threatening. On social media, young people in these friend circles had exhibited creative, aspirational, and hopeful attitudes toward new technologies and possibilities for social change, possibilities that in many cases have not borne out. How emerging technologies will unfold in conditions of growing illiberalism, as they become key sites for information manipulation and structural violence, remains unanswerable. But I hope it is clear that neither media technologies nor global connection will bring about the expansive futures we—scholars, tech critics, activists—envision, unless we put them to those ends, with a clear-eyed understanding of how such technologies work and what constitutes them as technologies. Scales can break apart; we must decide whether and how to remake them.

Notes

INTRODUCTION

1. Martin Reiter, "Art House Tacheles," interview by Rory MacLean, *Meet the Germans—Typically German*, Goethe Institut, May 2010, http://www.goethe.de/ins/gb/lp/prj/mtg/men/kun/tac/enindex.htm.

2. All names are pseudonyms. Some figures are composites to protect the identity and privacy of my research participants.

3. See, for example, Felix Denk and Sven von Thülen, *Der Klang der Familie* (Books on Demand, 2014).

4. According to Richard Florida (2004), "creativity" was a new economic force in the late 1990s and early 2000s, especially among young professionals in diverse, but ultimately gentrifying, urban centers.

5. All of my interlocutors were born before 1989; the Germans in my research were therefore from either West or East Germany, but most moved to Berlin after reunification.

6. By 2018, the space remained empty and its future uncertain. See Taylor Lindsay, "Life after Tacheles: What's Become of the Artist Squatters?," *Exberliner*, May 27, 2018, http://www.exberliner.com/features/culture/life-after-tacheles/; also Nicholas Kulish, "Dressing Artists' Hub in Something Button-Down," *New York Times*, August 10, 2010, https://www.nytimes.com/2010/08/11/world/europe/11berlin.html.

7. The extensive public transit system, for example, now linked up East and West Berlin underground (U-Bahn) lines, although the streetcar lines had been decommissioned in the West (see, for example, Eckard Wolf 2004; Peters 2010).

8. As Quinn Slobodian explains: "Unlike the ordoliberals, who called for an 'economic constitution' at the level of the nation, the Geneva School neoliberals called for an economic constitution for the world. I argue that we can understand the proposal of the Geneva School as a rethinking of ordoliberalism at the scale of the world. We might call it ordoglobalism" (2018, 11–12).

9. This multinational policy established a common area in which people from a number of EU (and some non-EU) states can travel without visas.

10. Peter Gumbel, "Hip Berlin: Europe's Capital of Cool," *Time*, November 16, 2009.

11. International Telecommunication Union 2024c, 2024e; Statista 2024. In 2010, 26.2 percent of inhabitants had mobile broadband, compared to 71.2 percent in 2015 (International Telecommunication Union 2024a).

12. See Burgess, Marwick, and Poell 2017, which defines social media as "digital platforms, services and apps built around the convergence of content sharing, public communication, and interpersonal connection" (1).

13. Statcounter Global Stats, "Social Media Stats in Germany," https://gs.statcounter.com/social-media-stats/all/germany. YouTube meanwhile rose from no market share in September 2009 to 34 percent in November. By October 2014, Facebook had reached a high of 90 percent market share, while most other social media plummeted.

14. We Are Social Global Digital Statistics, 2014, https://datareportal.com/reports/digital-2014-global-social-media-users-pass-2-billion-mark. 32 percent of residents had a Twitter account, by contrast, and only 8 percent had used it within the past month.

15. "These terms focused on the way in which the new media seemed able to constitute spaces or places *apart from* the rest of social life ('real life' or offline life), spaces in which new forms of sociality were emerging, as well as bases for new identities, such as new relations to gender, 'race,' or ontology" (D. Miller and Slater 2000, 4).

16. Videos on large screens overhead showed blank dominoes being distributed to international students and artists to paint. Some dominoes sported corporate logos as well.

17. Other scholars have commented on the similarities between the Federation in the *Star Trek* films and TV series and twentieth-century geopolitics, particularly the Cold War (e.g., Weldes 1999; Booker 2008, 2018). The United Federation of Planets was formed by four allied planets after a major war and eventually makes an alliance with the militant Klingon Empire, ushering in a period of peace and exploration. As M. Keith Booker explains, technological development is key to this future of unity: "In Star Trek, interstellar travel has led to the establishment of a vast United Federation of Planets, presumably a benevolent and voluntary alliance of advanced planetary civilizations (the most important criterion for advancement is technological, in particular the achievement of warp drive engines for interstellar travel) that have joined to promote peace, cooperation, and the pursuit of scientific knowledge" (2008, 196).

18. From 2012 to 2016, for example, the percentage of adult internet users in the US who were on Facebook increased from about 67 percent to 79 percent (Shannon Greenwood, Andrew Perrin, and Maeve Duggan, "Social Media Update 2016," Pew Research Center, November 2016), although the number has not increased significantly since (Andrew Perrin and Monica Anderson, "Share of US Adults Using Social Media, Including Facebook, Is Mostly Unchanged since 2018," Pew Research Center, April 10, 2019, https://www.pewresearch.org/fact-tank/2019/04/10/share-of-u-s-adults-using-social -media-including-facebook-is-mostly-unchanged-since-2018/).

By late 2013, anthropologist Daniel Miller declared that Facebook was no longer cool among young people in the United Kingdom, partly because their parents and other adults were joining ("Facebook's So Uncool, but It's Morphing into a Different Beast," *Conversation*, December 19, 2013, https://theconversation.com/facebooks-so-uncool-but-its-mor phing-into-a-different-beast-21548).

Facebook surpassed a billion active users (those who have logged on to Facebook in the past thirty days) in 2012, up from 100,000 in 2008; that number exceeded 1.5 billion in 2015 (J. Clement, "Facebook: Number of Monthly Active Users Worldwide 2008–2019," Statista, July 31, 2019, https://www.statista.com/statistics/264810/number-of-monthly -active-facebook-users-worldwide/) and currently stands at over 3 billion S. J. Dixon, "Number of Monthly Active Facebook Users Worldwide as of 4th Quarter 2023," *Statista*, May 21, 2024, https://www.statista.com/statistics/264810/number-of-monthly-active-face book-users-worldwide/.

19. And furtively backed by Russia, which appeared to have interfered via an extensive disinformation campaign online, and a decentralized army of far-right internet trolls.

20. As reported, for example, by Catherine Hickley, "'Poor but Sexy' No More: Property Boom Drives Out Berlin's Artists," *Art Newspaper*, October 9, 2018, https://www.theartnews paper.com/feature/poor-but-sexy-no-more-property-boom-drives-out-berlin-s-artists.

21. Charly Wilder, "In Berlin, a Grass-Roots Fight against Gentrification as Rents Soar," *New York Times*, March 18, 2017, https://www.nytimes.com/2017/03/18/world/europe /berlin-rent-fight-against-gentrification.html.

22. This pattern is described in detail by Thomas Frank (1997) in *The Conquest of Cool*, where he argues that the "co-optation" view of youth culture misses the ways that novelty already drives capital accumulation. This is emblematic of a nostalgia for the late 1990s and 2000s in Berlin, which Katrina Sark (2019) terms "nostalgia for Babylon," in contrast to the "Ostalgie" and "Westalgie" for the lost East (and West) German pasts.

1. LOCATING EMERGING MEDIA

1. A text-based, public internet standard that supported early web boards.

2. In the early 2000s, internet access, particularly broadband, expanded rapidly in the United States, as well as in Europe. According to Pew Internet, for example, 52 percent of adults in the United States, where the public internet first originated, used the internet (in some form) in 2000; 76 percent did by the time of my fieldwork in 2009–10, and 90 percent did as of 2019 (*Internet/Broadband Fact Sheet*, Pew Research Center, June 12, 2019). In the European Union, 66 percent of households had internet access as of 2009, up to 87 percent by 2017 (Eurostat, "Internet Usage in Europe," *Statista*, March 2018, https://www.statista .com/statistics/377585/household-internet-access-in-eu28/), reaching 93 percent in 2023 (Statista Research Department, "Household Internet Access in the European Union (EU) 2010-2023," *Statista*, July 31, 2024, https://www.statista.com/statistics/377585/household -internet-access-in-eu28/).

3. "A continuous dialectical tacking between the most local of local detail and the most global of global structure in such a way as to bring both into view simultaneously" (Geertz 1974, 43).

4. Readers of science fiction in the early twentieth century, for example, created networks through the letter pages of science fiction magazines, as Francesca Coppa chronicles (Coppa 2014, 41), and in that sense, constituted an early print-based virtual community. The current concept of "fandom," however, is closely associated with the advent of *Star Trek* conventions, fan fiction, and fanzines in the 1960s and 1970s (see Verba 2003).

5. On the contrary, it is possible to argue that early private computer networks were quite local, or only connected some places, and that the global connection made possible by the commercial internet is a product of globalizing forces, not the cause.

6. In lieu of screenshots, both to protect user privacy and to adhere to Facebook's restrictions on how researchers can share such images.

7. See, for example, Allison Solberg, "The Evolution of the Facebook Algorithm: What It Means for Your Social Strategy," *Social Media Today*, August 28, 2015, https:// www.socialmediatoday.com/social-business/iamsolberg/2015-08-27/evolution-face book-algorithm-what-it-means-your-social. Tracking changes to Facebook's algorithm has spawned an entire industry of marketers and analysts trying to optimize advertisements and engagement.

8. Particularly places accessible by train or car. Berlin was especially popular as a weekend nightlife destination among many young Europeans. Budget airlines also increasingly made weekend travel around Europe affordable.

9. The building, spanning a city block, was constructed as a department store and shopping arcade in the early 1900s and was repurposed many times over the ensuing years, serving as a prison for the Nazi Party and central office for the SS and later as a trade union during the German Democratic Republic years. Parts were demolished eventually because of structural concerns, but an artists' collective established itself there in 1990 when it was slated for further demolition. The artists succeeded in declaring it a historic landmark and converted the space into an art and exhibition center, which they named Tacheles, allegedly Yiddish for "straight talking." Their lease ended in 2008, however, and the art center closed down in 2012 when the artists were evicted (Taylor Lindsay, "Life after Tacheles: What's Become of the Artist Squatters?," *ExBerliner*, May 27, 2018, https:// www.exberliner.com/berlin/life-after-tacheles/; Mathieu Durget, "The Story of Kunsthaus Tacheles—The Home of the Spirit of Art," *Berlin Street Art*, March 15, 2016, https://berlin streetart.com/kunsthaus-tacheles-berlin/).

10. "What we were observing was not so much people's use of 'the Internet' but rather how they assembled various technical possibilities that added up to *their* Internet" (Miller and Slater 2000, 14).

11. The word I have translated as "foreigners" is *Ausländer*, sometimes a term for Turkish Germans but here mainly for those from the European Union and Anglophone countries like the United States, the United Kingdom, and Australia.

12. Statista defines a household as having "at least one member aged between 16 and 74 years" and includes both "stationary and mobile broadband connections" ("Share of Households with Broadband Internet Access in Germany from 2003 to 2018," *Statista*, December 2018, https://www.statista.com/statistics/460163/broadband-internet-household -penetration-germany/).

13. *Statista*, "Share of Households."

14. In Tom Boellstorff's ethnographic monograph on Second Life, he argues that the persistence of virtual worlds as separate spaces constitutes them as worlds, as envisioned first by Myron Krueger, who developed Videoplace, likely the first virtual world, in 1983: "This characteristic of persistence has been fundamental to virtual worlds ever since. A conference call ends when everyone hangs up, and a virtual world like Second Life can go permanently offline, but while they exist as virtual worlds they persist beyond the logging off of any single resident" (2008, 47).

2. MULTIPLE MOBILITIES

1. "Mobile Cellular Subscriptions per 100 Inhabitants in Germany from 2000 to 2021," Taylor Petroc, *Statista*, July 2023 [source ITU, survey by Ofcom], https://www.statista .com/statistics/640154/mobile-cellular-subscriptions-per-100-inhabitant-germany/.

2. One theory was that Handy derived from a term for handheld radios, but according to Dietmar Pieper writing for *Spiegel Online* in 2007, linguistic experts at the Institute for German Language in Mannheim contested that origin. They instead speculated that Handy simply derives from the English *handy*. Dietmar Pieper, "*Ein Wort und seine Geschichte: Woher kommt das Handy?*" [A word and its history: Where does Handy come from?], *Spiegel Online*, June 29, 2007, https://www.spiegel.de/kultur/gesellschaft/ein-wort -und-seine-geschichte-woher-kommt-das-handy-a-491413.html.

3. As Pieper notes, Handy "sounds English and international" ("*was englisch klingt und also irgendwie international*").

4. In the Soviet Union, *rootless cosmopolitan* was a term of denigration for Jews, who embody the kind of pathological nomadism Malkki analyzes (e.g., M. Miller and Ury 2010).

5. "But it was the development of microelectronics-based digital communication, advanced telecommunication networks, information systems, and computerized transportation that transformed the spatiality of social interaction by introducing simultaneity, or any chosen time frame, in social practices, regardless of the location of the actors engaged in the communication process. This new form of spatiality is what I conceptualized as the space of flows: the material support of simultaneous social practices communicated at a distance" (Castells [1996] 2011, xxxii).

6. And paralleling literature in cultural geography on scalemaking (e.g., Brenner 1998, 2001; Cox 1998; Marston 2000; Marston, Jones, and Woodward 2005; Swyngedouw 1996, 2004).

7. See, for example, MacPherson's theory of "possessive individualism" in liberal enlightenment thinking, in which the possessive individual, typically an elite, is the "proprietor of the self, owing nothing to society" (1962, 3); see also Pincus 1998.

8. While in theory users can share their account with friends or family, this entails sharing information many understand as private and can generate further problems because typically a user account is associated with one email address or mobile number.

9. Compare to the ways many people in the Global South first used mobile phones when adoption rates were still low, often sharing or renting limited handsets, as seen in Tenhunen 2008; Donner 2007.

10. And recalling prior ways East Germans had shared landlines, which were not available in every household, in the GDR era (Schnöring and Szafran 1994, 462).

3. MULTISCALAR PUBLICS

1. This notion does not make such distinctions irrelevant—the binary between digital or virtual and real or actual remains crucial to meaning-making practices online, as Tom Boellstorff (e.g., 2008, 2012) argues.

N. Katherine Hayles views materiality as a "a dynamic quality that *emerges* from the interplay between the text as a physical artifact, its conceptual content, and the interpretive activities of readers and writers" (2004, 72, emphasis in original; see also chapter 5 of this book).

2. The algorithm has changed over the years, prioritizing things like how many comments a post attracts, how much "engagement" (likes and, for links or images, click-throughs) there is, how frequently a given person posts, how recently you added them as a friend, and so on.

3. Anderson writes, for example: "An American will never meet, or even know the names of more than a handful of his 240,000,000-odd fellow-Americans. He has no idea of what they are up to at any one time. But he has complete confidence in their steady, anonymous, simultaneous activity" ([1983] 1991, 26).

4. In 2013, Facebook altered the algorithm driving the News Feed, its central feature, to promote news stories, as part of a broader shift to encourage people to consume, discuss, and share news through Facebook. In Kraemer 2016 and 2017, I assess the consequences of this shift for how events such as the 2015 *Charlie Hebdo* attack in Paris unfolded, linking online and offline spaces in new ways.

5. Comparable to the practice of "Facestalking" among Australian users in a study by Young (2011, 26–27).

6. Compare to Light 1999 on women computers and ENIAC in the early 1940s and Hicks 2017 on the history of women in computing, particularly at Bletchley Park.

7. Idealized friendship here parallels other examples of what Latour (2005) called purification, such as science when viewed as a domain separate from society or art markets and cultural consumption. According to Bourdieu (1984), separation or distance from market relations confers maximum value, which can be converted to economic capital. In Silver's account of friendship, liberal thinkers construed prior understandings of friendship as exchange based, grounded in practical reciprocity. Medieval Europeans, for example, could not engage in disinterested mutual attachments free from market relations because all such relations were calculated (e.g., Silver 1990, 1484).

4. NETWORKED NATIONAL FEELINGS

This chapter appeared as an article in *Anthropological Quarterly* in 2018: "Of Spargel and Spiegel: Networked National Feelings in Berlin," *Anthropological Quarterly* 91, no. 4 (2018): 1385–416.

1. According to the Reuters Institute (Newman 2012), as of 2012 more Germans got news from "traditional" sources like TV (87 percent in the past week) and print media (68 percent) than did those in the United Kingdom, United States, France, and Denmark, though print news declined to 64 percent as of 2015 (Newman et al. 2015). In the United States, younger people consume news least of all age groups, regardless of source; this has changed little over twenty years. US print news consumption halved between 2000 and

2012, to 23 percent from 47 percent, more so than that of magazines or books, largely because news reading had shifted to online and digital sources (Doherty 2012).

2. "Thus, while capital must on one side strive to tear down every spatial barrier to intercourse, i.e., to exchange, and conquer the whole earth for its market, it strives on the other side to annihilate this space with time, i.e. to reduce to a minimum the time spent in motion from one place to another. The more developed the capital, therefore, the more extensive the market over which it circulates, which forms the spatial orbit of its circulation, the more does it strive simultaneously for an even greater extension of the market and for greater annihilation of space by time" (Marx [1973] 1993, 539).

3. *Patriotische Europäer gegen die Islamisierung des Abendlandes* (Patriotic Europeans against the Islamization of the West).

4. For more on the social construction of scale, see Marston (2000, but cf. Marston, Jones, and Woodward 2005).

5. Even as extremist groups were having a political resurgence (e.g., D. Holmes 2000).

6. This was mitigated by the similarities of their regional speech to Berlinerisch, which was not as stigmatized in Berlin.

7. Deutsche Demokratische Republik, the official name of the East German state.

8. Examples can be found in the Archiv für Alternativ Kultur in the Institut für Europäisches Ethnologie, Humboldt Universität, which I visited in 2010.

9. Not Saxony-Anhalt.

10. According to *Reuters Institute Digital News Report* (Newman, David, and Nielsen 2015).

11. Nor did they spend time on laptops; cafés were mainly popular for meeting friends.

12. Despite my observations, TV-news watching remained high in Germany, even among young adults (Newman 2012; Newman, David, and Nielsen 2015), but not among those I studied in Berlin.

13. *Spiegel.de* was the most popular German news website by a large margin; *Die Zeit* and FAZ.net less so.

14. As I detail in Kraemer 2014.

15. And reworks understandings of private and public (see Lange 2007).

16. Also see Ilana Gershon's (2010a, 2010b) work on media ideologies and morality.

17. An inversion of "rootless cosmopolitans," used to denigrate Jews in the Soviet Union under Stalin because of their alleged disconnection from place, similar to representations of refugees as disloyal, immoral, and without culture in Malkki's (1992) analysis.

18. Though, as Malkki (1992) argues, this risks reproducing dominant arboreal metaphors of place and belonging.

19. For more on emerging European transnationalist sentiment, see Kraemer 2017.

5. SCALING MEDIA INFRASTRUCTURES

1. Kevin O'Brien, "Royalty Dispute Stops Music Videos in Germany," *New York Times*, April 2, 2009, http://www.nytimes.com/2009/04/03/technology/internet/03youtube.html.

2. International Telecommunication Union 2024a, 2024b, 2024d, 2024e.

3. International Telecommunication Union 2024a, 2024b, 2024c, 2024d, 2024e.

4. Ways of managing this infrastructure also recall what Nikhil Anand (2011) describes in analyzing the political engagements generated by poor water pressure in Mumbai's municipal water system.

5. In 2001, Apple was the first computer company to open consumer retail operations, making computer buying a carefully "curated" experience, with minimalist tables displaying the company's signature streamlined laptops, iPods, and more.

6. Germany had some of the lowest food prices in Europe, while electronics were proportionately more expensive than in places like the United States.

7. According to Wikipedia, ".to is one of the few ccTLDs that (officially) do not maintain a (public) WHOIS database providing registrant information" (https://en.wikipedia.org/wiki/.to, accessed May 17, 2024). This is likely why the country code domain is popular with illicit services, though it also attracts licit URL-shortening services, similar to bit.ly or ow.ly (.ly is the country code for Libya, as Sandvig [2013] discusses).

8. See, for example, Jonathan Hutchison, "Megaupload Founder Goes from Arrest to Cult Hero," *New York Times*, July 3, 2012, https://www.nytimes.com/2012/07/04/technology/megaupload-founder-goes-from-arrest-to-cult-hero.html.

9. Another option was to use a VPN service, which can connect to the internet through a server in another country, like the United States, but these were typically pay services and were not always reliable.

10. HBO's *Game of Thrones* a few years later, for example, was distributed extensively over BitTorrent, partly because it aired only on premium cable and, initially, HBO offered no digital-only subscription option.

11. Initially after the Wende, mobile telephony was not available in former East Germany, even as it became popular elsewhere in Germany and Europe, because the Russian military was still using the necessary frequencies (Schnöring and Szafran 1994, 465–66).

12. US law changed in 2014, when then president Obama signed the Unlocking Consumer Choice and Wireless Competition Act (S.517), requiring providers to allow users to unlock their devices. Previously, phone unlocking was considered a violation of the 1998 Digital Millennium Copyright Act (DMCA). See Marguerite Reardon, "President Signs Cell Phone Unlocking Bill into Law," CNET.com, August 1, 2014, https://www.cnet.com/news/president-signs-cell-phone-unlocking-bill-into-law/.

6. PUBLIC MEDIA IN URBAN SPACE

1. See https://www.imdb.com/title/tt1034419/releaseinfo?ref_=tt_dt_dt.

2. Kai-Uve Altermann, "Wave Gothic Meeting 2008," *Terrorverlag: Alternative Music Webzine*, 2008, accessed May 17, 2024, https://www.terrorverlag.com/konzertberichte/wave-gotik-treffen-2008-leipzig-wgt/.

3. Many East Berliners moved westward for work, while many East Berlin buildings were not well repaired or maintained in the postwar years, and their ownership was not always known (e.g., Schnöring and Szafran 1994).

4. According to my own receipts and recollection. Groceries were particularly inexpensive in Germany compared to other European nations, but other goods, like household electronics, especially computer equipment and imported brands, were much more expensive.

5. Martin Reiter, "Art House Tacheles," interview by Rory MacLean, *Meet the Germans—Typically German*, Goethe Institut, May 2010, http://www.goethe.de/ins/gb/lp/prj/mtg/men/kun/tac/enindex.htm.

6. Hayles argues in particular that denying the materiality of digital media enacts the exclusion of bodies marked by gender and race in virtual spaces, where white masculinity becomes the implicit norm.

7. And which may be related to the term *WAG* (wives and girlfriends), a British term that came into circulation around the 2006 World Cup; see https://en.wikipedia.org/wiki/WAGs.

EPILOGUE

1. Steven Castle and Jack Ewing, "Europe Unifies to Assist Greece with Line of Aid," *New York Times*, April 11, 2010, https://www.nytimes.com/2010/04/12/business/global/12drachma.html.

2. Wolfgang Ischinger, "Germans Love Europe, but Not the Euro," *New York Times*, October 11, 2011, https://www.nytimes.com/2011/10/12/opinion/germans-love-europe-but -not-the-euro.html.

3. E.g., Dan Bilefsky and David Jolly, "Greek Workers Protest Austerity Plan," *New York Times*, May 4, 2010, https://www.nytimes.com/2010/05/05/world/europe/05greece.html.

4. "Anti-Islam 'Pegida' March in German city of Dresden," BBC News, December 16, 2014, http://www.bbc.com/news/world-europe-30478321; Lizzie Deardon, "Germany Anti -Islam Protests: Biggest Pegida March Ever in Dresden as Rest of Germany Shows Disgust with Lights-Out," *Independent*, January 6, 2015, http://www.independent.co.uk/news /world/europe/germany-anti-islam-protests-biggest-pegida-march-ever-in-dresden-as -rest-of-germany-shows-disgust-9959301.html.

5. The group messaging feature might have solved this problem, but I do not recall it being available yet.

6. Slate.com, for example, found that their traffic from Facebook dropped 87 percent between 2017 and 2018, owing to yet another change in the News Feed prioritizing content from "friends, family, and groups" over "public content" like news articles (Laura Hazard Owen, "Slate's Facebook Traffic Has Dropped by 87 Percent since 2017," NiemanLab.org, June 27, 2018, https://www.niemanlab.org/2018/06/slates-facebook-traf fic-has-dropped-by-87-percent-since-2017/; see also Laura Hazard Owen, "Facebook Drastically Changes News Feed to Make It 'Good for People' (and Bad for Most Publishers)," *NiemanLab.org*, January 11, 2018, https://www.niemanlab.org/2018/01/facebook-dra stically-changes-news-feed-to-make-it-good-for-people-and-bad-for-most-publishers/).

7. Varun Kacholia, "News Feed FYI: Showing More High Quality Content," *Facebook Business*, August 23, 2013, https://www.facebook.com/business/news/News-Feed -FYI-Showing-More-High-Quality-Content; see also Lars Backstrom, "News Feed FYI: A Window into News Feed," *Facebook Business*, August 6, 2013, https://www.facebook.com /business/news/News-Feed-FYI-A-Window-Into-News-Feed.

8. In 2013, fewer than half of US Facebook users reported consuming news on the site (47%, around 30% of the US population at the time, compared to 52% of Twitter users and 62% of Reddit users), and even fewer intentionally sought news there (Jesse Holcomb, Jeffrey Gottfried and Amy Mitchell, "News Use across Social Media Platforms," Pew Research Center, November 14, 2013, https://www.pewresearch.org/journal ism/2013/11/14/news-use-across-social-media-platforms/). By 2018, that number had doubled—about two-thirds of Americans got news on Facebook (Katerina Eva Matsa and Elisa Shearer, "News Use across Social Media Platforms 2018," Pew Research Center, September 10, 2018, https://www.journalism.org/2018/09/10/news-use-across-social -media-platforms-2018/). In 2012, a higher proportion of Germans consumed news from "traditional" sources like TV (87% in the preceding week) and print media (68%), compared to those in the United Kingdom, United States, France, and Denmark (Newman 2012). Print news declined to 64 percent by 2015 (Newman et al. 2015).

9. A pseudonym.

References

Abu-Lughod, Lila. 2005. *Dramas of Nationhood: The Politics of Television in Egypt.* Chicago: University of Chicago Press.

Abu-Lughod, Lila. 2012. "Living the 'Revolution' in an Egyptian Village: Moral Action in a National Space." *American Ethnologist* 39 (1): 21–25. https://doi.org/10.1111/j .1548-1425.2011.01341.x.

Ackerman, Mark. 2000. "The Intellectual Challenge of CSCW: The Gap between Social Requirements and Technical Feasibility." *Human-Computer Interaction* 15 (2): 179–203. https://doi.org/10.1145/245108.245122.

Agre, Philip E. 2002. "Cyberspace as American Culture." *Science as Culture* 11 (2): 171–89.

Akkaya, Aslihan. 2014. "Language, Discourse, and New Media: A Linguistic Anthropological Perspective." *Language and Linguistics Compass* 8 (7): 285–300. https:// doi.org/10.1111/lnc3.12082.

Alper, Meryl. 2017. *Giving Voice: Mobile Communication, Disability, and Inequality.* Cambridge, MA: MIT Press.

Alyanak, Oğuz. 2022. "Blaming Kehl: Muslim Turkish Men and Their Moral Journey in the Franco-German Borderland." *City & Society* 34 (1): 111–34. https://doi.org /10.1111/ciso.12419.

Amit, Vered, and Nigel Rapport. 2002. *The Trouble with Community: Anthropological Reflections on Movement, Identity and Collectivity.* Sterling, VA: Pluto.

Amrute, Sareeta. 2015. *Encoding Race, Encoding Class: Indian IT Workers in Berlin.* Durham, NC: Duke University Press, 2016.

Anand, Nikhil. 2011. "Pressure: The Politechnics of Water Supply in Mumbai." *Cultural Anthropology* 26 (4): 542–64. https://doi.org/10.1111/j.1548-1360.2011.01111.x.

Anderson, Ben, and Paul Harrison. 2010. *Taking-Place: Non-representational Theories and Geography.* Burlington, VT: Ashgate Farnham.

Anderson, Benedict. (1983) 1991. *Imagined Communities.* London: Verso.

Ang, Ien. 1985. *Watching Dallas: Soap Opera and the Melodramatic Imagination.* Translated by Della Couling. London: Methuen.

Appadurai, Arjun. 1981. "Gastro-Politics in Hindu South Asia." *American Ethnologist* 8 (3): 494–511. https://doi.org/10.1525/ae.1981.8.3.02a00050.

Appadurai, Arjun. 1990. "Disjuncture and Difference in the Global Cultural Economy." *Public Culture* 2 (2): 1–24.

Appadurai, Arjun. 1996. *Modernity at Large: Cultural Dimensions of Globalization.* Minneapolis, MN: University of Minnesota.

Bakshy, Eytan, Itamar Rosenn, Cameron Marlow, and Lada Adamic. 2012. "The Role of Social Networks in Information Diffusion." In *Proceedings of the 21st International Conference on World Wide Web*, 519–28. Lyon, France: ACM. https://doi .org/10.1145/2187836.2187907.

Barad, Karen. 2003. "Posthumanist Performativity: Toward an Understanding of How Matter Comes to Matter." *Signs* 28 (3): 801–31.

Baron, Naomi S. 1998. "Letters by Phone or Speech by Other Means: The Linguistics of Email." *Language and Communication* 18:133–70.

Bauer, Karin, and Jennifer Hosek. 2019. *Cultural Topographies of the New Berlin*. New York: Berghahn Books.

Baym, Nancy. 2007. "The New Shape of Online Community: The Example of Swedish Independent Music Fandom." *First Monday* 12 (8). https://journals.uic.edu/ojs /index.php/fm/article/view/1978/1853.

Baym, Nancy K. 2010. *Personal Connections in the Digital Age*. Malden, MA: Polity.

Bell, Genevieve, and Paul Dourish. 2006. "Yesterday's Tomorrows: Notes on Ubiquitous Computing's Dominant Vision." *Personal and Ubiquitous Computing* 11 (2): 133–43. https://doi.org/10.1007/s00779-006-0071-x.

Benjamin, Walter. 1962. "Theses on the Philosophy of History." In *Illuminations*, edited by Walter Benjamin, 253–64. New York: Schocken.

Berdahl, Daphne. 1999. *Where the World Ended*. Berkeley: University of California Press.

Berdahl, Daphne. 2000. "Introduction: An Anthropology of Postsocialism." In *Altering States: Ethnographies of Transition in Eastern Europe and the Former Soviet Union*, edited by Daphne Berdahl, Matti Bunzl, and Martha Lampland, 1–13. Ann Arbor: University of Michigan Press.

Berdahl, Daphne, Matti Bunzl, and Martha Lampland. 2000. *Altering States: Ethnographies of Transition in Eastern Europe and the Former Soviet Union*. Ann Arbor: University of Michigan Press.

Berger, Dan, Peter Funke, and Todd Wolfson. 2011. "Communications Networks, Movements and the Neoliberal City: The Media Mobilizing Project in Philadelphia." *Transforming Anthropology* 19 (2): 187–201. https://doi.org/10.1111/j.1548-7466 .2011.01128.x.

Berghahn, Volker R. 1982. *Modern Germany: Society, Economy, and Politics in the Twentieth Century*. Cambridge: Cambridge University Press.

Berlant, Lauren. 2008. *The Female Complaint: The Unfinished Business of Sentimentality in American Culture*. Durham, NC: Duke University Press.

Berlant, Lauren, and Michael Warner. 1998. "Sex in Public." *Critical Inquiry* 24 (2): 547–66.

Bernal, Victoria. 2006. "Diaspora, Cyberspace and Political Imagination: The Eritrean Diaspora Online." *Global Networks* 6 (2): 161–79. https://doi.org/10.1111/j.1471-03 74.2006.00139.x.

Bernal, Victoria. 2014. *Nation as Network: Diaspora, Cyberspace, and Citizenship*. Chicago: University of Chicago Press.

Bijker, Wiebe E., Trevor Pinch, and Thomas Parke Hughes. 1989. *The Social Construction of Technological Systems: New Directions in the Sociology and History of Technology*. Cambridge, MA: MIT Press.

Billig, Michael. 1995. *Banal Nationalism*. London: Sage.

Blanchette, Jean-François. 2011. "A Material History of Bits." *Journal of the American Society for Information Science and Technology* 62 (6): 1042–57.

Boellstorff, Tom. 2003. "Dubbing Culture: Indonesian Gay and Lesbi Subjectivities and Ethnography in an Already Globalized World." *American Ethnologist* 30 (2): 225–42.

Boellstorff, Tom. 2008. *Coming of Age in Second Life: An Anthropologist Explores the Virtually Human*. Princeton, NJ: Princeton University Press.

Boellstorff, Tom. 2012. "Rethinking Digital Anthropology." In *Digital Anthropology*, edited by Heather A. Horst and Daniel Miller, 39–60. London: Berg.

Boellstorff, Tom, Bonnie Nardi, Celia Pearce, and T. L. Taylor. 2012. *Ethnography and Virtual Worlds*. Princeton, NJ: Princeton University Press.

Bonfadelli, Heinz. 1993. "Adolescent Media Use in a Changing Media Environment." *European Journal of Communication* 8 (2): 225–56. https://doi.org/10.1177/026 7323193008002005.

Bonilla, Yarimar, and Jonathan Rosa. 2015. "#Ferguson: Digital Protest, Hashtag Ethnography, and the Racial Politics of Social Media in the United States." *American
Ethnologist* 42 (1): 4–17. https://doi.org/10.1111/amet.12112.

Booker, M. Keith. 2008. "The Politics of *Star Trek*." In *The Essential Science Fiction Television Reader*, edited by J. P. Telotte. Lexington: University Press of Kentucky.

Booker, M. Keith. 2018. *"Star Trek": A Cultural History*. Lanham, MD: Rowman & Littlefield.

Boone, Kofi. 2015. "Disembodied Voices, Embodied Places: Mobile Technology, Enabling
Discourse, and Interpreting Place." In "Critical Approaches to Landscape Visu-
alization." Special issue, *Landscape and Urban Planning* 142:235–42. https://doi
.org/10.1016/j.landurbplan.2015.07.005.

Bordi, Ivonne Vizcarra. 2006. "The 'Authentic' Taco and Peasant Women: Nostalgic
Consumption in the Era of Globalization." *Culture & Agriculture* 28 (2): 97–107.
https://doi.org/10.1525/cag.2006.28.2.97.

Borneman, John. 1992. *Belonging in the Two Berlins: Kin, State, Nation*. Cambridge: Cambridge University Press.

Borneman, John, and Nick Fowler. 1997. "Europeanization." *Annual Review of Anthropology* 26 (1): 487–514. https://doi.org.10.1146/annurev.anthro.26.1.487.

Borneman, John, and Stefan Senders. 2000. "Politics without a Head: Is the 'Love Parade'
a New Form of Political Identification?" *Cultural Anthropology* 15 (2): 294–317.

Bourdieu, Pierre. 1977. *Outline of a Theory of Practice*. Cambridge, UK: Cambridge University Press.

Bourdieu, Pierre. 1984. *Distinction: A Social Critique of the Judgement of Taste*. Cambridge, MA: Harvard University Press.

boyd, danah. 2008. "Why Youth ♥ Social Network Sites: The Role of Networked Publics
in Teenage Social Life." In *Youth, Identity, and Digital Media*, edited by David
Buckingham, 119–42. Cambridge, MA: MIT Press.

boyd, danah. 2010. "Social Network Sites as Networked Publics: Affordances, Dynamics, and Implications." In *A Networked Self: Identity, Community, and Culture on
Social Network Sites*, edited by Zizi Papacharissi, 39–58. New York: Routledge.

boyd, danah. 2011. "White Flight in Networked Publics? How Race and Class Shaped
American Teen Engagement with MySpace and Facebook." In *Race after the
Internet*, edited by Lisa Nakamura and Peter A. Chow-White, 203–22. New York:
Routledge.

boyd, danah. 2014. *It's Complicated*. New Haven, CT: Yale University Press.

boyd, danah, and Nicole B. Ellison. 2008. "Social Network Sites: Definition, History,
and Scholarship." *Journal of Computer Mediated Communication* 13 (1): 210–30.

Boyer, Dominic. 2005. "Welcome to the New Europe." *American Ethnologist* 32 (4): 521–
23. https://doi.org/10.1525/ae.2005.32.4.521.

Boyer, Dominic. 2006a. "Conspiracy, History, and Therapy at a Berlin 'Stammtisch.'"
American Ethnologist 33 (3): 327–39.

Boyer, Dominic. 2006b. "Ostalgie and the Politics of the Future in Eastern Germany."
Public Culture 18 (2): 361–81. https://doi.org/10.1215/08992363-2006-008.

Boyer, Dominic. 2012. "From Media Anthropology to the Anthropology of Mediation."
In *The SAGE Handbook of Social Anthropology*, 411–22. London: SAGE. https://
doi.org/10.4135/9781446201077.N66.

Boym, Svetlana. 2008. *The Future of Nostalgia*. New York: Basic Books.

Brenner, Neil. 1998. "Between Fixity and Motion: Accumulation, Territorial Organization and the Historical Geography of Spatial Scales." *Environment and Planning
D* 16:459–81.

Brenner, Neil. 2001. "The Limits to Scale? Methodological Reflections on Scalar Struc-
turation." *Progress in Human Geography* 25 (4): 591–614.

Breuilly, John, and Ronald Speirs. 2005. *Germany's Two Unifications: Anticipations, Experiences, Responses*. Houndmills, Basingstoke: Palgrave Macmillan.

Briggs, Asa, and Peter Burke. 2009. *A Social History of the Media: From Gutenberg to the Internet*. 3rd ed. Cambridge, UK: Polity.

Brown, Timothy Scott, and Lorena Anton. 2011. *Between the Avant-Garde and the Everyday: Subversive Politics in Europe from 1957 to the Present*. Vol. 6. New York: Berghahn Books.

Brubaker, Jed R., Mike Ananny, and Kate Crawford. 2014. "Departing Glances: A Sociotechnical Account of 'Leaving' Grindr." *New Media and Society* 18 (3): 373–90. https://doi.org/10.1177/1461444814542311.

Brutt-Griffler, Janina. 2002. *World English: A Study of Its Development*. Clevedon, UK: Multilingual Matters.

Bucher, Taina, and Anne Helmond. 2019. "The Affordances of Social Media Platforms." In *The SAGE Handbook of Social Media*, 233–53. London: SAGE. https://doi.org/10.4135/9781473984066.n14.

Bucholtz, Mary. 1999. "'Why Be Normal?': Language and Identity Practices in a Community of Nerd Girls." *Language in Society* 28 (2): 203–23.

Bucholtz, Mary. 2000. "Language and Youth Culture." *American Speech* 75 (3).

Bucholtz, Mary. 2002. "Youth and Cultural Practice." *Annual Review of Anthropology* 31:525–52.

Bucholtz, Mary, and Kira Hall. 2004. "Language and Identity." In *A Companion to Linguistic Anthropology*, edited by Alessandro Duranti, 369–94. Malden, MA: Blackwell.

Bucholtz, Mary, and Kira Hall. 2005. "Identity and Interaction: A Sociocultural Linguistic Approach." *Discourse Studies* 7 (4–5): 585–614.

Buckingham, David, ed. 2008. *Youth, Identity, and Digital Media*. Cambridge, MA: MIT Press.

Bunzl, Matti. 2005. "Between Anti-semitism and Islamophobia: Some Thoughts on the New Europe." *American Ethnologist* 32 (4): 499–508. https://doi.org/10.1525/ae.2005.32.4.499.

Burgess, Jean, Alice E. Marwick, and Thomas Poell. 2017. *The SAGE Handbook of Social Media*. London: SAGE.

Burrell, Jenna. 2012. *Invisible Users: Youth in the Internet Cafes of Urban Ghana*. Cambridge, MA: MIT Press.

Burrell, Kathy. 2008. "Materialising the Border: Spaces of Mobility and Material Culture in Migration from Post-Socialist Poland." *Mobilities* 3 (3): 353–73. https://doi.org/10.1080/17450100802376779.

Butler, Judith. 1997. *The Psychic Life of Power: Theories in Subjection*. Stanford, CA: Stanford University Press.

Cansoy, Mehmet, and Juliet B. Schor. 2017. "Who Gets to Share in the "Sharing Economy"?: Racial Inequalities on Airbnb." Working paper, Boston College, Boston.

Carlson, Jennifer D., and Kathleen C. Stewart. 2014. "The Legibilities of Mood Work." *New Formations* 82 (1): 114–33. https://doi.org/10.3898/NewF.82.07.2014.

Castells, Manuel. (1996) 2011. *The Rise of the Network Society*. Malden, MA: Blackwell.

Certeau, Michel de. 1984. *The Practice of Everyday Life*. Berkeley: University of California Press.

Chakrabarty, Dipesh. 2000. *Provincializing Europe: Postcolonial Thought and Historical Difference*. Princeton, NJ: Princeton University Press.

Chalmers, Matthew, and Ian MacColl. 2003. "Seamful and Seamless Design in Ubiquitous Computing." In *Workshop at the Crossroads: The Interaction of HCI and Systems Issues in UbiComp*, vol. 8.

Chesluk, Benjamin. 2004. "'Visible Signs of a City Out of Control': Community Policing in New York City." *Cultural Anthropology* 19 (2): 250–75.

Chu, Julie Y. 2010. *Cosmologies of Credit.* Durham, NC: Duke University Press.

Clifford, James. 1988. *The Predicament of Culture: Twentieth-Century Ethnography, Literature, and Art.* Cambridge, MA: Harvard University Press.

Clifford, James. 1992. "Traveling Cultures." In *Cultural Studies*, edited by Lawrence Grossberg, Cary Nelson, and Paula A Treichler, 96–116. New York: Routledge.

Clifford, James, and George E. Marcus. 1986. *Writing Culture: The Poetics and Politics of Ethnography.* Berkeley: University of California Press.

Clough, Patricia Ticineto, Jean Halley, Hosu Kim, and Jamie Bianco. 2007. *The Affective Turn: Theorizing the Social.* Durham, NC: Duke University Press.

Cócola Gant, Agustín. 2016. "Holiday Rentals: The New Gentrification Battlefront." *Sociological Research Online* 21 (3): 112–20. https://doi.org/10.5153/sro.4071.

Coleman, E. Gabriella. 2010. "Ethnographic Approaches to Digital Media." *Annual Review of Anthropology* 39 (1): 487–505. https://doi.org/10.1146/annurev.anthro.012809.104945.

Coleman, James S. 1988. "Social Capital in the Creation of Human Capital." In "Organizations and Institutions: Sociological and Economic Approaches to the Analysis of Social Structure." Supplement, *American Journal of Sociology* 94:S95–S120.

Collins, Jane. 2012. "Theorizing Wisconsin's 2011 Protests: Community-Based Unionism Confronts Accumulation by Dispossession." *American Ethnologist* 39 (1): 6–20. https://doi.org/10.1111/j.1548-1425.2011.01340.x.

Cook, Susan E. 2004. "New Technologies and Language Change: Toward an Anthropology of Linguistic Frontiers." *Annual Review of Anthropology* 33 (1): 103–15. https://doi.org/10.1146/annurev.anthro.33.070203.143921.

Coppa, Francesca. 2014. "Writing Bodies in Space: Media Fanfiction as Theatrical Performance." In *Fan Fiction Studies Reader*, edited by Karen Hellekson and Kristina Busse, 218–238. Iowa City: University of Iowa Press.

Costa, Elisabetta. 2018. "Affordances-in-Practice: An Ethnographic Critique of Social Media Logic and Context Collapse." *New Media and Society* 20 (10): 3641–56. https://doi.org/10.1177/1461444818756290.

Cox, Kevin R. 1998. "Spaces of Dependence, Spaces of Engagement and the Politics of Scale, or: Looking for Local Politics." *Political Geography* 17 (1): 1–23.

Crabtree, Andy, and Tom A. Rodden. 2008. "Hybrid Ecologies: Understanding Cooperative Interaction in Emerging Physical-Digital Environments." *Personal and Ubiquitous Computing* 12:481–93.

Cresswell, Tim. 2006. *On the Move.* New York: Routledge.

Crystal, David. (1997) 2003. *English as a Global Language.* 2nd ed. Cambridge: Cambridge University Press.

Crystal, David. 1999. "The Future of Englishes." *English Today* 15 (2): 10–20.

Crystal, David. 2001. *Language and the Internet.* Cambridge: Cambridge University Press.

Cvetkovich, Ann. 2007. "Public Feelings." *South Atlantic Quarterly* 106 (3): 459–68.

Dalsgaard, Steffen. 2015. "The Ethnographic Use of Facebook in Everyday Life." *Anthropological Forum* 26 (1): 96–114. https://doi.org/10.1080/00664677.2016.1148011.

DeNicola, Lane. 2012. "Geomedia: The Reassertion of Space within Digital Culture." In *Digital Anthropology*, edited by Heather A. Horst and Daniel Miller, 80–98. London: Berg.

Derrida, Jacques. 1974. *Of Grammatology*, translated by Gayatri Chakravorty Spivak. Baltimore, MD: Johns Hopkins University Press.

Derrida, Jacques. 1994. *Spectres of Marx: The State of the Debt, the Work of Mourning, and the New International.* Translated by Peggy Kamuf. New York: Routledge.

de Souza e Silva, Adriana. 2013. "Location-Aware Mobile Technologies: Historical, Social and Spatial Approaches." *Mobile Media & Communication* 1 (1): 116–21. https://doi.org/10.1177/2050157912459492.

Dibbell, Julian. 1999. "A Rape in Cyberspace (or TINYSOCIETY, and How to Make One)." In *My Tiny Life: Crime and Passion in a Virtual World*. London: Fourth Estate.

DiMaggio, Paul, Eszter Hargittai, W. Russell Neuman, and John P. Robinson. 2001. "Social Implications of the Internet." *Annual Review of Sociology* 27:307–36.

Doherty, Carroll. 2012. "Changing News Landscape, Even Television Is Vulnerable: Trends in News Consumption, 1991–2012." Pew Research Center, September 9, 2012.

Donath, Judith. 2007. "Signals in Social Supernets." *Journal of Computer-Mediated Communication* 13 (1): 231–51. https://doi.org/10.1111/j.1083-6101.2007.00394.x.

Donner, Jonathan. 2007. "The Rules of Beeping: Exchanging Messages via Intentional 'Missed Calls' on Mobile Phones." *Journal of Computer-Mediated Communication* 13 (1): 1–22. https://doi.org/10.1111/j.1083-6101.2007.00383.x.

Dourish, Paul. 2006. "Re-space-ing Place: 'Place' and 'Space' Ten Years On." In *Proceedings of the 2006 20th Anniversary Conference on Computer Supported Cooperative Work*, 299–308. Banff: ACM. https://doi.org/10.1145/1180875.1180921.

Dourish, Paul, Ken Anderson, and Dawn Nafus. 2007. "Cultural Mobilities: Diversity and Agency in Urban Computing." In *Lecture Notes in Computer Science*, vol. 4663, 1–14. Berlin: Springer.

Dourish, Paul, and Genevieve Bell. 2007. "The Infrastructure of Experience and the Experience of Infrastructure: Meaning and Structure in Everyday Encounters with Space." *Environment and Planning B: Planning and Design* 34 (3): 414–30. https://doi.org/10.1068/b32035t.

Dourish, Paul, and Melissa Mazmanian. 2013. "Media as Material: Information Representations as Material Foundations for Organizational Practice." In *How Matter Matters: Objects, Artifacts, and Materiality in Organization Studies*, edited by Paul R Carlile, Davide Nicolini, and Ann Langley, 92–118. Oxford: Oxford University Press.

Dunnewijk, Theo, and Staffan Hultén. 2007. "A Brief History of Mobile Communication in Europe." *Telematics and Informatics* 24 (3): 164–79. https://doi.org/10.1016/j.tele.2007.01.013.

Durham, Deborah. 2004. "Disappearing Youth: Youth as a Social Shifter in Botswana." *American Ethnologist* 31 (4): 589–605.

Durham, Deborah. 2008. "Review: New Horizons: Youth at the Millennium." *Anthropological Quarterly* 81 (4): 945–57. https://doi.org/10.2307/25488248.

Eckert, Penelope. 2006. "Communities of Practice." In *Encyclopedia of Language & Linguistics*, edited by Keith Brown, 683–85. 2nd ed. Oxford: Elsevier.

Ellison, Nicole B, Cliff Lampe, and Charles Steinfield. 2009. "Social Network Sites and Society: Current Trends and Future Possibilities." *Interactions* 16 (1): 6–9. https://doi.org/10.1145/1456202.1456204.

Ellison, Nicole, Charles Steinfield, and Cliff Lampe. 2006. "Spatially Bounded Online Social Networks and Social Capital." *International Communication Association*, 36:1–37.

Ellison, Nicole B., Charles Steinfield, and Cliff Lampe. 2007. "The Benefits of Facebook 'Friends': Social Capital and College Students' Use of Online Social Network Sites." *Journal of Computer-Mediated Communication* 12 (4): 1143–68.

Ellison, Nicole B., Charles Steinfield, and Cliff Lampe. 2011. "Connection Strategies: Social Capital Implications of Facebook-Enabled Communication Practices." *New Media and Society* 13 (6): 873–92. https://doi.org/10.1177/1461444810385389.

English-Lueck, J. A. 2002. *Cultures@Silicon Valley*. Stanford, CA: Stanford University Press.

Eriksen, Thomas Hylland. 2007. "Nationalism and the Internet." *Nations and Nationalism* 13 (1): 1–17.

Erling, Elizabeth J. 2002. "'I Learn English since Ten Years': The Global English Debate and the German University Classroom." *English Today* 18 (2): 8–13.

Erling, Elizabeth J. 2007. "Local Identities, Global Connections: Affinities to English among Students at the Freie Universität Berlin." *World Englishes* 26 (2): 111–30. https://doi.org/10.1111/j.1467-971x.2007.00497.x.

Erling, Elizabeth J., and Alan Walton. 2007. "English at Work in Berlin." *English Today* 23 (1): 32–40.

Escobar, Arturo. 2007. "The 'Ontological Turn' in Social Theory: A Commentary on 'Human Geography without Scale,' by Sallie Marston, John Paul Jones II and Keith Woodward." *Transactions of the Institute of British Geographers* 32 (1): 106–11. https://doi.org/10.1111/j.1475-5661.2007.00243.x.

Escobar, Arturo, David Hess, Isabel Licha, Will Sibley, and Marilyn Strathern. 1994. "Welcome to Cyberia: Notes on the Anthropology of Cyberculture [and Comments and Reply]." *Current Anthropology* 35 (3): 211–31.

Ewing, Katherine Pratt. 2006. "Between Cinema and Social Work: Diasporic Turkish Women and the (Dis)Pleasures of Hybridity." *Cultural Anthropology* 21 (2): 265–94. https://doi.org/10.1525/can.2006.21.2.265.

Ewing, Katherine Pratt. 2008. *Stolen Honor: Stigmatizing Muslim Men in Berlin*. Redwood City, CA: Stanford University Press.

Gray, Mary L. 2009. *Out in the Country: Youth, Media, and Queer Visibility in Rural America*. NYU Press.

Featherstone, Mike, and Roger Burrows. 1996. *Cyberspace/Cyberbodies/Cyberpunk: Cultures of Technological Embodiment*. London: SAGE.

Fehérváry, Krisztina. 2013. *Politics in Color and Concrete: Socialist Materialities and the Middle Class in Hungary*. Bloomington: Indiana University Press.

Ferguson, Charles A. 1992. "Foreword to the First Edition." In *The Other Tongue: English across Cultures (English in the Global Context)*, edited by Braj B. Kachru, xiii–xvii. Urbana: University of Illinois Press.

Florida, Richard L. 2004. *The Rise of the Creative Class: And How It's Transforming Work, Leisure, Community and Everyday Life*. New York: Basic Books.

Forche, Christian R. 2012. "On the Emergence of Euro-English as a Potential European Variety of English—Attitudes and Interpretations." *Jezikoslovlje* 13 (2): 447–78.

Foucault, Michel. 1977. *Discipline and Punish: The Birth of the Prison*. New York: Pantheon Books.

Foucault, Michel. 1988. *Care of the Self: The History of Sexuality*. Vol. 3. New York: Vintage Books.

Foucault, Michel. 1997. "Technologies of the Self." In *Ethics: Subjectivity and Truth*, edited by Paul Rabinow, translated by Robert Hurley, 223–52. New York: New Press.

Frank, Thomas. 1997. *The Conquest of Cool: Business Culture, Counterculture, and the Rise of Hip Consumerism*. Chicago: University of Chicago Press.

Franklin, M. I. 2010. "Digital Dilemmas: Transnational Politics in the Twenty-First Century." *Brown Journal of World Affairs* 16 (2): 67–85.

Frith, Jordan. 2015. *Smartphones as Locative Media*. Cambridge: Polity.

Fuchs, Christian. 2010. "Labor in Informational Capitalism and on the Internet." *Information Society* 26 (3): 179–96. https://doi.org/10.1080/01972241003712215.

Fukuyama, Francis. 1992. *The End of History and the Last Man*. New York: Free Press.

Gal, Susan. 2002. "A Semiotics of the Public/Private Distinction." *Differences: A Journal of Feminist Cultural Studies* 13 (1): 77–95.

Gal, Susan, and Judith T. Irvine. 2000. "Language Ideology and Linguistic Differentiation." In *Regimes of Language Ideologies, Polities, and Identities,* edited by Paul V. Kroskrity, 35–82. Santa Fe: School of American Research Press.

Garcia, Luis-Manuel. 2013a. "Crowd Solidarity on the Dancefloor in Paris and Berlin." In *Music Performance and the Changing City: Post-industrial Contexts in Europe and the United States,* edited by Fabian Holt and Carsten Wergin, 227–55. New York: Routledge.

Garcia, Luis-Manuel. 2013b. "Guest Editor's Introduction: Doing Nightlife and EDMC Fieldwork." *Dancecult* 5 (1): 3–17. https://doi.org/10.12801/1947-5403.2013.05.01.01.

Garcia, Luis-Manuel. 2015. "At Home, I'm a Tourist: Musical Migration and Affective Citizenship in Berlin." *Journal of Urban Cultural Studies* 2 (1): 121–34. https://doi .org/10.1386/jucs.2.1-2.121_1.

Garcia, Luis-Manuel. 2016. "Techno-Tourism and Post-industrial Neo-Romanticism in Berlin's Electronic Dance Music Scenes." *Tourist Studies* 16 (3): 276–95. https:// doi.org/10.1177/1468797615618037.

Geertman, Stephanie, and Julie-Anne Boudreau. 2018. "'Life as Art': Emerging Youth Networks in Hanoi and the Tree Hug Movement." *Visual Anthropology Review* 30 (2): 210–36. https://doi.org/10.1111/ciso.12162.

Geertz, Clifford. 1974. "'From the Native's Point of View': On the Nature of Anthropological Understanding." *Bulletin of the American Academy of Arts and Sciences* 28 (1): 26–45. https://doi.org/10.2307/3822971.

Gellner, Ernest. 1983. *Nations and Nationalism.* Ithaca, NY: Cornell University Press.

Gershon, Ilana. 2010a. "Breaking Up Is Hard to Do: Media Switching and Media Ideologies." *Journal of Linguistic Anthropology* 20 (2): 389–405. https://doi.org/10.1111 /j.1548-1395.2010.01076.x.

Gershon, Ilana. 2010b. "Media Ideologies: An Introduction." *Journal of Linguistic Anthropology* 20 (2): 283–93. https://doi.org/10.1111/j.1548-1395.2010.01070.x.

Gildart, Keith, Anna Gough-Yates, Sian Lincoln, Bill Osgerby, Lucy Robinson, John Street, Pete Webb, and Matthew Worley, eds. 2018. *Ripped, Torn and Cut: Pop, Politics and Punk Fanzines from 1976.* Manchester: Manchester University Press.

Goddard, Victoria A., Josep R. Llobera, and Cris Shore. 1994. *The Anthropology of Europe: Identity and Boundaries in Conflict.* Oxford: Berg.

Goffman, Erving. 1963. *Behavior in Public Places.* New York: Free Press.

Goffman, Erving. 1972. *Relations in Public.* New York: Penguin.

Goggin, Gerard. 2006. *Cell Phone Culture: Mobile Technology in Everyday Life.* London: Routledge.

Goggin, Gerard, and Larissa Hjorth. 2014. *The Routledge Companion to Mobile Media.* New York: Routledge.

Goggin, Gerard, and Mark McLelland. 2017. *The Routledge Companion to Global Internet Histories.* Florence, UK: Routledge.

Graeber, David. 2014. "Anthropology and the Rise of the Professional-Managerial Class." *HAU: Journal of Ethnographic Theory* 4 (3): 73–88. https://doi.org/10.14318/hau4 .3.007.

Graham, Mark. 2013. "Geography/Internet: Ethereal Alternate Dimensions of Cyberspace or Grounded Augmented Realities?" *Geographical Journal* 179 (2): 177–82. https://doi.org/10.1111/geoj.12009.

Granovetter, Mark S. 1973. "The Strength of Weak Ties." *American Journal of Sociology* 78 (6): 1360–80.

Green, Nicola. 2002. "On the Move: Technology, Mobility, and the Mediation of Social Time and Space." *Information Society* 18 (4): 281–92. https://doi.org/10.1080/019 72240290075129.

Gupta, Akhil, and James Ferguson. 1992. "Beyond 'Culture': Space, Identity, and the Politics of Difference." *Cultural Anthropology* 7 (1): 6–23. https://doi.org/10.1525/can .1992.7.1.02a00020.

Gupta, Akhil, and James Ferguson. 1997. *Anthropological Locations: Boundaries and Grounds of a Field Science.* Berkeley: University of California Press.

Guttentag, Daniel. 2014. "Airbnb: Disruptive Innovation and the Rise of an Informal Tourism Accommodation Sector." *Current Issues in Tourism* 18 (12): 1192–217. https://doi.org/10.1080/13683500.2013.827159.

Hakken, David. 1993. "Computing and Social Change: New Technology and Workplace Transformation, 1980–1990." *Annual Review of Anthropology* 22:107–32.

Hakken, David. 1999. *Cyborgs@Cyberspace? An Ethnographer Looks to the Future.* New York: Routledge.

Halegoua, Germaine R. 2020. *The Digital City: Media and the Social Production of Place.* New York: New York University Press.

Hall, Stuart, and Tony Jefferson, eds. (1975) 1993. *Resistance through Rituals: Youth Subcultures in Post-war Britain.* London: Routledge.

Hannerz, Ulf. 1996. *Transnational Connections: Culture, People, Places.* London: Routledge.

Haraway, Donna. 1990. "A Cyborg Manifesto." In *Simians, Cyborgs and Women: The Reinvention of Nature,* 149–81. New York: Routledge.

Hargittai, Eszter, and Amanda Hinnant. 2008. "Digital Inequality: Differences in Young Adults' Use of the Internet." *Communication Research* 35 (5): 602–21. https://doi .org/10.1177/0093650208321782.

Harrison, Steve, and Paul Dourish. 1996. "Re-place-ing Space: The Roles of Place and Space in Collaborative Systems." In *Proceedings of the 1996 ACM Conference on Computer Supported Cooperative Work,* 67–76. New York: Association for Computing Machinery. https://doi.org/10.1145/240080.240193.

Harvey, David. 1989. *The Condition of Postmodernity: An Enquiry into the Origins of Cultural Change.* Oxford: B. Blackwell.

Hayles, N. Katherine. 1999. *How We Became Posthuman.* Chicago: University of Chicago Press.

Hayles, N. Katherine. 2004. "Print Is Flat, Code Is Deep: The Importance of Media-Specific Analysis." *Poetics Today* 25 (1): 67–90. https://doi.org/10.1215/03335372-25-1-67.

Haythornthwaite, Caroline. 2005. "Social Networks and Internet Connectivity Effects." *Information, Community & Society* 8 (2): 125–47. https://doi.org/10.1080/136911 80500146185.

Hebdige, Dick. 1979. *Subculture: The Meaning of Style.* London: Methuen.

Heller, Chaia. 2007. "Techne versus Technoscience: Divergent (and Ambiguous) Notions of Food 'Quality' in the French Debate over GM Crops." *American Anthropologist* 109 (4): 603–15. https://doi.org/10.1525/aa.2007.109.4.603.

Henry, Eric. 2007. "The Anthropology of Global English." *Anthropology News* 48 (6): 39–40. https://doi.org/10.1525/an.2007.48.6.39.

Herring, Susan C. 2004. "Slouching toward the Ordinary: Current Trends in Computer-Mediated Communication." *New Media and Society* 6 (1): 26–36. https://doi.org /10.1177/1461444804039906.

Herz, Andreas, and Claudia Olivier. 2014. "Transnational Social Networks—Current Perspectives." *Transnational Social Review* 2 (2): 115–19. https://doi.org/10.1080 /21931674.2012.10820729.

Hesse, Kurt. 1990. "Cross-Border Mass Communication from West to East Germany." *European Journal of Communication* 5 (2): 355–71.

Hicks, Marie. 2017. *Programmed Inequality: How Britain Discarded Women Technologists and Lost Its Edge in Computing.* Cambridge, MA: MIT Press.

Hine, Christine. 2000. *Virtual Ethnography*. London: SAGE.

Hjorth, Larissa, and Sarah Pink. 2014. "New Visualities and the Digital Wayfarer: Reconceptualizing Camera Phone Photography and Locative Media." *Mobile Media & Communication* 2 (1): 40–57. https://doi.org/10.1177/2050157913505257.

Ho, Karen. 2005. "Situating Global Capitalisms: A View from Wall Street Investment Banks." *Cultural Anthropology* 20 (1): 68–96. https://doi.org/10.1525/can.2005.20.1.068.

Hobsbawm, Eric. 1992. *Nations and Nationalism since 1780: Programme, Myth, Reality*. Cambridge: Cambridge University Press.

Holmes, Douglas R. 2000. *Integral Europe: Fast-Capitalism, Multiculturalism, Neofascism*. Princeton, NJ: Princeton University Press.

Holmes, Seth M., and Heide Castañeda. 2016. "Representing the 'European Refugee Crisis' in Germany and Beyond: Deservingness and Difference, Life and Death." *American Ethnologist* 43 (1): 12–24. https://doi.org/10.1111/amet.12259.

Horst, Heather A., and Daniel Miller. 2006. *The Cell Phone: An Anthropology of Communication*. Oxford; New York: Berg.

Horst, Heather A., and Daniel Miller. 2012a. *Digital Anthropology*. New York: Berg.

Horst, Heather A., and Daniel Miller. 2012b. "Normativity and Materiality: A View from Digital Anthropology." *Media International Australia* 145 (1): 103–11. https://doi.org/10.1177/1329878X1214500112.

Humphreys, Lee. 2007. "Mobile Social Networks and Social Practice: A Case Study of Dodgeball." *Journal of Computer-Mediated Communication* 13 (1): 341–60. https://doi.org/10.1111/j.1083-6101.2007.00399.x.

Humphreys, Lee. 2010. "Mobile Social Networks and Urban Public Space." *New Media and Society* 12 (5): 763–78. https://doi.org/10.1177/1461444809349578.

Huyssen, Andreas. 1997. "The Voids of Berlin." *Critical Inquiry* 24 (1): 57–81.

Ingold, Tim. 2007. "Materials against Materiality." *Archaeological Dialogues* 14 (1): 1–16. https://doi.org/10.1017/S1380203807002127.

Ingold, Tim. 2012. "Toward an Ecology of Materials." *Annual Review of Anthropology* 41 (1): 427–42. https://doi.org/10.1146/annurev-anthro-081309-145920.

International Telecommunication Union. 2024a. "Germany: Active Mobile-Broadband Subscriptions, 2007–2023." ITU *DataHub*. Geneva, Switzerland: ITU. https://datahub.itu.int/data/?e=DEU&i=11632&v=chart.

International Telecommunication Union. 2024b. "Germany: Households with Access to Internet, by Type of Service, 2003–2021." International Telecommunication Union, Geneva, Switzerland, 2024, https://datahub.itu.int/data/?e=DEU&i=100001&v=chart.

International Telecommunication Union. 2024c. "Germany: Households with a Computer, 2000–2017." *ITU DataHub*. Geneva, Switzerland: ITU. https://datahub.itu.int/data/?e=DEU&i=12046&v=chart.

International Telecommunication Union. 2024d. "Germany: Households with Internet Access at Home." International Telecommunication Union, Geneva, Switzerland, 2024, https://datahub.itu.int/data/?e=DEU&i=12047&v=chart.

International Telecommunication Union. 2024e. "Germany: Mobile-cellular Subscriptions per 100 People, 2000–2023." *ITU DataHub*. Geneva, Switzerland: ITU. https://datahub.itu.int/data/?e=DEU&i=178&v=chart&u=per+100+people.

Ito, Mizuko. 1997. "Virtually Embodied: The Reality of Fantasy in a Multi-user Dungeon." In *Internet Culture*, edited by David Porter, 87–109. New York: Routledge.

Ito, Mizuko, Sonja Baumer, Judd Antin, Megan Finn, Heather A. Horst, Arthur Law, Annie Manion, Sarai Mitnick, David Schlossberg, and Sarita Yardi. 2009. *Hanging Out, Messing Around, and Geeking Out: Kids Living and Learning with New Media*. Cambridge, MA: MIT Press.

Ito, Mizuko, Daisuke Okabe, and Misa Matsuda. 2005. *Personal, Portable, Pedestrian: Mobile Phones in Japanese Life*. Cambridge, MA: MIT Press.

Jain, Sarah S. 1999. "The Prosthetic Imagination: Enabling and Disabling the Prosthesis Trope." *Science, Technology & Human Values* 24 (1): 31–54.

Jakobson, Roman. 1963. *Essais de linguistique générale* [Essay in general linguistics]. Vol. 1, *Les fondations du langage*. Paris: Éditions de Minuit.

Jarrett, Kylie. 2016. *Feminism, Labour and Digital Media: The Digital Housewife*. New York: Routledge.

Jenkins, Henry. 2006. *Convergence Culture: Where Old and New Media Collide*. New York: NYU Press.

Jones, Graham M., and Bambi B. Schieffelin. 2009a. "Enquoting Voices, Accomplishing Talk: Uses of Be+Like in Instant Messaging." *Language and Communication* 29 (1): 77–113. https://doi.org/10.1016/j.langcom.2007.09.003.

Jones, Graham M., and Bambi B. Schieffelin. 2009b. "Talking Text and Talking Back: 'My BFF Jill' from Boob Tube to YouTube." *Journal of Computer-Mediated Communication* 14 (4): 1050–79. https://doi.org/10.1111/j.1083-6101.2009.01481.x.

Jones, Graham M., Beth Semel, and Audrey Le. 2015. "'There's No Rules. It's Hackathon.': Negotiating Commitment in a Context of Volatile Sociality." *Journal of Linguistic Anthropology* 25 (3): 322–45. https://doi.org/10.1111/jola.12104.

Juris, Jeffrey S. 2012. "Reflections on #Occupy Everywhere: Social Media, Public Space, and Emerging Logics of Aggregation." *American Ethnologist* 39 (2): 259–79. https://doi.org/10.1111/j.1548-1425.2012.01362.x.

Kafer, Alison. 2013. *Feminist, Queer, Crip*. Bloomington: Indiana University Press.

Katz, James E. 2003. *Machines That Become Us: The Social Context of Personal Communication Technology*. New Brunswick, NJ: Transaction.

Katz, James E. 2006. "Mobile Communication and the Transformation of Daily Life: The Next Phase of Research on Mobiles." *Knowledge, Technology & Policy* 19 (1): 62–71. https://doi.org/10.1007/s12130-006-1016-4.

Katz, James E., and Satomi Sugiyama. 2006. "Mobile Phones as Fashion Statements: Evidence from Student Surveys in the US and Japan." *New Media and Society* 8 (2): 321–37. https://doi.org/10.1177/1461444806061950.

Khabeer, Su'ad Abdul. 2016. *Muslim Cool: Race, Religion, and Hip Hop in the United States*. New York: New York University Press.

Kilborn, Richard. 1993. "Towards Utopia—or Another Anschluss? East Germany's Transition to a New Media System." *European Journal of Communication* 8 (4): 451–70. https://doi.org/10.1177/0267323193008004003.

Klumbytė, Neringa. 2010. "The Soviet Sausage Renaissance." *American Anthropologist* 112 (1): 22–37. https://doi.org/10.1111/j.1548-1433.2009.01194.x.

Kosnick, Kira. 2000. "Building Bridges: Media for Migrants and the Public-Service Mission in Germany." *European Journal of Cultural Studies* 3 (3): 319–42.

Kosnick, Kira. 2007. *Migrant Media: Turkish Broadcasting and Multicultural Politics in Berlin*. Bloomington: Indiana University Press.

Kraemer, Jordan. 2014. "Friend or Freund: Social Media and Transnational Connections in Berlin." *Human-Computer Interaction* 29 (1): 53–77. https://doi.org/10.1080/07 370024.2013.823821.

Kraemer, Jordan. 2016. "Doing Fieldwork, Brb: Locating the Field on and with Emerging Media." In *eFieldnotes: The Makings of Anthropology in the Digital World*, edited by Roger Sanjek and Susan Tratner, 58:e42–e48. Philadelphia, Penn.: University of Pennsylvania Press.

Kraemer, Jordan. 2017. "When Social Media Are the News." *Anthropology News* 58 (1): e42–e48. https://doi.org/10.1111/an.286.

Kraemer, Jordan. 2018. "Of Spargel and Spiegel: Networked National Feelings in Berlin." *Anthropological Quarterly* 91 (4): 1385–1416. https://doi.org/10.1353/anq.2018.0069.

Kraemer, Jordan. 2021a. "The Gender of the Interface: Coding Masculinity, Crafting Femininity among Berlin's Creative Class." *Catalyst: Feminism, Theory, Technoscience* 7 (2): 1–28.

Kraemer, Jordan. 2021b. "Virtually Gendered: Materiality and Interface Design on Transnational Social Media." *Global Perspectives* 2 (1): 1–7.

Kraemer, Jordan. 2022. "The Materiality of the Virtual in Urban Space." In *The Routledge Companion to Media Anthropology*, edited by Elisabetta Costa, Patricia G. Lange, Nell Haynes, and Jolynna Sinanan, 187–201. Abingdon: Routledge.

Kroskrity, Paul V. 2000. *Regimes of Language*. Santa Fe: School of American Research Press.

Kruse, Holly. 2003. *Site and Sound: Understanding Independent Music Scenes*. New York: P. Lang.

Lambek, Michael. 2011. "Catching the Local." *Anthropological Theory* 11 (2): 197–221.

Langan, Celeste. 2001. "Mobility Disability." *Public Culture* 13 (3): 459–84.

Lange, Patricia G. 2007. "Publicly Private and Privately Public: Social Networking on YouTube." *Journal of Computer-Mediated Communication* 13 (1): 361–80. https://doi.org/10.1111/j.1083-6101.2007.00400.x.

Larkin, Brian. 1997. "Indian Films and Nigerian Lovers: Media and the Creation of Parallel Modernities." *Africa: Journal of the International African Institute* 67 (3): 406–40.

Larkin, Brian. 2004. "Degraded Images, Distorted Sounds: Nigerian Video and the Infrastructure of Piracy." *Public Culture* 16 (2): 289–314.

Larkin, Brian. 2008. *Signal and Noise: Media, Infrastructure, and Urban Culture in Nigeria*. Durham, NC: Duke University Press.

Larkin, Brian. 2013. "The Politics and Poetics of Infrastructure." *Annual Review of Anthropology* 42:327–43.

Latour, Bruno. 1993. *We Have Never Been Modern*. Translated by Catherine Porter. Cambridge, MA: Harvard University Press.

Latour, Bruno. 2005. *Reassembling the Social: An Introduction to Actor-Network-Theory*. Oxford: Oxford University Press.

Lave, Jean. 1991. "Situating Learning in Communities of Practice." In *Perspectives on Socially Shared Cognition*, edited by Lauren B. Resnick, John M. Levine, and Stephanie D. Teasley, 63–82. Washington, DC: American Psychological Association. https://doi.org/10.1037/10096-000.

Lave, Jean, and Etienne Wenger. 1991. *Situated Learning: Legitimate Peripheral Participation*. Cambridge: Cambridge University Press.

Law, John. 1992. "Notes on the Theory of the Actor-Network: Ordering, Strategy, and Heterogeneity." *Systemic Practice and Action Research* 5 (4): 379–93.

Law, John. 2010. "The Materials of STS." In *The Oxford Handbook of Material Culture Studies*, edited by Dan Hicks and Mary C Beaudry, 173–88. Oxford: Oxford University Press. https://doi.org/10.1093/oxfordhb/9780199218714.013.0006.

Law, John, and Annemarie Mol. 1995. "Notes on Materiality and Sociality." *Sociological Review* 43 (2): 274–94. https://doi.org/10.1111/j.1467-954X.1995.tb00604.x.

Lee, Helen. 2007. "Transforming Transnationalism: Second Generation Tongans Overseas." *Asian and Pacific Migration Journal* 16 (2): 157–78.

Lefebvre, Henri. 1991. *The Production of Space*. Oxford: Blackwell.

Leitch, Alison. 2003. "Slow Food and the Politics of Pork Fat: Italian Food and European Identity." *Ethnos* 68 (4): 437–62. https://doi.org/10.1080/0014184032000160514.

Leitner, Helga. 1997. "Reconfiguring the Spatiality of Power: The Construction of a Supranational Migration Framework for the European Union." *Political Geography* 16 (2): 123–43.

Leitner, Helga, and Byron Miller. 2007. "Scale and the Limitations of Ontological Debate: A Commentary on Marston, Jones and Woodward." *Transactions of the Institute of British Geographers*, 32:116–25. https://doi.org/10.1111/j.1475-5661.2007.00 236.x.

Lenhart, Amanda, Mary Madden, Alexandra Rankin Macgill, and Aaron Smith. 2007. "Teens and Social Media." Pew Internet & American Life Project. Washington, DC: Pew Internet & American Life Project.

Leppänen, Sirpa. 2007. "Youth Language in Media Contexts: Insights into the Functions of English in Finland." *World Englishes* 26 (2): 149–69.

Licoppe, Christian. 2004. "'Connected' Presence: The Emergence of a New Repertoire for Managing Social Relationships in a Changing Communication Technoscape." *Environment and Planning D: Society and Space* 22 (1): 135–56. https://doi.org /10.1068/d323t.

Licoppe, Christian. 2016. "Mobilities and Urban Encounters in Public Places in the Age of Locative Media. Seams, Folds, and Encounters with 'Pseudonymous Strangers.'" *Mobilities* 11 (1): 99–116. https://doi.org/10.1080/17450101.2015.1097035.

Liechty, Mark. 2003. *Suitably Modern: Making Middle-Class Culture in a New Consumer Society*. Princeton, NJ: Princeton University Press.

Light, Jennifer. 1999. "When Computers Were Women." *Technology and Culture* 40 (3): 455–83.

Livingstone, Sonia. 2003. "On the Challenges of Cross-National Comparative Media Research." *European Journal of Communication* 18 (4): 477–500. https://doi.org /10.1177/0267323103184003.

Low, Setha M. 1996. "The Anthropology of Cities: Imagining and Theorizing the City." *Annual Review of Anthropology* 25:383–409.

Low, Setha M. 2000. *On the Plaza: The Politics of Public Space and Culture*. Austin: University of Texas Press.

Low, Setha M. 2009. "Towards an Anthropological Theory of Space and Place." *Semiotica* 2009 (175): 21–37. https://doi.org/10.1515/semi.2009.041.

Low, Setha M. 2014. "Spatializing Culture: An Engaged Anthropological Approach to Space and Place." In *The People, Place, and Space Reader*, edited by Jen Jack Gieseking and William Mangold, 34–38. New York: Routledge.

Low, Setha M. 2017. *Spatializing Culture: The Ethnography of Space and Place*. London: Routledge.

Lu, Weixu, and Keith N. Hampton. 2015. "Beyond the Power of Networks: Differentiating Network Structure from Social Media Affordances for Perceived Social Support." *New Media and Society* 19 (6): 861–79. https://doi.org/10.1177/1461444815 621514.

Luvaas, Brent. 2010. "Designer Vandalism: Indonesian Indie Fashion and the Cultural Practice of Cut 'n' Paste." *Visual Anthropology Review* 26 (1): 1–16. https://doi.org /10.1111/j.1548-7458.2010.01043.x.

MacDougall, Carla. 2011. "In the Shadow of the Wall: Urban Space and Everyday Life in Kreuzberg." In *Between the Avant-Garde and the Everyday: Subversive Politics in Europe from 1957 to the Present*, edited by Timothy Scott Brown and Lorena Anton, 154–73. New York: Berghahn Books.

MacKenzie, Donald A., and Judy Wajcman. 1999. *The Social Shaping of Technology*. Buckingham: Open University Press.

Macpherson, C. B. 1962. *Political Theory of Possessive Individualism: Hobbes to Locke.* Oxford: Clarendon.

Madianou, Mirca, and Daniel Miller. 2013. "Polymedia: Towards a New Theory of Digital Media in Interpersonal Communication." *International Journal of Cultural Studies* 16 (2): 169–87. https://doi.org/10.1177/1367877912452486.

Majchrzak, Ann, Samer Faraj, Gerald C. Kane, and Bijan Azad. 2013. "The Contradictory Influence of Social Media Affordances on Online Communal Knowledge Sharing." *Journal of Computer-Mediated Communication* 19 (1): 38–55. https://doi.org/10.1111/jcc4.12030.

Malinowski, Bronislaw. (1922) 2014. *Argonauts of the Western Pacific.* London: Routledge.

Malkki, Liisa. 1992. "National Geographic: The Rooting of Peoples and the Territorialization of National Identity among Scholars and Refugees." *Cultural Anthropology* 7 (1): 24–44. https://doi.org/10.1525/can.1992.7.1.02a00030.

Mandel, Ruth. 2008. *Cosmopolitan Anxieties: Turkish Challenges to Citizenship and Belonging in Germany.* Durham, NC: Duke University Press.

Mankekar, Purnima. 1999. *Screening Culture, Viewing Politics: An Ethnography of Television, Womanhood, and Nation in Postcolonial India.* Durham, NC: Duke University Press.

Mannitz, Sabine. 2006. "The Grand Old West: Mythical Narratives of a Better Past before 1989 in Views of West-Berlin Youth from Immigrant Families." In *Crossing European Boundaries*, edited by Jaro Stacul, Christina Moutsou, and Helen Kopnina, 83–102. New York: Berghahn Books.

Marston, Sallie A. 2000. "The Social Construction of Scale." *Progress in Human Geography* 24 (2): 219–42.

Marston, Sallie A., John Paul Jones III, and Keith Woodward. 2005. "Human Geography without Scale." *Transactions of the Institute of British Geographers* 30 (4): 416–32.

Marvin, Carolyn. 1990. *When Old Technologies Were New: Implementing the Future.* Cary, NC: Oxford University Press.

Marwick, Alice E. 2015. "Instafame: Luxury Selfies in the Attention Economy." *Public Culture* 27 (1 [75]): 137–60. https://doi.org/10.1215/08992363-2798379.

Marx, Karl. (1973) 1993. *Grundrisse: Foundations of the Critique of Political Economy* (Rough Draft). Translated by Nicolaus Martin. London: Penguin Books in association with New Left Review.

Massey, Doreen. 1993. "Power Geometry and a Progressive Sense of Place." In *Mapping the Futures: Local Cultures, Global Change*, edited by Jon Bird, Barry Curtis, Tim Putnam, George Robertson, and Lisa Tickner, 59–69. London: Routledge.

Massumi, Brian. 1995. "The Autonomy of Affect." *Cultural Critique*, no. 31 (Autumn): 83–109. https://doi.org/10.2307/1354446.

Massumi, Brian. 2002. *Parables for the Virtual: Movement, Affect, Sensation.* Durham, NC: Duke University Press.

Maurer, Bill. 2000. "A Fish Story: Rethinking Globalization on Virgin Gorda, British Virgin Islands." *American Ethnologist* 27 (3): 670–701. https://doi.org/10.1525/ae.2000.27.3.670.

Mazzarella, William. 2004. *Shoveling Smoke: Advertising and Globalization in Contemporary India.* Durham, NC: Duke University Press.

McGuigan, Jim. 2005. "The Cultural Public Sphere." *European Journal of Cultural Studies* 8 (4): 427.

McLuhan, Marshall. (1964) 2003. *Understanding Media: The Extensions of Man.* Corte Madera, CA: Gingko.

McRobbie, Angela. 1993. "Shut Up and Dance: Youth Culture and Changing Modes of Femininity." *YOUNG* 1 (2): 13–31. https://doi.org/10.1177/110330889300100202.

Melhuish, Clare, Monica Degen, and Gillian Rose. 2016. "'The Real Modernity That Is Here': Understanding the Role of Digital Visualisations in the Production of a New Urban Imaginary at Msheireb Downtown, Doha." *City & Society* 28 (2): 222–45. https://doi.org/10.1111/ciso.12080.

Miller, Daniel, Elisabetta Costa, Nell Haynes, Tom McDonald, Razvan Nicolescu, Jolynna Sinanan, Shriram Venkatraman, Juliano Spyer, and Xinyuan Wang. 2016. *How the World Changed Social Media.* London: University College London Press.

Miller, Daniel, and Don Slater. 2000. *The Internet: An Ethnographic Approach.* Oxford: Berg.

Miller, Michael L., and Scott Ury. 2010. "Cosmopolitanism: The End of Jewishness?" *European Review of History: Revue Européenne D'histoire* 17 (3): 337–59. https://doi.org/10.1080/13507486.2010.481923.

Mintz, Sydney W. 1985. *Sweetness and Power: The Place of Sugar in Modern History.* New York: Viking.

Morley, David, and Kevin Robins. 1989. "Spaces of Identity: Communications Technologies and the Reconfiguration of Europe." *Screen* 30 (4): 10–34.

Mukerji, Chandra. 2009. *Impossible Engineering: Technology and Territoriality on the Canal Du Midi.* Princeton, NJ: Princeton University Press.

Munn, Nancy. 1986. *The Fame of Gawa: A Symbolic Study of Value Transformation in a Massim (Papua New Guinea) Society.* Cambridge: Cambridge University Press.

Muñoz, José Esteban. 2000. "Feeling Brown: Ethnicity and Affect in Ricardo Bracho's 'The Sweetest Hangover (and Other STDs).'" *Theatre Journal* 52 (1): 67–79.

Nafus, Dawn. 2003. "The Aesthetics of the Internet in St. Petersburg: Why Metaphor Matters." *Communication Review* 6 (3): 185–212. https://doi.org/10.1080/107144 20390226252.

Nakamura, Lisa. 1995. "Race in/for Cyberspace: Identity Tourism and Racial Passing on the Internet." *Works and Days* 13 (1–2): 181–93.

Newman, Nic. 2012. "Reuters Institute Digital News Report 2012: Tracking the Future of News." Reuters Institute for the Study of Journalism, Oxford University, Oxford, UK.

Newman, Nic, A. L. David, and Rasmus Kleis Nielsen. 2015. "Reuters Institute Digital News Report 2015: Tracking the Future of News." Reuters Institute for the Study of Journalism, Oxford University, Oxford, UK.

Nye, Sean. 2013. "Minimal Understandings: The Berlin Decade, the Minimal Continuum, and Debates on the Legacy of German Techno." *Journal of Popular Music Studies* 25 (2): 154–84. https://doi.org/10.1111/jpms.12032.

Partridge, Damani J. 2008. "We Were Dancing in the Club, Not on the Berlin Wall: Black Bodies, Street Bureaucrats, and Exclusionary Incorporation into the New Europe." *Cultural Anthropology* 23 (4): 660–87. https://doi.org/10.1111/j.1548-1360.2008 .00022.x.

Partridge, Damani J. 2012. *Hypersexuality and Headscarves: Race, Sex, and Citizenship in the New Germany.* Bloomington: Indiana University Press.

Partridge, Damani J. 2013. "Occupying American 'Black' Bodies and Reconfiguring European Spaces—the Possibilities for Noncitizen Articulations in Berlin and Beyond." *Transforming Anthropology* 21 (1): 41–56. https://doi.org/10.1111/traa .12006.

Paxson, Heather. 2010. "Locating Value in Artisan Cheese: Reverse Engineering Terroir for New-World Landscapes." *American Anthropologist* 112 (3): 444–57.

Pearson, Charles Anthony. 2013. "Tea Party Technologies and Imaginaries: The Emergence of a Conservative Network Politics." ProQuest Dissertations and Theses. PhD dissertation, University of California, Davis.

Pearson, Erika. 2009. "All the World Wide Web's a Stage: The Performance of Identity in Online Social Networks." *First Monday* 14 (3).

Pécoud, Antoine. 2002. "Cosmopolitanism and Business among German-Turks in Berlin." *Journal of the Society for the Anthropology of Europe* 2 (3): 2–12. https://doi.org/10.1525/jsae.2002.2.1.2.

Pécoud, Antoine. 2004. "Do Immigrants Have a Business Culture? The Political Epistemology of Fieldwork in Berlin's Turkish Economy." *Journal of the Society for the Anthropology of Europe* 4 (2): 19–25. https://doi.org/10.1525/jsae.2004.4.2.19.

Peebles, Gustav. 2011. *The Euro and Its Rivals: Currency and the Construction of a Transnational City.* Bloomington: Indiana University Press.

Peters, Deike. 2010. "Rail City Berlin: Rail Infrastructure Development and Intermodality in the Reunified German Capital." *Transportation Research Record: Journal of the Transportation Research Board* 2146 (1): 60–68.

Pfaffenberger, Bryan. 1988. "The Social Meaning of the Personal Computer: Or, Why the Personal Computer Revolution Was No Revolution." *Anthropological Quarterly* 61 (1): 39–47.

Pincus, Steve. 1998. "Neither Machiavellian Moment nor Possessive Individualism: Commercial Society and the Defenders of the English Commonwealth." *American Historical Review* 103 (3): 705–36.

Pink, Sarah, Elisenda Ardévol, and Débora Lanzeni. 2016. *Digital Materialities Design and Anthropology.* London: Bloomsbury Academic.

Pink, Sarah, Heather A. Horst, John Postill, Larissa Hjorth, Tania Lewis, and Jo Tacchi. 2016. *Digital Ethnography: Principles and Practice.* Los Angeles: SAGE.

Platt, John, Heidi Weber, and Mian Lian Ho. 1984. *The New Englishes.* London: Routledge and Kegan Paul.

Porter, David, ed. 1997. *Internet Culture.* London: Routledge.

Postill, John. 2014. "Democracy in an Age of Viral Reality: A Media Epidemiography of Spain's Indignados Movement." *Ethnography* 15 (1): 51–69.

Quan-Haase, Anabel, and Barry Wellman. 2004. "How Does the Internet Affect Social Capital?" In *Social Capital and Information Technology*, edited by Marleen Huysman and Volker Wulf, 113–31. Cambridge, MA: MIT Press.

Rapp, Tobias. 2010. *Lost and Sound.* Frankfurt am Main: Suhrkamp.

Rasmussen, Terje. 2013. "Internet-Based Media, Europe and the Political Public Sphere." *Media, Culture & Society* 35 (1): 97–104. https://doi.org/10.1177/0163443712464563.

Rheingold, Howard. 1993. *The Virtual Community: Homesteading on the Electronic Frontier.* Cambridge, MA: MIT Press.

Ribes, David, and Janet Vertesi. 2019. *DigitalSTS: A Field Guide for Science & Technology Studies.* Princeton, NJ: Princeton University Press.

Rosenblat, Alex. 2018. *Uberland: How Algorithms Are Rewriting the Rules of Work.* Oakland: University of California Press.

Rosner, Daniela, Jean-François Blanchette, Leah Buechley, Paul Dourish, and Melissa Mazmanian. 2012. "From Materials to Materiality: Connecting Practice and Theory in HC." In *CHI '12 Extended Abstracts on Human Factors in Computing Systems (CHI EA '12)*, 2787–90. https://doi.org/10.1145/2212776.2212721.

Ryan, Johnny. 2010. *A History of the Internet and the Digital Future.* London: Reaktion Books.

Sahlins, Peter. 1989. *Boundaries: The Making of France and Spain in the Pyrenees.* Berkeley: University of California Press.

Sandvig, Christian. 2013. "The Internet as Infrastructure." In *The Oxford Handbook of Internet Studies*, edited by William H. Dutton, 86–106. Oxford: Oxford University Press.

Sark, Katrina. 2019. "Cultural History of Post-Wall Berlin: From Utopian Longing to Nostalgia for Babylon." In *Cultural Topographies of the New Berlin*, edited by Karin Bauer and Jennifer Hosek, 25–52. New York: Berghahn Books.

Schiller, Nina Glick, Linda Basch, and Cristina Szanton Blanc. 1995. "From Immigrant to Transmigrant: Theorizing Transnational Migration." *Anthropological Quarterly* 68 (1): 48. https://doi.org/10.2307/3317464.

Schnöring, Thomas, and Uwe Szafran. 1994. "Telecommunications in Eastern Germany a Success Story of East-West Integration." *Telecommunications Policy* 18 (6): 453–69. https://doi.org/10.1016/0308-5961(94)90014-0.

Schüll, Natasha Dow. 2012. *Addiction by Design*. Princeton, NJ: Princeton University Press.

Shankar, Shalini, and Jillian R. Cavanaugh. 2012. "Language and Materiality in Global Capitalism." *Annual Review of Anthropology* 41 (1): 355–69. https://doi.org/10.1146/annurev-anthro-092611-145811.

Sheller, Mimi, and John Urry. 2006. "The New Mobilities Paradigm." *Environment and Planning A* 38 (2): 207–26. https://doi.org/10.1068/a37268.

Shore, Cris. 2012. "The Euro Crisis and European Citizenship: The Euro 2001–2012—Celebration or Commemoration?" *Anthropology Today* 28 (2): 5–9.

Sicko, Dan. 2010. *Techno Rebels: The Renegades of Electronic Funk*. Detroit: Wayne State University Press.

Silver, Allan. 1989. "Friendship and Trust as Moral Ideals: An Historical Approach." *European Journal of Sociology* 30 (2): 274–97.

Silver, Allan. 1990. "Friendship in Commercial Society: Eighteenth-Century Social Theory and Modern Sociology." *American Journal of Sociology* 95 (6): 1474–1504.

Slobodian, Quinn. 2018. *Globalists: The End of Empire and the Birth of Neoliberalism*. Cambridge, MA: Harvard University Press.

Slobodian, Quinn, and Michelle Sterling. 2013. "Sacking Berlin: How Hipsters, Expats, Yummies, and Smartphones Ruined a City." *Baffler* 23 (July): 138–46. https://doi.org/10.1162/BFLR_a_00185.

Smith, Anthony. 1971. *Theories of Nationalism*. London: Duckworth.

Smith, Neil. 1992. "Geography, Difference and the Politics of Scale." In *Postmodernism and the Social Sciences*, edited by Joe Doherty, Elspeth Graham, and Mo Malek, 57–79. London: Palgrave Macmillan UK. https://doi.org/10.1007/978-1-349-22183-7_4.

Smith-Hefner, Nancy J. 2007. "Youth Language, Gaul Sociability, and the New Indonesian Middle Class." *Visual Anthropology Review* 17 (2): 184–203. https://doi.org/10.1525/jlin.2007.17.2.184.

Spitulnik, Debra. 1996. "The Social Circulation of Media Discourse and the Mediation of Communities." *Journal of Linguistic Anthropology* 6 (2): 161–87. https://doi.org/10.1525/jlin.1996.6.2.161.

Staab, Andreas. 1998. *National Identity in Eastern Germany: Inner Unification or Continued Separation?* Westport, CT: Praeger.

Star, Susan Leigh. 1999. "The Ethnography of Infrastructure." *American Behavioral Scientist* 43 (3): 377–91. https://doi.org/10.1177/00027649921955326.

Statista 2024. "Share of Internet Users in Germany from 2001 to 2023." *Initiative D21*. Statista: April 22. https://www.statista.com/statistics/380514/internet-usage-rate-germany/.

Stewart, Janet. 2002. "Das Kunsthaus Tacheles: The Berlin Architecture Debate of the 1990s in Micro-historical Context." In *Recasting German Identity: Culture, Politics, and Literature in the Berlin Republic*, edited by Stuart Taberner and Frank Finlay, 51–66. Rochester, NY: Camden House.

Stewart, Kathleen. 2007. *Ordinary Affects*. Durham, NC: Duke University Press.

Stocking, George W., Jr. 1966. "Franz Boas and the Culture Concept in Historical Perspective." *American Anthropologist* 68 (4): 867–82. https://doi.org/10.1525/aa.1966.68.4.02a00010.

Stone, Allucquere Rosanne (Sandy). 1991. "Will the Real Body Please Stand Up? Boundary Stories about Virtual Cultures." In *Cyberspace: First Steps*, edited by Michael Benedikt, 81–118. Cambridge, MA: MIT Press.

Strathern, Marilyn. 1988. *The Gender of the Gift: Problems with Women and Problems with Society in Melanesia*. Berkeley: University of California Press.

Strathern, Marilyn. 2000. *Audit Cultures: Anthropological Studies in Accountability, Ethics, and the Academy*. London: Routledge.

Stryker, Susan. 2000. "Transsexuality: The Postmodern Body and/as Technology." In *The Cybercultures Reader*, edited by David Bell and Barbara Kennedy, 588–97. London: Routledge.

Subrahmanyam, Kaveri, Stephanie M. Reich, Natalia Waechter, and Guadalupe Espinoza. 2008. "Online and Offline Social Networks: Use of Social Networking Sites by Emerging Adults." *Journal of Applied Developmental Psychology* 29 (6): 420–33. https://doi.org/10.1016/j.appdev.2008.07.003.

Swinehart, Karl F. 2008. "The Mass-Mediated Chronotope, Radical Counterpublics, and Dialect in 1970s Norway: The Case of Vømmøl Spellmanslag." *Journal of Linguistic Anthropology* 18 (2): 290–301. https://doi.org/10.1111/j.1548-1395.2008.00023.x.

Swyngedouw, Erik. 1996. "Reconstructing Citizenship, the Re-scaling of the State and the New Authoritarianism: Closing the Belgian Mines." *Urban Studies* 33 (8): 1499–521.

Swyngedouw, Erik. 2004. "Scaled Geographies: Nature, Place, and the Politics of Scale." In *Scale and Geographic Inquiry: Nature, Society, and Method*, edited by Eric Sheppard and Robert McMaster, 129–53. Malden, MA: Blackwell. https://doi.org/10.1002/9780470999141.ch7.

Sykes, Karen. 2007. "Interrogating Individuals: The Theory of Possessive Individualism in the Western Pacific." *Anthropological Forum* 17 (3): 213–24. https://doi.org/10.1080/00664670701637669.

Tarrow, Sidney. 2001. "Rooted Cosmopolitans: Transnational Activists in a World of States." Working paper, Workshop on Transnational Contention, Madison, WI, November 2, 2001.

Tenhunen, Sirpa. 2008. "Mobile Technology in the Village: ICTs, Culture, and Social Logistics in India." *Journal of the Royal Anthropological Institute* 14 (3): 515–34. https://doi.org/10.1111/j.1467-9655.2008.00515.x.

Thornton, Sarah. 1996. *Club Cultures: Music, Media and Subcultural Capital*. Middletown, CT: Wesleyan University Press.

Treitler, Inga. 2016. "Thinking about Refugee Integration in Berlin." *Anthropology News* 5 (57): e81–e82. https://doi.org/10.1111/j.1556-3502.2016.570533.x.

Tsing, Anna. 2000. "The Global Situation." *Cultural Anthropology* 15 (3): 327–60.

Tsing, Anna. 2005. *Friction: An Ethnography of Global Connection*. Princeton, NJ: Princeton University Press.

Tufekci, Zeynep. 2014. "Social Movements and Governments in the Digital Age: Evaluating a Complex Landscape." *Journal of International Affairs* 68 (1): 1–18.

Tufekci, Zeynep. 2017. *Twitter and Tear Gas: The Power and Fragility of Networked Protest*. New Haven, CT: Yale University Press.

Turner, Fred. 2005. "Where the Counterculture Met the New Economy: The WELL and the Origins of Virtual Community." *Technology and Culture* 46 (3): 485–512.

Turner, Fred. 2006. *From Counterculture to Cyberculture: Stewart Brand, the Whole Earth Network, and the Rise of Digital Utopianism*. Chicago: University of Chicago Press.

Udupa, Sahana. 2012. "News Media and Contention over 'the Local' in Urban India." *American Ethnologist* 39 (4): 819–34. https://doi.org/10.1111/j.1548-1425.2012.01 397.x.

Urry, John. 2000. *Sociology beyond Societies: Mobilities for the Twenty-First Century*. London: Routledge.

Van Dijck, José, and Thomas Poell. 2013. "Understanding Social Media Logic." *Media and Communication* 1 (1): 2–14. https://doi.org/10.12924/mac2013.01010002.

Verba, Joan Marie. 2003. *Boldly Writing: A Trekker Fan and Zine History, 1967–1987*. Minnetonka, MN: FTL.

Verdery, Katherine. 1996. *What Was Socialism, and What Comes Next?* Princeton, NJ: Princeton University Press.

Vertesi, Janet. 2019. "From Affordances to Accomplishments: PowerPoint and Excel at NASA." In *DigitalSTS: A Field Guide for Science & Technology Studies*, edited by Janet Vertesi and David Ribes, 369–92. Princeton, NJ: Princeton University Press.

Vertovec, Steven. 2001. "Transnationalism and Identity." *Journal of Ethnic and Migration Studies* 27 (4): 573–82. https://doi.org/10.1080/13691830120090386.

Vertovec, Steven. 2004. "Cheap Calls: The Social Glue of Migrant Transnationalism." *Global Networks* 4 (2): 219–24. https://doi.org/10.1111/j.1471-0374.2004.00088.x.

Ward, Simon. 2019. "Reconfiguring the Spaces of the 'Creative Class' in Contemporary Berlin." In *Cultural Topographies of the New Berlin*, edited by Karin Bauer and Jennifer Hosek, 113–29. New York: Berghahn Books.

Warner, Michael. 2002. *Publics and Counterpublics*. Brooklyn: Zone Books.

Watters, Ethan. 2003. *Urban Tribes*. New York: Bloomsbury.

Weidman, Amanda. 2010. "Sound and the City: Mimicry and Media in South India." *Journal of Linguistic Anthropology* 20 (2): 294–313. https://doi.org/10.1111/j.1548 -1395.2010.01071.x.

Weldes, Jutta. 1999. "Going Cultural: *Star Trek*, State Action, and Popular Culture." *Millennium: Journal of International Studies* 28 (1): 117–34. https://doi.org/10.1177 /03058298990280011201.

Wellman, Barry. 2001. "Computer Networks as Social Networks." *Science* 293 (5537): 2031–34. https://doi.org/10.1126/science.1065547.

Wellman, Barry, and Milena Gulia. 1997. "Net Surfers Don't Ride Alone: Virtual Communities as Communities." In *Communities in Cyberspace*, edited by Marc Smith and Peter Kollock, 167–94. New York: Routledge.

Wellman, Barry, Anabel Quan-Haase, James Witte, and Keith Hampton. 2001. "Does the Internet Increase, Decrease, or Supplement Social Capital?" *American Behavioral Scientist* 45 (3): 436–55. https://doi.org/10.1177/00027640121957286.

Wenger, Etienne. 1999. *Communities of Practice: Learning, Meaning, and Identity*. Cambridge: Cambridge University Press.

Werry, Christopher C. 1996. "Linguistic and Interactional Features of Internet Relay Chat." In *Computer-Mediated Communication: Linguistic, Social, and Cross-Cultural Perspectives*, edited by Susan C. Herring, 47–64. Pragmatics and Beyond New Series 39. Amsterdam: John Benjamins.

Wesch, Michael. 2007. "What Is Web 2.0? What Does It Mean for Anthropology? Lessons from an Accidental Viral Video." *Anthropology News* 48 (5): 30–31. https://doi .org/10.1525/an.2007.48.5.30.2.

Weszkalnys, Gisa. 2010. *Berlin, Alexanderplatz*. New York: Berghahn Books.

White, Jenny B. 1996. "Belonging to a Place: Turks in Unified Berlin." *City & Society* 8 (1): 15–28. https://doi.org/10.1525/ciso.1996.8.1.15.

Wilf, Eitan. 2013. "Toward an Anthropology of Computer-Mediated, Algorithmic Forms of Sociality." *Current Anthropology* 54 (6): 716–39. https://doi.org/10.1086/673321.

Wilk, Richard R. 1999. "'Real Belizean Food': Building Local Identity in the Transnational Caribbean." *American Anthropologist* 101 (2): 244–55. https://doi.org/10.1525/aa.1999.101.2.244.

Williams, Dmitri. 2006. "On and Off the 'Net: Scales for Social Capital in an Online Era." *Journal of Computer-Mediated Communication* 11 (2): 593–628. https://doi.org/10.1111/j.1083-6101.2006.00029.x.

Williams, Raymond. 1977. *Marxism and Literature*. Oxford: Oxford University Press.

Willis, Paul E. (1981) 1990. *Learning to Labor: How Working Class Kids Get Working Class Jobs*. New York: Columbia University Press.

Wilson, Samuel, and Leighton Peterson. 2002. "The Anthropology of Online Communities." *Annual Review of Anthropology* 31:449–67.

Wolbert, Barbara. 2001. "The Visual Production of Locality: Turkish Family Pictures, Migration and the Creation of Virtual Neighborhood." *Visual Anthropology Review* 17 (1): 21–35. https://doi.org/10.1525/var.2001.17.1.21.

Wolf, Eckard. 2004. "Berlin Shaped by History, Planning, and Economic Forces." In *European Cities: Insights on Outskirts; From Helsinki to Nicosia; Eleven Case Studies & Synthesis*, edited by Geneviève Dubois-Taine, 157–86. Brussels: METL/PUCA, Blanchard Printing.

Wolf, Eric. 1982. *Europe and the People without History*. Berkeley: University of California Press.

Woolard, Kathryn. 1998. "Language Ideology as a Field of Inquiry." In *Language Ideologies: Practice and Theory*, edited by Bambi Schieffelin, Kathryn Woolard, and Paul Kroskrity, 3–50. Oxford: Oxford University Press.

Wulff, Helena, and Vered Amit. 1995. *Youth Cultures: A Cross-Cultural Perspective*. London: Routledge.

Yates, Simoen J. 1996. "Oral and Written Linguistic Aspects of Computer Conferencing." In *Computer Mediated Communication: Linguistic, Social and Cross-Cultural Perspectives*, edited by Susan C. Herring, 29–46. Amsterdam: John Benjamins.

Young, Kirsty. 2011. "Social Ties, Social Networks, and the Facebook Experience." *International Journal of Emerging Technologies and Society* 9 (1): 20–34.

Yurchak, Alexei. 2006. *Everything Was Forever, Until It Was No More: The Last Soviet Generation*. Princeton, NJ: Princeton University Press.

Zhan, Mei. 2009. *Other-Worldly: Making Chinese Medicine through Transnational Frames*. Durham, NC: Duke University Press.

Zillien, Nicole, and Eszter Hargittai. 2009. "Digital Distinction: Status-Specific Types of Internet Usage." *Social Science Quarterly* 90 (2): 274–91. https://doi.org/10.1111/j.1540-6237.2009.00617.x.

Index

Page numbers in *italics* refer to figures.

www.ingramcontent.com/pod-product-compliance
Lightning Source LLC
Chambersburg PA
CBHW030221260325
24092CB00002B/87